BY CARL SANDBURG

ABRAHAM LINCOLN: THE PRAIRIE YEARS
ABRAHAM LINCOLN: THE WAR YEARS
MARY LINCOLN: WIFE AND WIDOW
THE AMERICAN SONGBAG
STEICHEN THE PHOTOGRAPHER
STORM OVER THE LAND
HOME FRONT MEMO

Poems

SMOKE AND STEEL
SLABS OF THE SUNBURNT WEST
CHICAGO POEMS
CORNHUSKERS
GOOD MORNING, AMERICA
SELECTED POEMS. Edited by Rebecca West
THE PEOPLE, YES

For Young Folks

ROOTABAGA STORIES
ROOTABAGA PIGEONS
ABE LINCOLN GROWS UP

CARL SANDBURG

HOME FRONT MEMO

NEW YORK
HARCOURT, BRACE AND COMPANY

first edition

This book is manufactured in conformity
with government regulations for saving
in the use of paper. The saving in no
way affects the contents of the book.

This collection of pamphlets, speeches, broadcasts, news-paper columns, poems, legends, photograph texts, now as-sembled and made available in one carry-all volume—this is

Dedicated

to the life, works, and memory of

STEPHEN VINCENT BENÉT

who knew the distinction between pure art and propa-ganda in the written or spoken word. He could sing to give men music, consolation, pleasure. He could intone chant or prayer pointing the need for men to act. He illus-trated the code and creed of those writers who seek to widen the areas of freedom for all men, knowing that men of ideas vanish first when freedom vanishes. He saw that a writer's silence on living issues can in itself constitute a propaganda of conduct leading toward the deterioration or death of freedom. He wrote often hoping that men would act because of his words. He could have been Olympian, whimsical, seeking to be timeless amid bells of doom not to be put off.

CONTENTS

THE UNFATHOMED LINCOLN

What would Lincoln do now?

Written for the Treasury Department as part of a series syndicated in news-papers, and given book publication in a volume entitled *There Were Giants in the Land*, published in the United States and Great Britain.

What would Lincoln do now? This question is heard. It is asked sometimes as though it could be answered in a few well-chosen words.

What did Lincoln do then—when he was alive and had many of the powers of a dictator? That, too, is a question. Often nobody but himself knew beforehand what he was going to do. And when he did it what happened? Take a look back and see what happened. We have a right to say there were times when what he did looked wrong to good men then.

To the men of his own party in Washington in early 1864 Lincoln looked wrong. Not a member of the United States Senate spoke out for him as good enough to have another term.

There were, as men go, some mighty good men in that Senate. But opinion at the national capital agreed with the *Detroit Free Press* correspondent at Washington writing: "Not a single Senator can be named as favorable to Lincoln's renomination for President." The Illinois Senator, Lyman Trumbull, always keen in reading political trends, wrote to a friend in February of '64: "The feeling for Mr. Lincoln's re-election *seems* to be very general, but much of it I discover is only on the surface. You would be surprised, in talking with public men we meet here, to find how few, when you come to get at their real sentiment, are for Mr. Lincoln's re-election. There is a distrust and fear that he is too undecided and inefficient. . . . You need not be surprised if a reaction sets in before the nomination, in favor of some man supposed to possess more energy."

This was the mild comment of an extraordinarily decent politician and statesman. What other Senators of Lincoln's own party

3

were saying and writing was neither mild nor decent. Thus the Senate. What of the House of Representatives? There only one member took the floor to say Lincoln was worth keeping in the White House.

A Pennsylvania editor visiting Washington said to Thaddeus Stevens, Chairman of the Ways and Means Committee and Republican-party floor leader, "Introduce me to some member of Congress friendly to Mr. Lincoln's renomination." Stevens took the editor to the desk of Isaac N. Arnold of Chicago, saying: "Here is a man who wants to find a Lincoln member of Congress. You are the only one I know, and I have come over to introduce my friend to you." "Thank you," said Arnold. "I know a good many such and I will present your friend to them, and I wish you, Mr. Stevens, were with us." Thus the very scrupulous Arnold recorded the incident. The other friends of Lincoln in Congress to whom Arnold referred were not named by him, nor did their wish to continue Lincoln as President show in their speeches.

Isaac N. Arnold, once a country schoolteacher in New York State, city clerk of Chicago in 1837, a practicing attorney at law, early in January of '64 took the floor to quote from Lincoln's "House Divided" speech, holding it prophetic, bold, honest, characteristic of "the man who, then obscure, has become already to-day, the foremost character in American history." Toward saving the Union, Lincoln had "labored and toiled through difficulties and obstacles known only to himself and God," said Arnold. "The great fault of his administration, the too tardy removal of incompetent men, has arisen from a too scrupulous care to be just."

Speaking to panels of skeptical faces, Arnold went on: "He has borne censure and denunciation for acts for which others were responsible, with a generosity which has extorted from his rivals the declaration, 'Of all men, Mr. Lincoln is the most unselfish.' I ask the ardent and impatient friends of freedom to put implicit faith in Abraham Lincoln. If you deem him slow, or if you think he has made mistakes, remember how often time has vindicated his wisdom. The masses of the people everywhere trust and love him. They know his hands are clean and his breast is pure. The people know that the devil has no bribe big enough, no temptation of gold, or place, or power, which can seduce the honest heart of Abraham Lincoln. They know that while he is President there is

4

no danger of a *coup d'état* . . . that their liberties and laws are safe in his hands. . . . You have a Chief Magistrate . . . somewhat rude and rough, it may be, but under this rough exterior you have the real and true hero."

And what light does this give us on what Lincoln would do now? About all we learn for sure is that he would expect trouble with Congress all the time and the best he could hope for would be to keep a smoldering volcano of impatience and frayed nerves from erupting into a volcano of straight-out antagonism. Lincoln so managed that he never got into open hostilities with the main body of Congress.

"The opposition to Mr. Lincoln," wrote Indiana Republican Congressman George W. Julian later, ". . . was secretly cherished by many of the ablest and most patriotic men of the day." Thaddeus Stevens in a letter written in '64 showed the mixed motives of himself and associates: "How little of the rights of war and the law of nations our Pres't knows! But what are we to do? Condemn privately and applaud publicly!"

And from this we learn that men who regard themselves among the ablest and most patriotic men of the day can privately cherish opposition they can't make public. We learn further that Lincoln now would expect to be dealing regularly with men as forthright and ruthless as Thad Stevens, who knew how to "condemn privately and applaud publicly."

Then how, against this smoldering and almost unanimous opposition in Senate and House, did Lincoln win renomination? By a national convention at Baltimore in June of '64 unanimous for him, the delegates responsive to a feeling among the mass of voters that Lincoln had handled a tough job pretty well and was worth another term in the White House. In March of '64 a Chicago newspaper had carried a paragraph: "A sturdy farmer from Oskaloosa, Iowa, one of the bone and sinew class, called upon us yesterday in relation to business matters. Before leaving, we asked him how Mr. Lincoln stood in Iowa. 'Stands?' said the old farmer, with glistening eyes and raising his brawny fist. 'Old Abe stands seventeen feet higher in Iowa than any other man in the United States!'"

Lincoln now in the White House would probably be considering that Iowa farmer as more important than the members of Congress. That farmer could understand better than official Washington what

John Bright of the British House of Commons told an American interviewer. Bright refused to worry over reports that Lincoln was too slow, adding, "Mr. Lincoln is like a waiter in a large eating house where all the bells are ringing at once; he cannot serve them all at once, and so some grumblers are to be expected."

Lincoln now would expect, whenever he was decisive, whenever he did something spectacular on a large scale, to be called tyrannical and despotic. Hundreds of speeches and editorials used the word "tyrant" and "despot" for him. Once as he read a sheaf of editorials Henry Ward Beecher had written and published in a religious weekly, the *Independent,* his one comment was "Is thy servant a dog?"

And when he was not decisive nor spectacular, what were the words for him? He was "slow," "indecisive," "vacillating." He lacked "vigor." A man of "more energy" was wanted. One persisting favorite adjective was "vacillating." When you try to walk a straight line chalked on a floor and you can't stick to the line you are vacillating.

In the spring of '61 he took to himself the powers of a dictator. He started a war without asking Congress, declared a blockade, called for troops to put down an insurrection, lifted for immediate use millions of dollars from the United States Treasury without authorized appropriation by Congress. And his call for Congress to meet and ratify these arbitrary acts of his named July 4, months ahead, as the date.

When his powers to do these things were bitterly questioned he asked whether he must stick strictly to the Constitution while trying to save the government of which the Constitution was the written instrument. They were dizzy days and he told his secretary John Hay one day, "My policy is to have no policy."

This same viewpoint stood forth in a letter made public in April of '64 written to a Kentucky man. It staggered some readers in its confession. "I claim not to have controlled events, but confess plainly that events have controlled me." What—no policy? Yes, that was what he was saying. Except on the one issue of saving the Union and no extension of slavery, he had no fixed paramount policy. He would have compromised on slavery forty ways for the saving of the Union. Events controlled him. Sometimes he prayed for an

6

event to happen, so he could do what could not be done till that event came.

What would Lincoln do now? Would he find the conflict between invested capital and organized labor as tough as the slavery issue of his own time? As Chief Magistrate of all the people he would hope, of course, to smooth out the differences among honest men, not to mention dealing with those he had in mind when writing: "Actual war coming . . . every foul bird comes abroad and every dirty reptile rises up. These add crime to confusion. Strong measures, deemed indispensable, but harsh at best, such men make worse by maladministration."

His own party then he saw split forty ways on what to do about slavery. The moderates divided into those who with Lincoln favored the government buying the slaves and setting them free and those who thought this wouldn't work. The radicals divided into the abolitionists who, like Wendell Phillips and Charles Sumner, called for an emancipation proclamation as soon as the war started and those like William Lloyd Garrison and Harriet Beecher Stowe who favored going slower and making sure. There were Douglas Democrats who wanted to save the Union and let slavery alone, many of them splendid fighting men. There were sections and factions always to be considered, as to principles and offices and patronage, and they tore their shirts when they didn't get what they wanted. There were cliques and individuals wanting contracts, subsidies, special favors. Some wanted greenbacks, others "hard money." The tariff, banking, and Pacific-railway blocs never stopped looking toward their particular goals.

Through this chaos of clashing ideas Lincoln had to ride. Every day came pressure and he had to say Yes or No. And in these pressures did he have a choice between right, on the one hand, and wrong, on the other? Hardly. Day after day and hour on hour he had to decide between what was partly right and partly wrong, on the one hand, and what, on the other hand, was partly right and partly wrong. Many a time when making his decision he admitted it was partly wrong but it was the best he could do. He had a word for this. He would point to what he would like to do that would be perfectly right and then show how what was perfectly right wouldn't work—in the end it would get worse results than another course which he termed "expedient."

7

The saving of the Union was the only major issue where he held his cause completely just as well as politic and expedient. On the other major issue, slavery, what did he do that was "expedient" rather than right? Look at his Emancipation Proclamation. It says plainly that he issues it because of "military necessity." He means the Union armies will win sooner if the slaves are made free. Of course, as he said later, he believed slavery to be wrong. He believed in freedom for the blacks bought and sold as livestock and assessed on the tax books as were cattle and sheep. But he didn't and felt he couldn't say so in the Emancipation Proclamation. There he said they were given freedom "as an act of justice warranted by the Constitution upon military necessity."

Did this mean that he freed all slaves in all slave states? No. In the states named in the Emancipation Proclamation the so-called Border States were left out. In the slave states of Missouri, Kentucky, Delaware, Maryland, were the slaves declared to be free? No. Those states had not seceded, were not "in rebellion," as he phrased it. And did he declare all slaves in the seceded states to be forever free? No, he made exceptions. He named thirteen parishes of the State of Louisiana, including the city of New Orleans, as exceptions. There the slaves were not declared free. Likewise in seven counties and two cities of the State of Virginia, including the forty-eight slave-soil counties of West Virginia, the slaves were not declared free. They were excepted.

Of course, he had reasons, arguments that look good today, for doing what was expedient rather than right. Lincoln now, if alive and effective, would often be doing the expedient thing rather than the right thing. Otherwise he would go down politically and be swept out of use, which didn't happen to Lincoln while he was alive. The mystery of justice tangled in realities stood forth in Horace Mann sniffing to Samuel J. May, "I hate your doctrine that we should think only of the right and not of the expedient," and May sniffing in return, "And I hate your doctrine that we should think of the expedient, and not only of the right."

Not merely day after day but month on month and year after year the two leading and most widely circulated newspapers of the country challenged, attacked, belittled Lincoln's course of action or inaction. These were the *New York Herald,* conservative and hating abolitionists, and the *New York Tribune,* radical and antislavery.

And the *Herald* nearly always saw Lincoln going too far while the *Tribune* hardly ever failed to find fault with Lincoln for not going far enough. The *Herald* in early '64 hoped to get Grant nominated for President instead of Lincoln. The *Tribune* named several who would make better candidates than Lincoln and said some other man ought to be nominated if only to respect "the salutary One Term principle."

Also day after day Lincoln was the target of slander, scandal, misrepresentation, vituperation, lies, false rumors, half-truths, insinuations, lampoons, caricatures from a free press that hated him and his ways. They poured it on him. He took it meekly and bowed low before it. He took it with laughter and cheer at times when on the face of it a lie couldn't get by. He writhed and twisted when he knew it harmed his cause and that of the boys who had answered his call to service. That was his mood when in Philadelphia at a Sanitary Fair dedication in April of '64 he said, "It is difficult to say a sensible thing nowadays." So much of what he had been saying was tortured into something else that he didn't mean. A hundred voices and as many journals over and again used the word "imbecile" to describe his administration.

When a military authority, without asking Lincoln about it, shut down a treasonable newspaper with a neurotic editor in Chicago, an editor at a later time declared by a jury to be "mentally unsound," Lincoln said nothing, did nothing. When coolheaded friends of Lincoln in Chicago pleaded with him to revoke the military order and let the Chicago newspaper run its free presses again, Lincoln issued the order, so the newspaper was again free to spread sedition and teach treason. When the same military authority arrested an Ohio Congressman on charges of giving comfort and aid to the enemy, Lincoln said he would have done it different if he had been asked about it—and then ordered the treason agitator sent to the Union Army lines, where he was marched on into the enemy lines, "banished" from Ohio and the United States of America. In each of these actions Lincoln was before and after denounced by his political opposition as "tyrant," "despot," "dictator," "imbecile." When the foremost Democratic-party newspaper, the *New York World,* published a bogus and forged defeatist proclamation as signed by the President, Secretary of State William H. Seward said that as a newspaper it had been published "a minute too long."

9

War Secretary Stanton wrote an order for its suppression. Lincoln signed the order. The paper was shut down, couldn't run its presses, couldn't print and sell because of Federal troops in possession of the plant. Then Lincoln issued another order and the *New York World* again printed its papers, packed with denunciations of the President.

Widely published was Lincoln's little query "Must I shoot a simple-minded soldier boy who deserts, while I must not touch a hair of a wily agitator who induces him to desert?" That is a terrible question. It carries its own answer. It was in the minds of some of the men who joined mobs that wrecked or burned a score of newspaper plants, dailies and weeklies, and came to no punishment from local or Federal authorities.

Lincoln now might not be hearing from supporters that he is "slow," "vacillating," and from enemies that he is "imbecile." He might not. And again he might. Human impulses have not changed particularly as between then and now. Certainly the politicians of the various sections and factions play the game much the same.

An Illinois politician and soldier who had for years watched Lincoln thought the best key to the man and his style as a statesman was in an odd little speech that Lincoln made aimed at this one man, John M. Palmer, a Union Democrat and a brave officer.

Palmer found Lincoln in the hands of the barber, and Lincoln called, "Come in, Palmer, come in. You're home folks. I can shave before you. I couldn't before those others, and I have to do it sometime." They chatted about politics, Palmer finally speaking in a frank and jovial mood. "Mr. Lincoln, if anybody had told me that in a great crisis like this the people were going out to a little one-horse town and pick out a one-horse lawyer for President I wouldn't have believed it." Lincoln whirled in his chair, his face white with lather, a towel under his chin. Palmer at first thought the President was angry. Sweeping the barber away, Lincoln leaned forward, put a hand on Palmer's knee, and said, "Neither would I. But it was a time when a man with a policy would have been fatal to the country. I have never had a policy. I have simply tried to do what seemed best as each day came."

The good woman Ida Tarbell read a thousand books on Lincoln and wrote more books of her own with fresh material about him and after years of studying him she said it is impossible to make either merely a saint or a hero out of him—he was too human, too wide-ranging. A New York clergyman of godly ways, with the ungodly name of Octavius Brooks Frothingham, wrote of how the costumers tried to make clothes and gloves for him but the bones always stuck out and "they could make nothing of him" because "he was a character—not a doll." So while his coffin traveled from Washington to Springfield "the country does not go wild over him; it silently weeps for him; it does not celebrate him as a demigod— it mourns for him as a friend. It gives him no noisy place in the hall of the heroes—it gives him a dear and still one in the chamber of the heart. . . . Ordinary human nature was honored in him, and so ordinary human nature weeps for him."

The words "responsible" and "responsibility" stick out from many of his letters. And he liked the word "thorough." He thought freedom worth men's dying for but he would like it that freemen could understand their freedom would be safer if they felt responsible about it and could be thorough in their work as freemen.

Often amid chaos and howls of shame and guilt he sat cool as death writing memoranda on what it was immediately possible to do. Or again, as when news came of a valued friend killed in combat, the tears ran down his face, and after the slaughters of two lost battles he was in grief near to agony. In one lull after a disaster he was full of jokes and told one fool story after another till he heard a question why he could be so light-minded, when he answered, "My God, man, don't you see that if I didn't laugh I would have to cry?" His personality held a wide range of the tragic and the comic. Perhaps democracy can best survive where men know the right moments for complete and solemn reverence or the nonsense that nourishes and the laughter that rests and may even heal.

The foremost humorists, the three leading comics of his time, Artemus Ward, Petroleum Vesuvius Nasby, Orpheus C. Kerr, were with him. They loved him. They enjoyed poking fun at him and kicking his dignity in the slats, sneaking in sidewise their affection and admiration for him. His opposition tried for it but could never come through with effective ridicule that had people laughing at the first authentic humorist to occupy the White House.

Lincoln now laughs. The ghost of his laughter is part of our inheritance. The people, who stood with him when the politicians in Washington wondered what was the matter with their constitu-

11

ents, understood he was laughing their own corn-on-the-cob mirth that helps when things go bad sometimes. Not until peace came did he allow himself to smile for a photographer. And behind the smile was a haggard weariness.

There were many fool talkers and writers in Lincoln's generation. They let themselves go. They had a good time and indulged their passions and their hate. Today their words look pathetic or ridiculous. We may read the *Congressional Globe* of the 1860's with amazement at how large a majority of Congressmen did not know the history in the making before their own eyes. We feel sorry they had such loose mouths and so little care and anxiety as to how their utterance would look in the future.

Lincoln was one of the few who had precisely and deeply that care and anxiety about what he said or wrote. He could be musical of speech, but there are times when he hedges and cribs and confines what he is saying till it seems crabbed and clumsy. What is he doing? He is circumscribing the area where he says he knows something for sure. He is taking care to mislead no one. So the people over the states trusted him when the Senate and the House and the *New York Herald* and the *New York Tribune* and the London *Times* didn't. He foreshadowed something. The people took him as a new figure of hope for them. This hope ranged around wider freedom, political and economic, for the common man. It might be long in coming. But Lincoln held the lights and the high torch for it.

The people of this and many other countries take Lincoln now for their own. He belongs to them. To many the word "freedom" or the word "democracy" is hard to get at. And the Constitution— sure, we're for the Constitution, though we're not sure what it means and we have even heard of lawyers who don't know what the Constitution means and they prove it by arguing and disputing about what it means.

But Lincoln—yes—he stands for decency, honest dealing, plain talk, and funny stories. Look where he came from—don't he know all us strugglers and wasn't he a kind of a tough struggler all his life right up to the finish?

Something like that you can hear in any near-by neighborhood— and across the seas in far continents. Millions there are who take Lincoln as a personal treasure. He had something they would like to see spread everywhere over the world. Democracy? We can't say exactly what it is, but he had it. In his blood and bones he carried it. In the breath of his speeches and writings it is there. Popular government? Republican institutions? Government where the people have the say-so, one way or another telling their rulers what they want? He had the idea. It's there in the lights and shadows of his personality, a mystery that can be lived but never fully spoken in words. A London *Spectator* writer tried to analyze Lincoln's message to Congress in December of 1862, found it having a "mystical dreaminess," and "The thoughts of the man are too big for his mouth."

Turmoils of an earlier day

One of the Once-a-Week Pieces for the Papers, February 14, 1943.

Early in 1864 the editor of the *Janesville Gazette* in Wisconsin was sure that if by military edict President Lincoln should adjourn Congress, he would be entitled to the thanks of the country.

He editorialized: "They are a set of gaseous, windy blatherskites who do little else but eat, drink, draw their pay and make Buncombe speeches."

Thus the *Gazette* editor relieved his feelings. What was pent up had vent. He probably knocked off for the day and went home to have a look at the baby's new tooth.

Likewise the chaplain of the United States Senate, the Reverend Dr. Byron Sutherland, whose prayers had been edging into politics so that various Senators had rebuked the chaplain. Before resigning to go to Paris and serve as pastor of an American congregation there, he offered up a curious invocation. Young Noah Brooks, writer of news letters to the *Sacramento Union* in California, heard the Senate's praying chaplain deliver these words into the ears of the listening honorable body: "O Lord, give us that Thou wilt in Thine infinite wisdom vouchsafe to our rulers and legislators in this Congress assembled more brains—more brains, Lord." So the chaplain felt better and was pleased he was leaving, many Senators appropriately saying "We wish you the same."

Moving adjournment one day, Thad Stevens remarked, "Everybody is offering Buncombe resolutions and I think we had better

13

adjourn." Stevens could say more in a sentence or two than any-body else in the House, one day railing, "Debate is exhausted on the amendment, and everybody here is exhausted with the debate," and still later that day: "I am opposed to the amendment. I do not know what the amendment is but I am opposed to it." The *New York World* saw eye to eye with those alleging that "whoever cracked Thaddeus Stevens' skull would let out the brains of the Republican party."

The *Detroit Free Press* in characterizing Stevens "an abusive and vulgar blackguard" nevertheless quoted his priceless rejoinder to another Congressman: "The gentleman who has just spoken need not fear that I will make any insinuations or sneer or thrust at him. There are some reptiles so flat that the common foot of man can-not crush them."

Manners in that war generation were much as manners now. So likewise were human motives. Among politicians and journalists were those who knew less, or at least no more, after the four-year war trial and ordeal than before. The valor, the toil, the agony, did nothing to them inside or out. Others kept growing, kept learn-ing, kept finding new strengths in silent meditation.

President Lincoln, as we all know, was one of those who grew, who, as one noted, was "always a learner." Of the many forces that helped shape Lincoln before he became President, there has come to be increasing respect for his father Thomas Lincoln. Each new and authenticated item of information about this father throws fa-vorable light on him. The present writer has seen in the collection of Oliver R. Barrett of Chicago a scrapbook kept by Nancy Hall, one of the grandchildren in the home of Thomas and Sarah Bush Lincoln at Goose Nest Prairie in Coles County, Illinois. Some of the newspaper clippings pasted in this scrapbook report stories and sayings among the Lincolns. Short-spoken, humble, and reverent was the blessing young Abraham often heard at table, if this brief account in one newspaper is correct:

"John Hall, a near relative of Abraham Lincoln's stepmother, says that Thomas Lincoln returned thanks at every meal, always using the same words, 'Fit and prepare us for humble service, we beg for Christ's sake. Amen.' "

A story not yet included in any Lincoln biography is reported in this same scrapbook of Nancy Hall. The evidence seems to be

14

that Thomas Lincoln was a worthy husband of Nancy Hanks, the mother of Abraham Lincoln who died when he was a child, and of Sally Bush, the beloved foster mother. But the only account we have from Thomas Lincoln in this regard is in this scrapbook. It reads:

"One day when alone with her husband, Mrs. Lincoln said, 'Thomas, we have lived together a long time and you have never yet told me whom you like best, your first wife or me.' Thomas replied, 'Oh, now, Sarah, that reminds me of old John Hardin down in Kentucky who had a fine-looking pair of horses, and a neighbor coming in one day and looking at them said, 'John, which horse do you like best?' John said, 'I can't tell; one of them kicks and the other bites and I don't know which is wust.' It is plain to see where Abraham Lincoln got his talent for wit and apt illustrations."

The latest light on Lincoln's religion

One of the Once-a-Week Pieces for the Papers, March 29, 1942.

Was Abraham Lincoln an infidel and a scoffer at the Christian religion? This question has been raised again and again and debated over and over for many years. Now today comes new light, for the first time statements written by Lincoln himself, early in his political career, where he records his answer to the question whether he was then a religious man. Neither private memoranda nor in a letter marked "Confidential," they were published in a newspaper on specific request of Lincoln.

In an old copy of the *Illinois Gazette* of Lacon, Illinois, dated August 15, 1846, Harry E. Pratt, secretary of the Abraham Lincoln Association at Springfield, Illinois, discovered these documents made public by Paul M. Angle, editor of the Association's quarterly magazine.

Angle rates them "the most explicit, fully authenticated statement Lincoln ever made on this perennially debated subject." They show how Lincoln's mind ranged with reference to religion. They reveal how Lincoln chose to handle a whispering campaign aimed

15

to beat him in his run for Congress. We get a look at Lincoln's patience with crazy rumors.

The circuit-riding Methodist preacher Peter Cartwright, running against Lincoln, knew that Lincoln belonged to no Christian church, knew too there were old Sangamon County neighbors of Lincoln who talked about him as a scoffer at religion and claimed he had said, "Christ was a bastard." That rumors, scandals, back-biting, and malice played their part in politics in those early horse-and-buggy days, even as now in this motorized age, is evident in the tone of Lincoln's letter to the *Illinois Gazette*, published after Lincoln had won the election.

"I was informed by letter from Jacksonville," he wrote to the editor, "that Mr. Cartwright was whispering the charge of infidelity against me in that quarter. I at once wrote a contradiction of it and sent it to my friends there, with the request that they should publish it or not, as in their discretion they might think proper, having in view the extent of the circulation of the charge, as also the extent of the credence it might be receiving. They did not publish it."

On later information from other neighborhoods Lincoln believed "nine persons out of ten" had not heard the charge against him. "Its extent of circulation was just such as to make a public notice of it uncalled for, while it was not entirely safe to leave it un-noticed." So he published a handbill for those neighborhoods.

This handbill, addressed to "Fellow Citizens," and dated July 31, 1846, when Lincoln was thirty-seven years of age, belongs on all shelves of basic Lincoln books and data. The handbill read:

"A charge having got into circulation in some of the neighbor-hoods of this district, in substance that I am an open scoffer at Christianity, I have by the advice of some friends concluded to notice the subject in this form. That I am not a member of any Christian church, is true; but I have never denied the truth of the Scriptures; and I have never spoken with intentional disrespect of religion in general, or of any denomination of Christians in par-ticular. It is true that in early life I was inclined to believe in what I understand is called the 'Doctrine of Necessity'—that is, that the human mind is impelled to action, or held in rest by some power, over which the mind itself has no control; and I have sometimes (with one, two or three, but never publicly) tried to maintain this opinion in argument. The habit of arguing thus, however, I have entirely left off for more than five years. And I add here, I have always understood this same opinion to be held by several of the Christian denominations. The foregoing is the whole truth, briefly stated, in relation to myself upon this subject.

"I do not think I could, myself, be brought to support a man for office whom I knew to be an open enemy of, and scoffer at, religion. Leaving the higher matter of eternal consequences between him and his Maker, I still do not think any man has the right thus to insult the feelings, and injure the morals, of the community in which he may live. If, then, I was guilty of such conduct, I should blame no man who should condemn me for it; but I do blame those, whoever they may be, who falsely put such a charge in circulation against me."

Lincoln's accompanying letter explained he wished to reach "some honest men" whom his opponent "had succeeded in deceiving." Lincoln had "little doubt" that "to slyly sow the seed in select spots was the chief object of his [Cartwright's] mission through your part of the district, at a time when he knew I could not contradict him, either in person or by letter, before the election."

Lincoln then took up the case of a rumormonger named Woodward, who had hoped to defeat Lincoln by spreading the word he was an infidel. "I can still suppose him to be a worthy man; he may have believed what he said; but there is, even in that charitable view of his case, one lesson in morals which he might, not without profit, learn of even me—and that is, never to add the weight of his character to a charge against his fellow man without knowing it to be true. I believe it is an established maxim in morals that he who makes an assertion without knowing whether it is true or false is guilty of falsehood, and the accidental truth of the assertion does not justify or excuse him. This maxim ought to be particularly held in view when we contemplate an attack upon the reputation of our neighbor."

In this campaign the story arose of Lincoln going to a meeting where Cartwright preached, in due time saying, "All who desire to lead a new life, to give their hearts to God, and go to heaven, will stand." A sprinkling of men, women, and children stood up. Then the preacher exhorted, "All who do not wish to go to hell will stand." All stood up—except Lincoln. Then said Cartwright in solemn tone: "I observe that many responded to the first invitation

17

to give their hearts to God and go to heaven. And I further observe that all of you save one indicated that you did not desire to go to hell. The sole exception is Mr. Lincoln, who did not respond to either invitation. May I inquire of you, Mr. Lincoln, where you are going?"

Lincoln slowly rose and slowly spoke: "I came here as a respectful listener. I did not know that I was to be singled out by Brother Cartwright. I believe in treating religious matters with due solemnity. I admit that the questions propounded by Brother Cartwright are of great importance. I did not feel called upon to answer as the rest did. Brother Cartwright asks me directly where I am going. I desire to reply with equal directness: I am going to Congress."

Birth dates of Lincoln folk authenticated

One of the Once-a-Week Pieces for the Papers, February 7, 1943.

When Abraham Lincoln's father died in a Goose Nest Prairie log cabin near Charleston, Illinois, on January 17, 1851, the son was not at the bedside. Shortly after, however, he visited his stepmother, Sarah Bush Lincoln, joining in a reunion of kith and kin. And they gave the best of their information and belief to a record of the marriages, births, and deaths of the Lincoln family.

In Abraham Lincoln's handwriting this record went into the family Bible. Time passed, and a few years after the death of President Lincoln his cousin Dennis Hanks, leaving Charleston for a visit with his daughter, removed from the family Bible the record leaf written by Abraham Lincoln. In 1888 this documentary page came into the hands of Jesse Weik, the young Hoosier collaborating with William H. Herndon on a biography of Lincoln, Weik noting, "Dennis tore out and wore out the Bible record."

Whether Dennis carried the priceless authoritative document of important dates in a hip or vest pocket we have no word. And though creased and worn, it still serves students and biographers.

I saw the original a few days ago when Oliver R. Barrett let it come out for a while from a fireproof vault.

Only in recent weeks has Barrett finished a research that tells us what it was that Abraham Lincoln wrote in the five lines of the upper right-hand corner of this Bible leaf, a creased corner that got worn or torn off and lost.

On those five lines Lincoln wrote the birth dates of his father Thomas Lincoln and his mother Nancy Hanks and the date of their marriage. Having this data, we are able now to correct the mistaken dates now chiseled on gravestone and memorial tablets and to fill in the blanks where several good and well-meaning biographers are vague or incomplete.

Naturally, too, it is well to have now the birth date of Lincoln's mother as he himself wrote it in the family Bible, inasmuch as the Historical Society of Spencer County, Indiana, has plans and hopes for a memorial stamp commemorating the hundred-and-twenty-fifth anniversary of the death of Nancy Hanks, the petition for such a stamp now having upward of a half-million signatures.

The missing five lines of the Bible leaf record as restored through the Barrett research read:

"Thos. Lincoln was born Jan. the 6th A. D. 1778 and was married June 12th 1806 to Nancy Hanks who was born Feb. 5th 1784.
Sarah Lincoln Daughter of Thos. and"

And how can we be sure these are the five lines torn or worn, lost and missing, from the Bible-leaf record that Lincoln wrote? By four separate and different pieces of evidence in the Barrett collection.

John D. Johnston, good-looking, well-spoken, and somewhat lazy and shiftless, a son of Sarah Bush Lincoln by her first marriage and a foster brother of Abraham Lincoln, was going to move to Arkansas. Johnston copied from the family Bible the entire record there made in Lincoln's handwriting. On a blank page of an account book Johnston entered the Bible-leaf record where it may be seen today, the outstanding item amid the record of numerous sales of whisky at 50 cents a gallon.

John J. Hall, a cousin of Lincoln, and a grandson of Sarah Bush Lincoln living with her at the time that Lincoln wrote the family Bible record, also made a copy of that record before Dennis Hanks removed it. Hall's copy was kept in the Lincoln cabin until 1891. Visitors to the cabin often saw this Hall copy of the Lincoln record.

On at least three occasions John J. Hall's copy of the Lincoln record was given publication. *The History of Coles County,* published in Chicago in 1879, has this entry: "While in the old cabin where he [Thomas Lincoln] lived and died, we were shown the family record copied by Mr. Hall from a leaf of the family Bible. . . . It reads Thomas Lincoln was born Jan. 6, 1778, and was married June 12, 1806, to Nancy Hanks, who was born Feb. 5, 1784."

In a large scrapbook where plain handwriting tells us it was "made by Nancy A. Hall, great-granddaughter of Sarah Bush Lincoln, Goose Nest Prairie, near Charleston, Ill.," is a clipping of one of a series of newspaper articles titled "Half Century in Coles County," by John Cunningham, Chapter 11, "Pleasant Grove, The Lincoln Family." The writer tells of relic-hunters carrying off family records, though "Mr. John Hall has a copy, however, of a leaf from the Lincoln family Bible, which I give entire."

Then follows the text with the birth dates identical with the record in the county history and the John D. Johnston account book, and there is still another newspaper clipping, this from the *St. Louis Globe-Democrat,* saying: "Mr. Hall retained nothing [of family relics] but a copy of the family record, the only genealogy kept by the Lincoln family, incomplete though it was, which is given in full below."

Maybe this all seems a little complicated, and possibly unnecessary, to some people. To others of us it is nice to have this record nailed down and secure. It throws out of the window and disposes securely of several loose-tongued writers and gossips of former generations. And if the Nancy Hanks memorial stamp is issued this year, the date of her birth, February 5, 1784, can be printed with confident accuracy.

And I am glad that one of our Chicago trial lawyers is an antiquarian with gifts of imagination and deduction that make his worn relics and faded records come alive for use and service.

Mr. Longfellow and his boy

Written February, 1941; published in *Collier's* June 14, 1941.

Mr. Longfellow, Henry Wadsworth Longfellow,
    the Harvard Professor,
    the poet whose pieces you see in all the schoolbooks,
"Tell me not in mournful numbers
    life is but an empty dream . . ."
Mr. Longfellow sits in his Boston library writing,
Mr. Longfellow looks across the room
    and sees his nineteen-year-old boy
propped up in a chair at a window,
home from the war,
a rifle ball through right and left shoulders.

In his diary the father writes about his boy:
    "He has a wound through him a foot long.
    He pretends it does not hurt him."
And the father if he had known
would have told the boy propped up in a chair
how one of the poems written in that room
    made President Lincoln cry.
And both the father and the boy
would have smiled to each other and felt good
about why the President had tears over that poem.

Noah Brooks, the California newspaperman,
could have told the Longfellows how one day
Brooks heard the President saying two lines:
    "Thou, too, sail on, O Ship of State!
    Sail on, O Union, strong and great!"
Noah Brooks, remembering more of the poem, speaks:

"Thou, too, sail on, O Ship of State!
Sail on, O Union, strong and great!
Humanity with all its fears,
With all the hopes of future years,
Is hanging breathless on thy fate!
We know what Master laid thy keel,
What Workmen wrought thy ribs of steel,
Who made each mast, and sail, and rope,
What anvils rang, what hammers beat,
In what a forge and what a heat
Were shaped the anchors of thy hope!
Fear not each sudden sound and shock,
'Tis of the wave and not the rock;
'Tis but the flapping of the sail,
And not a rent made by the gale!
In spite of rock and tempest's roar,
In spite of false lights on the shore,
Sail on, nor fear to breast the sea!
Our hearts, our hopes, are all with thee,
Our hearts, our hopes, our prayers, our tears,
Our faith triumphant o'er our fears,
Are all with thee—are all with thee!"

Noah Brooks sees Lincoln's eyes filled with tears,
        the cheeks wet.
They sit quiet a little while, then Lincoln saying:
"It is a wonderful gift to be able to stir men like that."
Mr. Longfellow—and his boy sitting propped up in a chair—
with a bullet wound a foot long in his shoulders—
would have liked to hear President Lincoln saying
        those words.

Now Mr. Longfellow is gone far away, his boy, too,
        gone far away,
and they never dreamed how seventy-eight years later
the living President of the United States, in the White House
        at Washington,
takes a pen, writes with his own hand on a sheet of paper

about the Union Ship of State sailing on and on—
    never going down—
how the President hands that sheet of paper
to a citizen soon riding high in the air, high over salt water,
high in the rain and the sun and the mist over
    the Atlantic Ocean,
riding, pounding, flying, everything under control,
crossing the deep, wide Atlantic in a day and a night,
coming to London on the Thames in England,
standing before the Prime Minister of the British
    Commonwealth of Nations
so the whole English-language world
from England across North America to Australia and
    New Zealand
can never forget Mr. Longfellow's lines:
    "Thou, too, sail on, O Ship of State!
    Sail on, O Union, strong and great!"

ON THE PLATFORM AND IN THE AIR WAVES

What is humanity's greatest need today?

Broadcast May 4, 1939, "America's Town Meeting of the Air."

The greatest need of mankind today is a combination of freedom and discipline holding sway over the earth among all nations and individuals. That sounds like something. But it doesn't mean a thing. Not unless first of all we come to a common agreement about what we mean by freedom and discipline. Lincoln saw this in his time when he said in '64 that "the sheep and the wolf are not agreed upon a definition of the word liberty." And in thousands of written and spoken words and by hundreds of acts and decisions Lincoln gave the world his definition of liberty: a mystic, melancholy, involved definition of liberty—not smooth, easy, and garrulous—as though you can't have liberty unless you are willing to pay a price for it—as though it costs you something every hour that you have it—and as though it is something that connects with human relations and human fellowship and your own personal development.

Plainly, too, Lincoln taught that you can't have liberty, under the present humanity, unless there are common understandings as to authority; with freedom of any kind must go discipline and a spirit of co-operation, of yielding to others, and in degree giving yourself. He was on involved ground, Lincoln was, when he said, "As labor is the common burden of our race, so the effort of some to shift their share of the burden onto the shoulders of others is the great durable curse of the race." Whatever is the opposite of that "great durable curse" is the greatest need of mankind now.

All of us would like to see an arrangement by which the idle rich and the idle poor could make a two-power pact to take care of each other. In this world of ours now is no common agreement on why either the idle rich or the idle poor are idle. When this lack of common agreement among us gets worse and worse till it explodes in the helpless violence of war or revolution, both men and nations, after the shooting is over, quote the old Kansas saying "We asked the cyclone to go around our barn—but it didn't." You might say that in this hour mankind's greatest need is a common agreement on the causes and conditions that have produced idlers at the top and the bottom of society. Such an agreement would have to consider the vast mass of unspeakable, inarticulate, woebegone human tragedy gathered under the head of that hideous but accurate phrase from the science of economics, "the technologically disemployed"—the people whose jobs have been abolished and destroyed by machines and new industrial processes and transitions.

The extent to which this stream of economic misery is answerable for national and international turmoil is beyond the reckoning of any current commentator, but will be cast up in the balances of future historians. The answers hide in the course of events as swayed by great forces which leaders merely exhibit. We need now and need sadly some common agreement as to where national territorial expansion or private profit in business and industry becomes just plain wolfish greed. Congressman Abraham Lincoln, when he took a stand against our country's starting a war with Mexico for the sake of territorial expansion, shared with his friends the story of a farmer accused of being greedy for land. And the farmer had an answer, "I ain't greedy for more land—no, I only want what jines mine."

While we are trying to negotiate the antagonisms and contradictions that seethe around us, whirling us toward a national fate that today hides behind fog banks, there is vast need of reverence for the human mind and spirit. Goethe called for *"mehr Licht"*— more light. Victor Hugo stressed the word "Light!" Thomas Jefferson hoped for a day when every newspaper would label its items under four heads: (1) truth, (2) probabilities, (3) possibilities, (4) lies. Some of us take it as a good sign that a score of leading universities and colleges have opened classes for study and discussion of propaganda, publicity, and advertising. Lincoln used the phrases "debauchery of public opinion," "drugging the public mind," referring to leaders of men having no hesitation about befouling the human mind with any motive, passion, or prejudice that will get results. Yet the supreme names beloved and lasting in human annals are those of men having reverence for the human mind, a respect and wonder over the resources of the human spirit. As one historian has it, "Civilization rests on uncoerced diversity of opinion."

Ben Franklin and others have put it another way: "Your doxy is orthodoxy, my doxy is heterodoxy, and it will be a bad day when neither of us can have whatever doxy he likes." And Lincoln added light to the American dream in once saying, "I have not willingly planted a thorn in any man's bosom," and once writing, "I shall do nothing in malice. What I deal with is too vast for malicious dealing."

Election-eve broadcast

This speech had the last five minutes of a two-hour nation-wide radio program ending at midnight, November 6, 1940. Eighty million listeners were supposed to be tuned in. This was the only speech on the program by a political independent.

Seventy-six years ago, early in the year 1864, nearly the entire Republican leadership in Washington took a stand against Abraham Lincoln having a second term as President. In the Senate and the House there were only two men who openly favored Lincoln for a second term. One of these was a brother of America's most sacred martyr to the cause of free speech and a free press, Elijah Lovejoy, whose printing press at Alton, Illinois, was thrown into a river and Lovejoy himself shot to death by members of a mob that came in the night and burned his printshop to the ground. His brother, the Reverend Owen Lovejoy of Princeton, Illinois, a Congressman and a radical, was on his deathbed when in February of 1864 he wrote a letter to William Lloyd Garrison saying: "I write you . . . to express to you my gratification at the position you have taken in reference to Mr. Lincoln. I am satisfied, as the old theologians used to say in reference to the world, that if he is not the best conceivable President he is the best possible. I have known something of the facts inside during his Administration. . . . And although he does not do everything that you and I would like, the question recurs, whether we can elect a man who would."

On Thanksgiving in the previous year, in 1863, the Reverend Henry Fowler in the Second Presbyterian Church in Auburn, New York, compared Lincoln with the prophet Samuel in Jewish history: "Such an epoch of perplexity, transition, change, is not often witnessed. In every such passage of a nation there ought to be a character like Samuel. Misunderstood and misrepresented at the time; attacked from both sides . . . charged with saying too much and saying too little, he slowly, conscientiously and honestly works out the mighty problem. He was not a founder of a new state of things like Moses; he was not a champion of the existing order of things like Elijah. He stood between the two; between the living and the dead; between the past and the present; between the old and the new; with that sympathy for each which at such a period is the best hope for any permanent solution of the questions which torment it. He has but little praise from partisans, but is the careful healer binding up the wounds of the age, in spite of itself; the good surgeon knitting together the dislocated bones of the disjointed times. . . . The explanation of his every act is this: He executes the will of the people. . . . His wisdom consists in carrying out the good sense of the nation. His growth in political knowledge, his steady movement . . . are but the growth and movement of the national mind. . . . He stands before you . . . a not perfect man and yet more precious than fine gold."

And for some of us, that goes, in the main, in the present hour of national fate, for Franklin Delano Roosevelt.

There are some independent voters in this country who belong to no political party, no faction, no political group open or secret in its operations. They are not in the service and pay of any organization public or private that brings social, or financial, or any kind of control over what they have to say in this hour of national fate. These independent voters may be wrong, but the final control over them is under their own hats. They make their final decisions in the deep silence of their own minds and the low whispered prayers of their own hearts. They will speak tomorrow.

A picture of the American people

Broadcast January 25, 1941, from the Metropolitan Opera House, New York City.

An eminent South American statesman, not long ago in a broadcast to the Western Hemisphere, ended his reference to democracy as being mystical. That was his word—mystical. He meant that it was one of the great, strange, holy words for which those who believe in it are willing to die. And he spoke of how the word "freedom" is important in connection with democracy. But there is another word—"discipline"—that must not be forgotten. When democracy gets going at its best, you will always find not freedom alone but discipline too. To the free man and the man disciplined in a democracy, there is always faith in people. I doubt whether any man can have health or even a little fun out of his democracy unless he has some deep-rooted faith in the people, a love of the people such as Abraham Lincoln had, loving and understanding them with all their faults and failings. In one passage of my sixth book of poetry, *The People, Yes,* I put a lot of proverbs made by the people. One way or another these proverbs have the breath of the people—the people who have made our country what it is.

The people is Everyman, everybody.
Everybody is you and me and all the others.
What everybody says is what we all say
            And what is it we say? . . .
                          Listen . . .
    We'll see what we'll see.
    Time is a great teacher.
    Today me and tomorrow maybe you.
What is bitter to stand against today may be sweet to remember
        tomorrow.
Whether the stone bumps the jug or the jug bumps the stone, it is
        bad for the jug.
One hand washes the other and both wash the face.
Better leave the child's nose dirty than wring it off.
We all belong to the same big family and have the same smell.
Handling honey, or tar, some of it sticks to the fingers. . . .
No matter how important you are, you may get the measles.
    Wash a dog, comb a dog, still a dog.
    Apes may put on finery but they are still apes.
    The liar comes to believe his own lies.
He who burns himself must sit on the blisters.
    God alone understands fools.
    What is bred in the bone will tell.

31

Between the inbreds and the cross-breeds the argument goes on.
You can breed them up as easy as you can breed them down.
"I don't know who my ancestors were," said a mongrel, "but
we've been descending for a long time."
"My ancestors," said the Cherokee-blooded Oklahoman, "didn't
come over in the Mayflower but we was there to meet the boat."
Always some dark horse never heard of before is coming under the
wire a winner.
A thoroughbred always wins against a scrub, though you never
know for sure; even thoroughbreds have their off days; new
blood tells; the wornout thoroughbreds lose to the fast young
scrubs.
Said Harmodius the Greek, "Your low birth puts you beneath
me," Iphicrates replying, "The difference between us is this.
My family begins with me. Yours ends with you."

And perhaps I may offer the closing passage of this long poem
entitled *The People, Yes* as having some breath of our American
Democracy in this hour.

The steel mill sky is alive.
The fire breaks white and zigzag
Shot on a sun-metal gloaming.
Man is a long time coming.
Man will yet win.
Brother may yet line up with brother:

This old anvil laughs at many broken hammers.
There are men who can't be bought.
There are women beyond purchase.
The fireborn are at home in fire.
The stars make no noise.
You can't hinder the wind from blowing.
Time is a great teacher.
Who can live without hope?
In the darkness with a great bundle of grief the people march.
In the night, and overhead a shovel of stars for keeps, the people
march:
"Where to? What next?
Where to . . . and what next . . . ?"

32

And these are the sayings of the people. To me they have some of the dark wisdom of the people, some of the deep vitality of the people—forces and motives operating in our way of living today. And they will be going on tomorrow, too.

Chicago Stadium speech

A mass meeting of 24,000 people crowded the Chicago Stadium on the night of June 7, 1941, to hear a program of music and speeches serving the cause of national unity (see page 69).

I hope you will excuse me for getting personal here on this platform tonight. It is a time when every American who prizes his citizenship is getting personal about it. He is asking himself where he stands and he is asking his friends and neighbors where they stand and he is asking some plain questions as to who is for America first and who isn't.

First of all, I might say that along with millions of other American citizens I am not a member of any committee to put us in war or keep us out. I am merely one of millions of political independents who judge the President of the United States by the question of whether he is trying to drag us into a war not our own or whether he is doing the best that can be done for America first by policies and decisions that every day and every hour must change because of changing events.

I have a suspicion, though I am not sure, that my own drifting and shifting on the question of whether we should throw all possible aid to Britain is somewhat the same story of exactly the same kind of drifting and shifting that has taken place in the minds and hearts of millions of Americans.

When the war began in 1939 I was for the strictest of neutrality. I hoped that France and Britain would in the end win the war, though along with this I had a hope that something might happen to all who had a hand in the strangling of democracy in Czechoslovakia and Spain.

The months passed and suddenly the so-called phony war broke into the wildest tornado of mechanized warfare that the human family had ever seen. April, May, June of last year saw one nation after another go down, one, two, three, four, five.

When the Republic of France was crushed in dust and shame I had fear and anxiety. The famous flyer who has quit flying and taken to talking, who is proud that he has ice instead of blood in his veins, he has no more notion of what has kept me awake when I wanted to sleep than a Greenland walrus has of the Negro spiritual "Swing Low, Sweet Chariot." He calls me hysterical. He sees others like me shaken and anxious at what has happened to human freedom under the "New Order" in Europe, under the wave of the future. And he calls them hysterical. He wishes us to understand that he is as cool as a surgeon making a diagnosis.

Very well, then we are hysterical. Very well, then the Declaration of Independence is hysterical, the Constitution of the United States is hysterical, the Bill of Rights is hysterical, the Gettysburg Speech and the Second Inaugural of Abraham Lincoln are hysterical—and the men who fought and died to establish those documents and give them meaning, they were all hysterical.

The famous flyer who has quit flying and taken to talking doesn't know that the hysteria he mentions is in part the same anxiety, the identical deep fear that men politically free have always had when there were forces on the horizon threatening to take away their political freedom.

When the famous flyer's picture was hung on the walls of high schools and colleges thirteen years ago, it was because he symbolized youth ready for risk and adventure, laughter in the face of death. Then, after thirteen years of fine Scandinavian silence, he breaks out in a rash of oratory where his advice to the youth of the country is all in the language of comfort, convenience, safety, feather beds, and breakfast at home with Mother every morning.

When the Republic of France was crushed in dust and shame I was one of millions of Americans who saw that Britain was next on the Nazi timetable. We saw the people of Britain in that hour, by democratic processes, throw out a government that had helped build up Hitler and put in a government that fought him, that for the first time stopped him in his tracks, that for the first time smashed his well-prepared timetable.

I was one of millions of Americans who saw that and drew closer

34

to Britain. We had been saying, "Let Europe fight her own wars—"
And we began changing into saying, "Don't let England, with all
her faults, go down, because after England, America will be first
on the Nazi timetable."

We saw that this was the fight of a people who had certain definite freedoms and rather than lose those freedoms they would as
soon die and be buried and forgotten. Rather than live in a Nazi
world, under the Hitler "New Order," they would prefer to die
fighting and have ever afterward the sweet forgetfulness of death.

What the British have been able to take and stand up under
shows that there is something to their claim that there are things
worse than death.

From month to month with millions of other Americans I saw
the "New Order" in Europe develop under the Nazis and I joined
with thousands of other Americans in saying it was neither an order
nor was it new.

To say this "New Order" is just a lot of spinach, to say it is cockeyed and lousy and it stinks, to say it is cold, cruel, inhuman, stupid,
infamous, doesn't cover the case. There are no words for this particular dream and nightmare of world conquest by a new procedure of organized murder, race hate, national frenzy, systematized
robbery, clockwork exploitation, and inconceivable degradation of
the human person and mind.

Meantime, from month to month the Royal Air Force took to
the air and proved to the world that man for man and machine for
machine they were better than the Nazis and all that the Schicklgruber cohorts had was superior numbers. Along with millions of
Americans, I hated to think of Britain going down because of one
thing, because she didn't have the planes, ships, and armament we
could supply. I was an insignificant unit among the millions whose
talk and feeling made possible the decisive vote in Congress by
which the Lend-Lease Bill was passed.

And now what? Now I have come slowly but surely to a feeling
that unless we see to it that the help we want to give Britain reaches
her shores, we are taking the risk of her going down, and if she
goes down we will have had a hand in it by our neglect and hesitation.

Having taken the British Isles, Hitler will have the Mediterranean, the Near East, Africa. On the continent of Europe he will

have no reckonable opposition in taking Portugal, Switzerland, Sweden, and Finland as part of his "New Order."

From then on we as a country and a people would just begin to get acquainted with how the Nazi machine works toward what it wants. The whole setup in this country would become something else again. It is a process for softening the inside before giving you the works from the outside. It speaks a language of comfort, convenience, safety first, breakfast at home with Mother.

We would either have to take shame after shame piled on us or we would have to fight a war to find out whether we are a self-determining nation of politically free people. In other words, I am one of the millions in this country who believe that if we now let Hitler tell us we can't do this or we can't do that, we will later either again let him tell us what we can or can't do—or in that later time we will take the only course open to us, that of fighting a long and bloody war.

Either way we go as a nation, there is going to be sacrifice and cost. I take the soothing babble of those who try to tell us that Hitler will let us alone as about the same thing the canary was saying to itself just before the cat swallowed it.

And when the famous flyer points me to his father having opposed the last world war, I ask him to read the words of a great statesman who was right there in Congress alongside his father in opposing the war. I refer to United States Senator George W. Norris of Nebraska, who believes it is the will and the vision of the people of this country that we should give aid to Britain, if necessary we should use patrols or convoys or any method that will ensure our planes and armament reaching Britain, and who goes farther and favors the bombing of every industrial plant in Germany producing planes, weapons, and war supplies.

As the wild and terrible scene in Europe zigzags on into new shapes we don't know what our eyes will see, to later fill our hearts with bitter regrets over what we might have done for the sake of America first.

The Battle of Ireland may come with a sudden swoop, by which the counties of Cork, Roscommon, and the rest of the Emerald Isle find themselves in the same stranglehold as the one that has Norway nailed down—we don't know and the dreambooks and the astrologers who read the stars can't tell us. The Battle of Britain may yet include the final resort to chemical warfare and the silent suffocation of civilian populations by poison gas—there is no book of rules worth reading on the subject.

The Nazis have their own way of doing things. They have been stopped at the English Channel because the British have their own way of doing things and because America has been doing one thing after another that the Nazis don't want done and because we did them in spite of the Nazis saying we mustn't do them.

I am for carrying that principle farther. And I am thankful we have a President of the United States who by speech and act has over and over done exactly the thing that the Nazis didn't want done.

If we are going to be a self-determining nation of politically free people, deciding on our own way of life in line with the best traditions of Jefferson and Lincoln, we are either going to throw in our help in Britain's fight now or at a later time we are going to have bitter regrets over what we might have done and failed to do.

I am merely one of millions of watchers trying to read what will be the next twist of a wild and stupendous hurricane of fate. The future is beyond any man's reading. We are moving into an adventure beyond the horizon, and I am taking my chances with those who say "God bless the President of the United States."

The dream that holds us

Speech at Madison Square Garden national-unity meeting under the auspices of the Council for Democracy, August 19, 1941, given over CBS network and WBBM, Chicago, September 9, 1941.

The Norwegian Henrik Ibsen, whose plays are now forbidden to be printed or circulated, forbidden to be read or acted, in the country where he was born and lived and died, once wrote, "There is no word that has been soiled with lies like that word 'love.'"

So we all know there are sacred words that can be soiled with lies. We are all well aware the word "democracy" has been soiled by many liars. Yet every one of us knows fairly well what either the word "love" or the word "democracy" means, even though no one, not even the most learned of men, has ever given us a definition, an explanation of love or democracy that is final and absolute.

When the question is asked, "Why do you favor the democratic system when it holds so much waste, corruption, demagoguery, and other evils?" we answer, "Because we have looked over all the other systems and found that they too have waste, corruption, demagoguery, and other evils, and we take our chances on the democratic system because of what it has that the other systems don't have."

We never know in a democracy whether the next blazing headline event will call for reverence or laughter. In a democracy both deep reverence and a sense of the comic are requisite. Who knows better than we who believe in the democratic system what are its wrongs and shadows? Who knows better than we who are believers in the democratic system the many precise points where it needs study and devotion, patience and prayer and kindly laughter? Yet we cling to it. Yet we fasten our faiths deeper and deeper in it.

Why? Because we have not yet seen a system that works better, because by the very nature of the workings of the democratic system in the long run it gives more people more chances to think, to speak, to decide on their way of life, to shape and change their way of life if they want to, than any other system. It has more give and take, more resilience, ductility, and malleability, more crazy foolishness and more grand wisdom, than any other system. It is never the same two days straight. It is one thing today and another tomorrow. It represents and celebrates man the seeker, man the restless experimenter and adventurer who bets that he will yet bring the Heavenly City into the places where now stand Chicago and Omaha, Philadelphia and Seattle.

Of course we can't answer the question "What is democracy?" smooth and easy like we answer "Where is the Union Station?" or "Which way to the post office?" Yet we know as definitely where democracy is not as we do where the Union Station is not or where the post office is not. It is like Charlie McCarthy being asked, "What do you know about air-conditioning?" and answering, "Well, I have to breathe, don't I?" In a sense and with some allowance we can say that the democratic system is the air-conditioning apparatus by and through which the political rights of free men function.

Under no other system can a man be so many different kinds of a fool—and get away with it—and get paid for it. So long as he isn't interfering with other fools he always has the alibi "This is a free country, ain't it?" Personal freedom, a wide range of individual expression, a complete respect for the human mind and the human personality—this is the ideal of the democratic system. In all the literature, the documents of democracy, you can find this respect, this hope, this attitude of reverence toward the fullest possible flowering of each human personality. President Lincoln enjoyed quoting the Irishman who said, "In this country every man is as good as the next one and for the matter of that a little better."

We are men, not angels—that is sure. Also we hope we are men and not mice. And sometimes we feel like mere worms of the dust, doing the best we can, moving a little soil of the earth from where it was to where it will be.

Never before was there such a world storm and never before was any one man or any one captain of men so insignificant before the sweep and the immensity of the storm. We have no time now for reading the epics of the past, because living men are fighting vaster epics on every continent. We would not listen to what any stone Sphinx of Egypt might choose to break his long silence with, because we doubt whether we could hear it for the noise of the droning air squadrons overhead. How many years the storm will howl before it goes down no man knows. We do know—and this we know deep and sure—that only terrific struggle and bloody fighting can now decide—that the next world order, including this Western Hemisphere, must not and shall not be dictated by monsters who divide the human family into Nazis, Nazi slaves, and democratic swine.

Ibsen knew who and what he meant when he said no word had been soiled with lies like the word "love." We know who and what we mean when we say there are those who soil the word "democracy" with lies. They are haters of political freedom for all men, scorners of religious freedom, race-haters, propagandists who believe they stand a chance of adding one hate movement to another till they have enough hates to discredit the democratic system so that the people will turn in desperation to something else, anything else. This has happened in other countries. And in this country these propagandists, serving alien causes though some of them are American-born, have found themselves checked and counterchecked by several forces, movements, organizations, whose work will go on. So long as it is needed it will go on.

War? Who wants war? Nobody. Only fools and idiots want war, only Nazi believers in the biological necessity of war. Yet sometimes the issue comes before a nation of people: Will you fight a war now, or would you deliberately choose another later inevitable war, another inevitable bloody struggle for the sake of not losing what we have now? Or would you rather go into a pleasant sleeping sickness and come out of it a paralyzed and punch-drunk stumblebum, as nations go, because of economic pressure from the outside and seething propaganda on the inside intended to soften us as a nation and a people? This last has happened. We have seen it happen. The pleasant sleeping sickness sometimes came from propaganda, apathy, and slack faith. Against these we throw our counterpropaganda, carrying on around such questions as What is this democratic system we live under? Can we help you to understand how and why it is in danger from the inside and the outside?

The Nazis have their own way of doing things. They have been stopped at the English Channel because the British have their own way of doing things. They have been stopped in their march to Moscow because the Russians have their own way of doing things. They are going to feel more and more the pressure of the American way of doing things the Nazis don't want done, and we shall do these things in spite of the Nazis saying we mustn't do them.

The dream that holds us will never come true to a perfect finish. The Man of Galilee once told his fellow fishermen "Be ye perfect," knowing well that they could never be perfect but knowing that they would go farther and find more peculiar treasures if they dreamed and tried to reach a perfect finish. And everything of this present hour considered, I am joining my hopes and taking my chances with those American citizens and those believers in democracy who say in this hour "God bless the President of the United States."

Wings for Norway

Speech broadcast over NBC, Chicago, April 18, 1942, and later given in Carnegie Hall, New York, June 13, 1942.

Most of you are aware that the country lying next to Sweden— people having a blood kinship with the Swedish people—is in the hands of an aggressor who came into Norway in a sneak attack, like the one of the Japanese at Pearl Harbor. The freedom of the people of Norway is gone—the independence of Norway as a nation is gone. Religious freedom, political freedom, personal freedom, is gone. The labor organizations have seen their funds and bank accounts taken away, their journals and newspapers told definitely what they can print or not print, their trade-union leaders and their most active organizers and believers in a free labor movement—all of them, by the hundreds, either sent to concentration camps or some of them, without trial or public hearing, stood up before a firing squad and shot, in a Nazi strategy of terror aimed at making shivering and cowering slaves out of men once free.

To the bishops and pastors of the Church in Norway have gone the Nazi edicts: Say Yes to what we tell you—and to these edicts, the answers of the bishops and pastors have been either No—and again No or "We have never learned to say Yes the way you want us to say Yes."

From month to month, while this procedure, aimed at making the Norwegians a slave people, has gone on, the Swedish people have been moved more and more deeply. From month to month, as inhuman deeds, atrocities almost beyond words, have gone on, the Swedish people have become more desperate as to their own preparations for avoiding the fate of Norway. From month to month, expressions have widened, until they include voices from practically all groups—spokesmen such as the Prime Minister, the Minister of War; and William, the King's younger son, a brother to the Crown Prince, made the declaration that Sweden will fight, if invaded, and that she will use all she has to fight for her freedom and her independence as a nation. The leading journals have made these declarations in great detail—there is no mistaking what they mean.

The Swedish Labor Congress last September, after a Nazi firing squad had shot to death two of the best-known representatives of the labor movement of Norway, passed resolutions of sympathy for their Norwegian brothers, with bitter denunciations of the needless cruelties of the Nazi regime.

And we Americans of Swedish descent who are alive to history in the making before our eyes—we feel a call of blood. We cannot look with cold indifference on the present scene in the Scandinavian

41

Peninsula. The very latest dispatches tell us of Jewish refugees from Germany being admitted into Sweden—and we are well aware that this is one more act of disobedience to the wishes of the Nazi regime in Berlin. The latest news further tells us of Communists laying away their red flags and marching publicly with the Social Democrats, this being only one sign in the many of Swedish national unity, good to look at.

The present plans for the contributions of Swedish-blooded Americans to pay for the training planes of Norwegian youth now in Canada, are partly a token and a sign of our feelings, a practical contribution to Norway, one of the twenty-six United Nations. Norwegian youth in Canada have nearly all of them made a dangerous journey across the North Sea to Britain and then across the Atlantic—or else by that long winding route across Asia and the Pacific Ocean. They have in their blood the deathless hate of free men for despots. They want to fly—they want to fight—if we give them transport and weapons, they will show the world a saga of valor and endurance. These boys, all they want is a chance to go up in the sky and flirt with death for the sake of freedom and independence for Norway. We, of course, will be doing nothing heroic— we will only be helping youth of heroic blood to fight for their homeland. This enterprise of Wings for Norway comes out of American soil and air and has no official connection with any government. Until some months ago Federal laws would not let us do as we are now doing in raising money. The answer now is to raise the funds that will guarantee the Norwegian youth the training planes they need. The big word is "Send those boys in Canada the training planes they are calling for."

Tribute to Bill Mahon and the Amalgamated

On September 17, 1942, the golden anniversary, the fiftieth year of age, was celebrated by the Amalgamated Association of Street, Electric Railway and Motor Coach Employes of America. This was my tribute to the organization and its president in a Blue Network broadcast.

Today—now—day and night—in all weathers—the Amalgamated Association membership of 125,000 is under a heavier load of work and care than any time in its fifty years, hauling more passengers, more riders on more kinds of wheels, taking them from their homes to the plants, shops, factories where guns, planes, bombs, and the stuff of war are being shaped for global conflict.

The Amalgamated Association of Street, Electric Railway and Motor Coach Employes of America is a peculiar organization on its fiftieth birthday. It is one of the labor unions of this country that has a good name. With labor—with management—with the public that uses transportation—it has a good name. Among street-railway workers, before the Amalgamated came, those workers took whatever was handed them and had no voice or recourse except that a man was free to quit his job. In those days they had, to use the words of Bill Mahon, who was starting to help them organize themselves, "wrongs and mistreatment, long hours and small pay." The driver of the horsecar sometimes worked eighteen hours in a day. No horse was allowed to work longer than four hours a day.

That was fifty years ago. In those fifty years much has happened. What in this field is the biggest single change that has come? Well, we probably won't go far wrong to say that the change is one in the human heart, the human spirit, that the change has come to both labor and management, that where in the first days of organization and negotiation there was "bad feeling" throughout the whole industry there is now by contrast "good feeling." It is possible that the entire history and development of the Amalgamated has its lesson for this hour.

To the extent that there is now *good* feeling instead of *bad,* it is due to the extent that on both sides, labor and management, there is a sense of responsibility to each other. When either side tries to get all it can and keep all it gets, when both sides are inflexible and there is no spirit of accommodation and basic respect, then there is certain to come a form of retribution, a mean, hard pay-off of strife instead of peace, of suspicion instead of trust.

Those who think they can have freedom without discipline, liberty without responsibility, they might try talking with Bill Mahon, who has been places in strife and negotiation. As the president of the Amalgamated for fifty years he has a good name for keeping contracts, for going out of his way to check and repress contract-breakers. I have known Mahon and the Amalgamated leadership for thirty years—and if anybody thinks I am saying they are a set of angels with nice white wings they had better go roll a peanut

43

around the corner and think again. What I am saying and stressing is that in this time of storm and in the more stormy days to come, human betterment and the dignity of the common man are not going to lose out if there is enough of decency and plain dealing, a readiness to fight against inequity and injustice—along with a sense of responsibility and a spirit of accommodation.

These are qualities that mark and distinguish the Amalgamated and William D. Mahon, the snow of eighty-one winters whitening on his venerable head, a philosopher, a humorist, a spokesman for plain workingmen and their families, a friendly man with a lighted face, a man of rare executive ability who has seen many millions of dollars pour through the treasury of his organization *without mis-handling,* a man whose personal wants and needs are easily met.

When the editor of the Amalgamated monthly magazine asked me for a little message for their fiftieth anniversary, for auld acquaintance' sake I sent him this:

"So the Amalgamated now comes fifty years old. 'Well and good,' say those familiar with its record, with the main trend of its policies and programs. It is an occasion to give salutations to Bill Mahon, his able leadership, his scrupulous accounting, his sagacity and plain ways of living that might to advantage have more and better imitators here and there in the American labor movement."

Meditation at Arlington

Broadcast on the G-E Mazda Lamp "Hour of Charm," February 7, 1943.

The shadow of Abraham Lincoln spreads far—far enough to reach and touch in either sunshine or moonlight any place in his country kept sacred with meanings for the American people. His shadow lingers and the implications of his words haunt the national capital of Washington, D.C., and Pennsylvania Avenue and the clouds of misgiving and the rainbows of hope over the Potomac and the marble shrine at Arlington where in bright weather or blowing sheets of rain day and night the sentries keep watch as though over an altar of freedom where only the light-minded and those soft of faith have no hope for tomorrow.

Each of the Allied nations of 1918 dedicated a memorial to its unknown soldier. Here at Arlington on the Potomac the American people have their tomb of their Unknown Soldier and the years have gone by while the living sentinels kept watch over the bones and memory of a soldier whose name is lost while his dust is kept.

A great war has its hundreds of heroes whose names stand out, blazed high on the public records. But they are only a handful and often what they did would not have been possible except for the hundreds of thousands, even the millions, who hammered out weapons, raised and transported food, passed along ammunition, wrote letters sending messages of faith, love, and hope—these anonymous ones too vast for the record, these and the loyal soldier who does his plain, humdrum duty—they and the Unknown Soldier belong to each other.

What if the sleeping one there at Arlington tonight should wake and speak to these anonymous ones? He might have any one of a thousand questions to ask, and perhaps not least would be "Wasn't the war we fought supposed to be a war to end war?"

And perhaps someone with a solemn face and a voice not free from grief and guilt would answer: "Yes, but when peace came we didn't know how to keep the peace. We made mistakes and we hope not to make those same mistakes this time. Some of us are praying, thinking, hoping, struggling. It looks like your war didn't end. This is the same war. The peace wasn't a peace. This time the answers are different. Maybe this time it will work out."

Today a great host holds a deep wish and a fathomless prayer that never again shall the nations of the earth make war. Now again often comes the cry that it would be wonderful if mankind could make this the last war.

Perhaps in this war there will be no betrayal of the Unknown Soldier who fights it and gives to it his all—even his life. Perhaps we have found the will and vision. It is a possibility (who knows?) that we have built our last tomb for the Unknown Soldier. Time will tell—time and our will and our vision.

45

ONCE-A-WEEK PIECES FOR THE PAPERS

"We can't see that far"

April 6, 1941

A favorite game thinkers play in these days is what you might call Alternatives. In case Britain does this and Germany does that, then you will see dese, dose, and dem—and from there you go to various points of the compass, depending on who plays the ace of spades or throws six sixes.

In this connection we may look at World War the First and take a little counsel that goes for now. Some of the shrewdest and ablest minds of the time took a hand in this game of Alternatives—and what they had to say then is not the basis of their excellent reputations now, including intellects as diverse as Woodrow Wilson and Nikolai Lenin.

Three events in the First World War came suddenly and came with such high decision that as soon as they happened all the predictors had to revise their predictions. Each stargazer had to fix him up a new horoscope. The numerologists had to take new numbers and guess again and try to guess better. The thinkers playing the game of Alternatives had to readjust their ifs, ands, and buts.

There was France, a victim of corruption, bribery, and conspiracy—a procedure Hitler now terms "softening." Then Clemenceau was put in as dictator. His purges and reorganizations earned him the name of Savior of France. Until he stepped in, France in one hour looked gone.

There was the time Germany had the Allies worn and sagging. "France bled white" was the descriptive phrase used. And about then the people of the United States elected, by a narrow margin, a President whose supporters urged votes for him on the brief and sweet explicit plea "He kept us out of war." The predictors had something to think about when the President so elected carried his country straight into the war and by that action gave the Allies their victory over Germany.

The point here is not whether that President was right or wrong in so doing. The point is that when that event came it was sudden, world-shaking, decisive, and nobody could have foretold a year or two years before that it would happen. It developed out of factors hard to weigh and measure. It arose out of a fog of imponderables where one man's guess was as good as another's.

Then there was the heavy and unforeseen smoke and flame known as the Russian Revolution. It came—and lasted. The Czar of Russia had entered the war with eight million soldiers, in man power the largest army in the world. With that many armed men the Czar might not win the war, but he would certainly have enough of a bodyguard to keep him and his government going. The country was backward in industry and its people submissive— so it was said—and when revolution came in Europe it would come thundering up somewhere else in a country where revolutionary parties were more thorough and methodical.

Yet the revolution came—from Petrograd to Vladivostok. So Germany had to fight only on the one Western front, no longer on two fronts. This was the least foreseen of all the terrific events that shaped the deep channels of the war. The aftermath of it is one of the foggiest incalculables of the present war.

What will Russia do if this or that happens?

This is one of the toughest enigmas on which those who play the game of Alternatives bump their hard and serious heads.

I have done some fooling with alternatives myself, trying to figure out who will get what if dese, dose, and dem arrive. I could write a book on alternatives—and nobody who is anybody would care.

If and when Hitler brings his blitzkrieg to Britain and the greatest and most decisive battle affecting ways and systems of human life on this planet is fought, will the President of the United States take his chances and throw the American fleet in? Nobody knows.

The President himself now says, "We can't see that far."

For a while we must drift

One reason why I understand some of my isolationist friends is because I know their language and why they talk like they talk.

Only a little more than a year ago I was using their same line of talk.

Even while Hitler was taking Denmark and Norway, Holland and Belgium, I believed there was a probability, a fighting chance, that once more France and Britain would be deadlocked in a long war like the last one—and the pattern of the war might take the same shape as the last one.

Chamberlain was still Prime Minister of Britain, Daladier at the helm in France, and the sickness and shame of the Munich four-power pact still evident.

The lassitude, stupidity, and shame involved in France and Britain handing over Czechoslovakia to Hitler—the infamy of France and Britain letting Loyalist Spain go down under the tanks and bombing planes of Hitler and Mussolini—I could not forget these—I remember them now and I hope to go on remembering.

Then France went down.

Then France came under the clammy paws of the Nazis.

Then Britain threw out her reactionaries and stood up and fought and took punishment and did a thing that amazed the world.

For the first time the Hitler timetable was wrecked.

The English Channel, the R.A.F., and the fleet stopped and held the swiftest and best co-ordinated war machine that had ever taken the field.

Then slowly across weeks and months the British defense kept on. And I found myself from day to day drifting, my blood and brain saying things they had not said before.

Day by day came the questions "If Hitler takes Britain, what kind of a world will it be for us of the United States to live in? Does any man know? If Britain goes down, Hitler takes over un-occupied France, Spain, Switzerland, Sweden, Finland, Yugoslavia, Greece, Turkey, with Italy and Spain as yes-saying partners—and why not? Who is to stop him? Then what? Who will give me a picture of what then follows for this country of ours?

"Who knows how long Soviet Russia then would keep certain oil lands and areas near Germany which Hitler has termed a 'rich bread basket'? Are not the Nazis a school, a cult, and a philosophy vastly different from that of the Kaiser and the Hohenzollerns? Have they not, as Cardinal Mundelein said, taken the children away from the teaching of the Church? And have they not active spokesmen and defenders in North and South America? And would not these voices be louder and more active than ever if Britain should fall and Hitler take over Europe?

"And what program of human betterments would have much of a chance while we operated as an isolated nation, so armed and so dedicated to national existence that it would not be long before we would have to fight alone a full-sized war or be one more country saying yes-yes to those who wish to regulate our national housekeeping for our own good?"

So I drifted along with those who favored all possible aid to Britain, short of war. From this point on I did more drifting. I believed that when we sent those fifty overage destroyers to Britain we were taking a chance. It spoke our wish that Britain should win enough of her war to still be standing as a nation. It was so near to a declaration of war on Nazi Germany that the point was merely technical as to whether we were in a war or not.

Now what? Now whither am I drifting? Now I find myself approving the war of nerves that President Roosevelt is using on the Nazis. He has given millions of white men, regimented into slavery on the continent of Europe, the hope that arms, planes, and supplies from this country may in the end break Hitler's power. Does this mean we send another A.E.F. to Europe? I doubt it, for several reasons. For a year to come—and so much can happen in a year—we will do well to equip all the men now over there anxious to have the use of all we can send. Furthermore, if there should be a call from over there for men, I believe the American volunteer is not extinct. From among our enlisted men, and outside, there could be had in sixty days, I would guess, a half-million young fighting wildcats. And in modern mechanized warfare this half-million would be equivalent to more than the A.E.F., each man in front combat service requiring forty mechanics, transport, and service and supply men to keep him going.

And there is nothing unusual, unique, or out of the ordinary about my driftings. At times I felt something almost uncanny about the way my driftings were registered in the periodic shifts and gains and losses of the two leading polls of public opinion.

Also I am well aware that the foregoing is an inadequate statement; that what I have tried to say here briefly would require a book with many shadings and modulations. But this is a time when writers ought to try to put on paper for their readers those things moving as shadows in their hearts—and which they are speaking frankly in talk with friends and neighbors.

I agree with my isolationist friends, the handsome Doc Hutchins, the sweet and unimpeachable Lillian Gish, the horselaughing Oscar Ameringer, that if and when we save Britain there will be terrific headaches over what kind of peace is possible to negotiate. They think they know Roosevelt is leading us into war and national suicide. I think they know very little—and maybe next to nothing—about what the picture will be a year from now, even a month from now.

I wish I knew more than I know. I go on drifting. The nation drifts. It is written for a while we must drift. By drifting I mean guessing as to where the national ship of state is going and what will happen to it in the end. Just now I am willing to throw in everything to save Britain. Beyond that I agree with anyone who has a headache.

Virginia Woolf's personal decision

April 20, 1941

Virginia Woolf left her home in England near the sea, and went for a walk. Her steps led her to the bank of a tidal river. She walked out into the sea till she became a part of the river and the sea. She was tired of the land. And being tired of time, too, she turned her back on it and walked into a timeless beyond named eternity. What she wrote in a little farewell note to her husband about why she was never coming back to him nor to anyone else on the land—this last testimony was not made public and it is better so because it is nobody's business.

Virginia Woolf knew what she was doing better than some who believe it easy to judge her to be one more easygoing suicide. For the nice strange, incalculable quality of her mind we may go read *Mrs. Dalloway*. It is dreamy and plays beautiful tricks with the human mind.

You don't know where you go from here. At moments the nonsense and thin airy fantasy is not ridiculous but sublime. The British Empire—her special and personal British Empire—floats and sways as a bundle of toy balloons. She was tall, gaunt, strong, resourceful, and could have outargued anyone who might have pleaded with her that she didn't know what she was doing.

Naturally, I am not here making a case in favor of suicide. If I favored suicide as a method of escape I would pick a suitable quiet and starlit night on the eastern shore of Lake Michigan, walk out into the black waters, slanting my eyes toward the haze of lights over Chicago, and then go on walking till my hat floated.

I am merely saying that in this hour of the world, the British Empire, and the smoke and stench over Europe, I hesitate about inquiring into the motives of Virginia Woolf. I can't help wondering what a book she would have written about why she wanted to belong to the sea forever, to be no more on the land.

She understood anyone of baffling ways. In *The Waves*, written more than ten years ago, she had Rhoda say: "That is my face in the looking-glass behind Susan's shoulder—that face is my face. But I will duck behind her to hide it, for I am not here. I have no face. Other people have faces; Susan and Jinny have faces; they are here. Their world is the real world. The things they lift are heavy. They say Yes, they say No; whereas I shift and change. . . ."

She wrote an imaginary biography. In a family castle in the days of Queen Elizabeth a child, a youth, a young nobleman, begins growing up, ending finally as a modern woman in our own times.

"This ivory dome of mine," Virginia Woolf seemed often to imply, "has pavilions and people who forget they belong to the regular and established order—they don't belong!" She was long-necked and lanky, having a touch in head and face of Rossetti's "The Blessed Damozel."

Why she walked into tidal waters of the sea for a fade-out no one can tell. My reverence for her mind and heart goes on. She represented things money cannot buy nor children be taught.

We shall hear, for a time, perhaps, of dark moods, in tone not unlike the letter of Sir James Mackintosh during the Napoleonic

Wars to a friend in Vienna: "I believe, like you, in a resurrection, because I believe in the immortality of civilization, but when, and by whom, and in what form, are questions which I have not the sagacity to answer.

"A dark and stormy night, a black series of ages may be prepared for our posterity, before the dawn that opens the more perfect day. Who can tell how long that fearful night may be before the dawn of a brighter to-morrow? The race of man may reach the promised land, but there is no assurance that the present generation will not perish in the wilderness."

Note: This piece was written before her husband made public Virginia Woolf's farewell note to him reading:

"I feel certain that I am going mad again. I feel we can't go through another of those terrible times. And I shan't recover this time."

Readers of Virginia Woolf will be interested to have this further explanation from Mr. Woolf: "She had had a mental breakdown about twenty-five years ago; the old symptoms began to return about three weeks before she took her life, and she thought that this time she would not recover. Like everyone else, she felt the general strain of the war, and the return of her illness was no doubt partly due to that strain. But the words of her letter and everything which she ever said prove that she took her life not because she could not 'carry on,' but because she thought she was going mad again and would not this time recover."

Neg Cochran and other independents

April 27, 1941

We have heard of independent editors and publishers. Negley D. Cochran of Toledo, Ohio, peace to his ashes, strictly belonged. His face had somewhat the look of Ben Franklin's and he had Franklin's habit of examining himself and finding that he was, like most other men, a sinner.

He trained as a young reporter under David R. Locke, alias

Petroleum Vesuvius Nasby, one of Lincoln's favorite authors, and could shift from the earnest and solemn into horseplay, satire, and pleasant mockery when his system needed it.

Once he spoke to Old Man Scripps about certain human improvements he thought possible, the old man snorting, "Neg, you're always talking about human improvements, but I tell you the human race is ninety-eight per cent brute and two per cent human and you'll be a thousand years making it one per cent more human."

He liked to tell of hearing others quote the Old Man, "That damned Neg Cochran is the only man in the organization who tells me where to get off."

Once on the old *Chicago Day Book* he told me of a constant reader asking him, "What do you do when you get off on the wrong foot?" and his answering, "I back up and start off on the other foot."

The independent human mind, going its own way hoping and praying that time will prove it right, is always worth study. I am still studying some words reported to me as coming from a rarely independent mind.

The friend who reports these words has for a long time known Governor Murray D. Van Wagoner of Michigan. And about mid-April he noted carefully these words from the Governor of the automotive state:

"I'm going to be a one-term governor and I don't give a damn. Ford hates me. He's out to get me. And the CIO is going to hate me before I'm done. I'm going to make them go back to work and I'm going to open that plant."

This, of course, was a case where the opening of the plant was the first consideration. Each party to the dispute had its arguments. The Governor took his stand on the big and main point that the arguments could go on while the plant operated. If in the future he loses his shirt, politically speaking, he will have the satisfaction that he helped national defense production get going and served his country well, though at personal cost.

Every executive or administrator, who must regularly say Yes or No on this and that, understands how seldom it is that he has a choice of deciding between two claimants, one of them perfectly right and the other perfectly wrong.

56

This hardly ever happens. The decision must be, in nearly all cases, in favor of one who is partly right and partly wrong as against another who is also partly right and partly wrong. Therefore the good executive often wins merely the ill will and the muttered razzberry from both sides.

President Lincoln believed his man General John M. Schofield was doing a pretty good job in running the State of Missouri in 1863 and 1864. He sent Schofield the advice:

"If both factions, or neither, shall abuse you, you will probably be about right. Beware of being assailed by one and praised by the other."

The national weather now is a good deal like it was when Lincoln gave one of his administrators that advice.

A long war or short?

May 4, 1941

There was the man who fell out of a window on the top floor of a skyscraper, and as he passed each floor on the way down called out, "All right so far!" That was a made-up story. Along with it we might consider the actual fact of two New York businessmen boarding a train in Connecticut, two friends and commuters. One said, "You are looking brighter than I have seen you for weeks," and the other, "Yes, I am feeling better than I have for months. I have decided it is going to be a long war."

Perhaps for those who like their wars short and convenient there is no consolation in the horizons to be scanned with expectant binoculars. The smoke gets in your eyes—now or later. And whenever the smoke does drift away and you can see clearly, you will be hearing things dark with fury. The eyes or the ears—or both—had better learn to take it. Not necessarily to eat it and like it—but to take it.

The man analyzed himself. He found a short war wasn't easy to think about. But a long war called for his reserves of patience and calm and humor. So he felt better.

Like you, my dear reader, if you are still with me, I wish I had the information, data, and judgment—or the deep dark clairvoyance—to tell how long the war will last. In so saying, I am considering those who believe we can keep out of war by letting Britain go down.

Suppose it should happen that next summer or fall Hitler and Göring and Goebbels and Hess ride through the ashes and rubble of what was the city of London. Suppose they hold exercises in London with blaring bands, parading Storm Troopers, radio broadcasts to the world, formally and ceremonially taking over the British Isles and the authority and domains of the British Empire.

That would be the end of the war? Would it? Or only an interlude, a short breathing spell?

We read the speeches, writings, doctrines of the Nazi leaders. We follow the zigzags of their past. We look at the controlling minds and personalities. And who has any faith in any peace to last even if and when the Nazis should take the British Isles? Can any country be named that has worked out a treaty or an understanding with Berlin, as of now, that has any operating trust or security?

The British Isles gone, Ireland follows, Switzerland follows, Sweden, Finland, Spain, Portugal. And we would be sitting pretty—yes, we would keep out of the war—with our fingers crossed—with our battle wagons and planes ready—waiting for a war sure to come.

For a long time now, a long time as struggle, bitter misunderstandings, suffering are measured, we shall know fog and smoke. By wish or will or national policy, we can keep out of the present war? If so, what of the one to come just after, the war to dispute would-be world conquerors who want to take us in their stride?

That particular war could be evaded, avoided, postponed, only by our becoming a little turtle nation saying "Yes, yes" over and over to a new world authority speaking a language we have never learned.

Only by Yankee Doodle becoming a pathetic yes-man or the American Eagle turning into a scared parrot repeating what is nice and safe to say, only so can the United States keep out of either the present war or the one to be offered just after.

That's my guess. And you, dear reader, of course are entitled to your guess.

Some of us understand completely that Connecticut commuter saying he now feels better and explaining, "I have decided it is going to be a long war."

Murderers of books

May 11, 1941

In a Library of Congress hall a peculiar little memorial program was given. And why not? Why shouldn't a living library, representing a nation and a people building an arsenal of democracy, memorialize certain books?

Over Nazified Europe these books have been put to death. With grimaces, jeers, maledictions, these books have been burned, banned, published as dead, cremated, and the epitaphs well chosen.

Einstein, the German Jew, the mathematician with a hair-trigger imagination, his works are verboten, three strikes and out. The little song of the Lorelei by Heinrich Heine, the wit, the lyric writer whose bittersweet is better than straight sweet, you can't read him nor sing him except behind closed doors with an eye and ear ready for the Gestapo, who might have heard about your personal taste in literature and music.

Karel Capek, the Czech who had something on the ball in drama and whimsy, who invented Rossum's Universal Robots, who put an ant colony on the stage as a forecast of the "New Order" and the wave of the future, who died in part of sheer heartbreak, not wanting to live any more after Czechoslovakia died its political death preparatory to dying other deaths—Capek is verboten, nix, his books legally and by decree dead as a dead mackerel in the moonshine.

And the living Thomas Mann, who got out while the going was good, when they read him in the original German as once published in what was then his country—when in Berlin, Bremen, Breslau, Munich they read Mann—they do it in secret and hide the forbidden book where they hope no informer might find it.

Many more authors and books could be named. The theory of the authorities is that these books are washed up and destroyed for all time, or at least a thousand years, the time limit calculated by the Leader.

Maybe this is so. Maybe not. Maybe this is partly what the shooting is about. At least in this United States of America an organization has well under way the reprinting and restoration of every book of permanent value officially destroyed, purged, assassinated, in Europe. These books have crossed the Atlantic Ocean for a rebirth and a resurrection, available in the original languages for any one the wide earth over who wishes to read them.

Among those who now favor all-out aid to Britain are men and women who can't think of human freedom except as it touches the human mind. They look at what has happened to the human mind in Nazified Europe and see it as a vast atrocity.

To kill the books of Heine and Capek is a more dirty and bloody form of human murder than leading handcuffed authors out to have their heads hacked off by an official axman with an official napkin for wiping the gore off the edge of the ax blade.

Why the murder of a book is worse than the murder of a man you may find argued well in the works of John Milton who is dead and Archibald MacLeish who is alive.

There are Irish books that will go down if and when Britain goes down and Ireland with her. There are Swiss, Swedish, and Finnish books that will meet the deaths now being given to Norwegian books in the latest Nazi bans in Oslo—if and when Britain goes down.

The "New Order" in Europe requires death, as public policy and surgical procedure, for all outspoken believers in freedom—along with death for the books of such believers.

One Washington correspondent quotes a church dignitary as charging that the majority of the 800,000 prisoners in German concentration camps are Catholics. This is an estimate that cannot be verified. What needs no verification is the dank and clammy fact that in the Nazi realm every book that advocates freedom of conscience and worship has been called in, made verboten, and when seized burned to a nice black and gray crisp that stinks.

It is well to say 1941 is not 1914 or 1915. The conflicting aims are not the same. The atrocities are different. The possible consequences are different. The time for crossing the Atlantic Ocean has been reduced since 1927, when the top record was thirty-three hours, to the month of March in 1941, when a bomber flew from Newfoundland to Britain in nine hours, a later flight making it in seven and a half hours.

60

Mental anguish, sincere people, and a mother with four sons

May 18, 1941

One eminent capitalist makes public a letter telling the country he favors all possible help for Britain. He reaches this decision, he tells us, at great cost of "mental anguish."

Plenty of us believe him. The phrase "mental anguish" is good and correct. Each of us, as citizens, must decide whether we want Britain to go down, whether Britain is worth saving, whether our help is actually needed for Britain, whether all the help we might now be able to send would be enough to save Britain, whether the aftermath of saving Britain would take us into world leadership and committals dizzy to think about.

A living ex-President of the United States tells us he is sure the English Channel and the British defenses can stop any Nazi invasion. He is contradicted by a famous aviator who swears by what he has seen of armament and planes in Europe that Britain had the war lost when she began it.

The ex-President does show in his words that he has had some degree of "mental anguish" in arriving at his judgments. The famous aviator, however, wishes us to know that he is not like other men he sees in the country who are victims of "hysteria."

While others have become lost in hysteria, he assures us, his own approach is that of the cool surgeon who performs a diagnosis without emotion. In his case, if we take his word for it, there is no "mental anguish."

As someone said when Ossip Gabrilowitsch went through perfect execution of a difficult concerto, "Oh! if he would just make one mistake!"

Or he might for a few moments behave like General Grant when a committee of Congressmen stepped into his headquarters tent and asked, "How are you going to take Richmond?"

The General lit his cigar once, twice, three times, and several times more. When finally Grant's mind had arrived at the answer he would give the committee, he quit striking match after match. He wasn't hysterical. He was slightly perturbed and mentally alive.

The mental anguish of the capitalist aforementioned had back-

61

grounds—a wife who hates war and has contributed to peace movements, several sturdy sons of draft age, a church pastor of unusual sincerity whose mental anguish has led him to a viewpoint opposed to his church member.

So it goes. Here and there friendships have gone on the rocks, families desolated in arguments and accusations. This is the turmoil of a nation finding itself, a country zigzagging toward an adventure beyond the horizon.

From a Wisconsin woman comes a letter. She has no murmur, only a dark and inexplicable gladness that two of her four boys are going to army camps in June. Both are Yale graduates and had their plans, which had to be discarded. And, she writes: "Another son the government has refused to take because he is doing what they feel is important work in engineering. My oldest boy was born deaf and is unable to serve. Four sons—my life and only contribution—one needs a sense of more than humor these days to keep heads up. The British War Relief keeps me going twelve or fourteen hours each day—that and books."

She is for war—all-out efforts to save Britain. And after that? Then her word is the same as the many of us, "We can't see that far."

Nations have been outfought—and outthought

May 25, 1941

Thomas Edison, the thinker, had suspicions. Mainly he himself was the suspect. By going along just as though nothing was happening in his mind, he would suddenly spring out from behind somewhere straight at himself—and so finding what? Finding precisely what he suspected, that nothing original was happening in his mind, that he was merely thinking he was thinking.

Often he wrote it or spoke to others of the rarest thing in the world, a man thinking, a man actually breaking away from what others tell him to think, from what the past and his own habits and inclinations tell him to think, and then by a combination of faith and works moving on to where he has an original idea and can prove it.

When a public-opinion pollster asks a man "What do you think?"

he usually means "What would you like to have other people think you think?" And many of us are well acquainted with the fellow who enjoys his positive opinions and sort of luxuriates in what he believes he knows for sure. And this fellow could be properly polled with the question "What are your prejudices?"

The professor had something on the ball in his confession "When I am not engaged in thought I am employed in recovering from its effects."

A faint violet smoke of high import is attached to the historian who lighted his pipe with the casual and unqualified proposition "The great events of the world take place in the brain."

Once in the city of Dayton, Ohio, I had a little talk with a man who with his brother used to run a bicycle repair shop. There was nothing loud about him. He was quiet-spoken, just a little shy. And on my asking him he told me a little about one of the greatest events of the world that had taken place in the brains of himself, Orville Wright, and his brother, Wilbur Wright.

First of all, in building a machine that would lift itself off the ground and stay in the air, with everything under control, they had to be sure about measurements of wind velocity. They made a few tests and found that the tables and figures existing had mistakes and could lead to broken necks. So they designed wind tunnels and worked out their own reliable measurements as to wings and wind pressure.

After many experiments they took off and stayed up and came down safe and alive. The whole world heard about it and came to them for flying lessons. They embodied the wonder that was never lost on Tom Edison—man thinking.

Orville Wright, when I left him, was still pondering on where we go from here. He and his brother were surprised to learn they could prove as to air transport "The faster you go, the less power you need." And he was puzzled and meditating aloud on the hidden forces lying beyond that word "attraction," saying: "What is 'attraction'? When will we learn 'why' things go when they go? What and where is the power?"

Edison once wrote "Look at the moon—it winks at the ignorance of the world." He meant that for the realm of science and invention and for the areas of politics and human relationships.

In an hour of national crisis any citizen might be asking himself "What do I do when I think?" In the present argument there is a minority of fanatics and ghost dancers on both sides. Also at each end of the argument are thinkers ready and willing to admit that either course of policy, intervention or isolation, has terrible risk—and neither side can prove which course has the greater risk.

The decisions President Roosevelt must make require him to think his way deep into what the mind of the nation is considering and what the will and vision of the country are ready to fight for. This is a heavy load. Events press. He says Yes here, No there, Not-yet further beyond. No precedents are at hand to guide him. He has merely the choice of war now to save Britain or war later to save an encircled United States of America.

Meantime, he must listen and consider the points presented by the honest advocates, the clean and sincere partisans who believe that by keeping out of the present war we can live in armed peace having nonaggression understandings with a Nazi regime controlling Europe, the British Isles, Africa, the Mediterranean, the Near East—and a Japan that would want nothing under the "New Order" except control of the Pacific.

The professor was correct. "The great events of the world take place in the brain." Nations have been outfought. And they have been outthought.

The kalsominer is still correct

June 1, 1941

Orators, preachers, speakers on solemn occasions, and columnists with a sense of timing often make use of the line "This too shall pass away."

As a precious line, it goes back to the king who hung up a bag of sweepstakes gold. The bag would go to any philosopher, hobo, or kalsominer who should come through with a line of wisdom, a phrase of savvy, so good, so sure, so guaranteed, that no matter what happened to who or what, at any time in a thousand years or ten thousand years, the line would stand true.

The idea was that whether you read the line today or your great-grandson's great-grandson's great-grandson reads it centuries after you, either of you could step back, and holding your left ear with

64

a contemplative thumb and forefinger, quietly murmur, "Ain't it the truth!"

And the prize-winner, the kalsominer to whom the king handed the sweepstakes gold—he won with the line "This too shall pass away."

The only comfort that some pessimists have been able to summon in the past year is the fact, freely admitted and publicly mentioned even among the highest and most sacrosanct of the Nazi High Command, that the Leader himself, Der Führer, will some day lay him down, breathe the word "Rosebud" or something equally enigmatic, and then die like any ordinary Aryan or non-Aryan worm of the dust.

What sort of biographies will then be written about him and circulated will depend mainly on who came out winner in the wars or revolutions on the map just before Der Führer passed out, got a rain check at the Hall of Valhalla, and climbing out of a battered Stuka at the Gate of Hell heard, as this folk tale runs, the Devil himself hissing, "All I got to say to you, Adolf, is that we're running this place different from your concentration camps—and the only thing for you to do is to go somewhere else and start a hell of your own."

Before marching on Poland to grind its people in dust and shame, Der Führer mentioned how he might at any given moment die. He spoke as though definitely aware that nothing is more certain than death and nothing more uncertain than the hour. In case he should bite the dust and be united in the fellowship of worms with the meanest of his Polish victims, he wished it known that Hermann Göring should follow him as Der Führer. Then as though Göring too is mortal and might at any moment bite the dust, he gave it as his wish that Rudolf Hess, the second beloved and valued, should be second in line, next only to Göring.

And now what? Now Hess is vanished. Not dead but gone. Not extinct but departed. Not buried but incommunicado.

Whatever counsels Hess might wish to speak to Der Führer are out, nothing doing, no can do. Out of the same sky into which the prophet Elijah vanished in a chariot of fire, Rudolf Hess dropped down heaven-sent to Scotland. Instead of a broken neck he had only a broken ankle.

In the scurrying at Berlin and the joint counsels around the

65

mahogany table there may have been muttering "Why wasn't it his neck and not the ankle? It's a bad break. He should have been less careful. Who would have thought he was the best amateur parachutist in the Reich? Without practice he made a perfect landing. Who told him he could do that? It isn't in the books."

For Hitler's purposes in Berlin and over the Continent, Hess is a once trusted lieutenant and bosom friend now buried alive—and perhaps talking. We may be sure the British caretakers are not slamming him over the head with a rubber truncheon and crying: "Now will you talk! Now will you tell us! When we get through with you you'll sing like a canary."

Mr. Hess can have food, ventilation, clean sheets, whatever he orders. He has class. For the time being he is the finest living specimen of the Man without a Country. He may have said, as reported of his landing in Scotland, "I have come to save humanity." And again he may not have spoken so fine a line. If he said it, he is for sure no longer a Nazi. The true Nazi is first for the Nazis, second for Germany, third for humanity and with the fingers crossed.

Hess represents the unexpected, the unpredictable. He is Mr. X, the odd number, the inexplicable. We know he vanished from his once beloved Germany and for the time and the hour it was bad for Nazi morale. Any cunning of evil he might try the British can solve. Their experts include Agatha Christie. And no one knows what possible and conceivable good may come out of what this spectacular prisoner may be telling those who talk with him. My guess joins those who believe that Berlin would pay high ransom to get him back.

The Axis had four high men, Hitler, Göring, Hess, Mussolini. Two of them, for Axis purposes, are gone, as good as dead. They have passed away. Hess and Mussolini no longer function. Two months ago, who would have believed it? Two down out of four. Who'll be the next to go? I will close with the toast of the old Whitechapel Club in Chicago, on news of one of the members passing on, "Hurrah for the next who goes!"

Postscript: The war will be won or lost or go to a stalemate by reason of events now beyond forecast. Who foresaw the dramatic, miscellaneous fighting for the island of Crete? Who outlined beforehand the Nazi zigzags toward Iraq and unlimited oil? What prophet told us that the first British superdreadnaught to go down with the whole crew would be trading shots with a German superdreadnaught up in the Arctic Zone near the North Pole? Or that the scurrying Nazi modern superdread would be tracked and buried?

Who would have expected that the isolationist sons of Robert M. La Follette, the senior, would be confronted by the convoy-favoring interventionist Senator George W. Norris of Nebraska, the most intimate and loyal colleague of their father when he opposed the American entry in the last world war? These old friends may salute each other with the line from Lincoln "I do not impugn the motives of those who are opposed to me."

Bruddah Thomas and our jitters

June 8, 1941

I listened the other night to Bruddah Norman Thomas. His subject was our national hysteria. About this and that, in connection with the well-known war, he finds as people we are far too hysterical. I could tell by the way he spoke of hysteria that it is not a good thing to have and he is in favor of our having less of it.

I gathered definitely, too, that he wished to convey the impression that here and there was John Doe or Richard Roe, sitting perfectly calm and enjoying the landscape, when all of a sudden comes along a warmonger. And no sooner had the aforesaid John Doe or Richard Roe taken an earful of what the warmonger was spilling than he lost his calm and began running around with a bad case of babbling, bombinating hysteria.

I have never gone in heavy for pathological psychology. And I didn't go on listening to Bruddah Thomas on account of what I know about either pathology or psychology. I took it that Bruddah Thomas would not mind if I assumed that hysteria is the jitters, and vice versa. He means that the warmongers have the jitters and the kind of talk warmongers spread has given too many good people the jitters.

On the other hand, however, he wished to convey the impression that the appeasers are cool, calm, collected, serene, well poised, considerate, reasonable, moderate, urbane, amiable—and if you know how to listen to them, your case of the jitters will pick up and improve right away and after a while you'll be a convalescent and you may even be completely cured.

As I listened on and on to the verbal cadenzas of Bruddah Thomas, I found he was grinding and gnashing some of his syllables. They came out of his vocal apparatus with all the dissonance of a self-starter quarreling with bad ignition complicated by an old-fashioned gear stripping itself. He began crescendo and tried to make the whole speech crescendo. He pulled out the diapason stops and tried for variations of sheet lightning, gargling thunder, and hoarse murder in the moonlight. I wished for Herb Graffis, for Lloyd Lewis, for Bugs Baer, for Bill Saroyan, to tell me whether you can cure the jitters with the jitters, or whether it does any good to hiccup in the face of someone who has the hiccups.

Likewise in the case of the Montana Senator, Wheeler by name. He meets hysteria over the country, sees it, hears it, smells it. So he combats hysteria. He would soften, lessen, soothe the hysteria he sees as an evil condition that may drag us into the war. And how would he mitigate, palliate, this hysteria? By telling it with his open mouth to the country that we have a President of the United States who wants a war that will "plow under" every fourth boy of draft age. By telling it in a nation-wide radio address that the President is under the influence of "the international bankers, the Rockefellers and Kuhn Loeb."

And the distinguished aviator, the fair-haired boy whose record of thirty-three hours crossing the Atlantic has been cut to seven and a half hours by flying bombers from Newfoundland to Britain, how is he on our hysteria? Like his colleagues, he says it is bad. He would allay and tone down our hysteria. And how? By telling us that England had the war lost when she declared it and when the Nazis come to take us we will wait till we can see the whites of their eyes and then shoot.

Also to quiet us he offers the advice that in the present crying-out-loud, when God only knows what is next on the timetable, we have a leadership that would be better if thrown out.

As near as I can figure these advocates of peace-it's-wonderful, these trumpet tongues who summarize a vast and tumultuous epoch in a few well-chosen words, they mean it is hysteria and the jitters if the other fellow has it.

What songs shall we sing?

June 15, 1941

Neither Niagara at dawn nor the Golden Gate in the evening nor any of the grand canyons on the Santa Fe or the Union Pacific is as awful and awesome to look at as the Chicago Stadium with its main floor and four galleries packed with a crowd of 24,000 people met for a single purpose, that of moving toward a national unity. The All-American Committee of two hundred sponsoring the rally had on its list just about all of the elements that figure in Earl Robinson's "Ballad of Americans." Mr. Robinson should understand that if there were any races, breeds, nationalities, religions, colors, and previous conditions of servitude left out it was because of an oversight, and there was no intention of slighting anyone.

Sam Levin and Leo Krycski of the CIO were there and John Fitzpatrick of the AFL. Also James F. Forgan of the First National Bank. Also John Alden Carpenter, the famous and original composer of music in the American, had arisen from a sickbed to be present. Also there was the University of Chicago professor Paul H. Douglas, a peculiar human specimen who is an efficient member of the city council and who, it is universally believed in Chicago, has never cared to pluck one dirty nickel out of the game of politics. And there was Ed Kelly, the mayor, under a spotlight shaking hands with Wendell L. Willkie who had blown in on an eastern breeze from his office at 15 Wall Street, New York.

The high spot of the evening for me was when a frail gal from Hollywood, li'l Judy Garland, stepped up to a mike and let her warm tremulous contralto go on the first line of "God Bless America." Before she had reached the second line, at least half of the audience on the main floor rose from their seats and joined in the singing. Not from anywhere came a hoot or a protest—not a sign of one person in a murmuring demurrer to Irving Berlin's song. Then the magnetic little Judy, beating time with the sway of her arrowlike figure, carried the song through to a massive choral effect.

In those moments I was nearer to tears than at any other time during a highly emotional evening. I could not forget that only a few weeks before, at an America First meeting in Orchestra Hall on the lake front, the singing of "God Bless America" was hooted and booed and howled down till those trying to sing it had to quit in confusion. Shortly after came the news of a like performance in Philadelphia.

This seems to show that in the America First organization there are men who believe in the merits of "God Bless America" as one of our national songs worth community singing no matter what the race of the author of the song. But the attempts of these good Americans to have it sung by an audience have been crossed up by an unwelcome element that comes in and does its rough stuff like the fanatics and hoodlums they are. The element is almost entirely Bundist and stems from the undercover Nazi propaganda groups.

These "racists," to use the Nazi term, are not Communist. One basic difference there is between Nazi and Communist doctrine. The Reds teach no race discrimination, no color line. And when "God Bless America" is howled down at an America First meeting in Chicago or Philadelphia, there may be innocents who believe it does not trace back to Herr Goebbels and his propaganda department in Berlin, but others see it as the work of a hideous, slimy, and subhuman crew operating in this country as they operated in each of the countries that went through a confusion and a "softening" process before Hitler took them over.

The usual America First query at this point is "Well, what do you propose? An invasion of Europe and the correction of race hate by force of arms?" That is another question. It does not touch the point that when the long arm of Nazi propaganda reaches from Berlin to Chicago and Philadelphia telling us what songs we can or can't sing, we are merely getting a little preview and foretaste of what that propaganda will hand us when its prestige and power have been fortified and buttressed to the extent we will surely see if and when the British Isles become a Nazi outpost through lack of what we might have determined to send.

I hope, then, for as few riots as possible over what songs we want to sing. And I still think there was something lovely about the way Judy Garland began singing her song and everybody joined in and the Chicago Stadium had for a moment all the venerable dignity of a cathedral not yet bombed.

Little commencement speech

June 22, 1941

Young men and women of the graduating class of 1941, you have been told "The world is before you." And some of you have answered: "Yes, and every day the map is wrecked and made into something else again. Where can we get a map this week that will be good next week?"

The answer to that depends on how the war goes and what happens when the shooting is over. Your eyes will see many things never to be known to your fathers and mothers. Your eyes will see who comes out winner or loser in this war, or whether all come out losers, or whether new dark ages fell on mankind, or whether some new birth of freedom came out of the sweat, blood, and tears.

You will see things hard to look at and easy to forget and better if forgotten. Some actions you take a hand in will have heroic struggle good to remember. Other affairs you mix in will have tragedy, loss, grief, even shame.

Have your books and teachers trained you to take loneliness and say it is not so bad?

Has your training ever helped you to sit in a quiet corner by yourself and ask what is happening in your mind? Have you sometimes gone on a walk by yourself and asked what your mind does when it thinks?

Or have you been afraid of loneliness and let others shape your decisions for you? Then the great books have been of little help to you—and you have merely learned to lean on others for the final decisions that make your personality what it is. In a room so silent you can hear the ticking of a wrist watch are the final decisions made.

One of my neighbors on the Lake Michigan shore line was a flyer in the Lafayette Escadrille in France in 1917 before this country entered the war. He told me a few days ago about a man back from Canada and visiting his boy, a graduate pilot soon to cross the Atlantic and join the Royal Air Force. The father put his arms around his boy, saying good-by, saying to the boy, "Well, son, when you get over there your life won't be worth a nickel." And the boy, smiling, "Well, dad, that last five cents will be worth it."

That boy, of course, had been educated by many different forces.

Propaganda, slogans, watchwords, catchwords, arguments, name-calling, had come to his ears. But in the end he made a personal decision, alone in a room so silent the ticking of a wrist watch could be heard.

That was a portentous line from Winston Churchill on the Royal Air Force last summer and fall saving Britain and its people, "Never have so many owed so much to so few." A lonely man speaking of lonely men—and none of them afraid of their loneliness.

Of fellowship in a human cause, of good companions, comrades, friends, the communions of like minds and like hearts, so much can be said in praise. In an hour of crisis, however, when personal decisions affect mankind at a dark and terrible crossroads, the stress is on loneliness. It takes little imagination to understand how and why in this hour the President of the United States is the loneliest man of all in his country. Should whimsical serenaders at the White House front this week sing Tschaikovsky's "None but the Lonely Heart" they would be more than half right.

The future, graduates of 1941, is revealed neither to the hard-boiled nor to the soft nor to those who are just plain good eggs. There is a pay-off, however, for those who have learned what it is to be lonely and how to take it. May you have good going, youth of America. May there be luck stars over you—and the care of a kind Providence.

Pure American hybrid

June 29, 1941

At a national unity meeting in the Chicago Stadium I made reference to "the famous flyer who has quit flying and taken to talking." So I am getting letters about how I should have not said that. Of course, it happens to be one of the few known and admitted facts in the present argument. You don't have to prove it. Who else is our foremost nonflying flyer?

The Associated Press, the United Press, the special and spot newswriters who get a by-line, they all tell us from day to day the famous flyer no longer flies and instead of flying steps out before audiences and microphones and opens his mouth and talks and talks.

A magazine editor in New York asked me didn't I think our

famous flyer has "intellectual integrity." I said, "Yes" and was reminded of a dinner in the old Palmer House of Chicago when Edgar Lee Masters asked a ward alderman, Dennis Egan, whether a certain politician was honest. Egan's eyes flashed, and from his decisive jowls came the answer, "Yes, for them he's with."

I take it as having meaning that the famous flyer writes a magazine article titled "The Rising Tide of Color," that he holds theories of race discrimination and the color line quite the opposite of those held by Thomas Jefferson and Abraham Lincoln on biology and breed with reference to democracy and popular government. His theories are not new. They are to be found, in their main tone and trend, in the declarations of the Know-Nothing party of Lincoln's generation, also in the pronouncements of the Ku Klux Klan of the early 1920's, and a little later in *Mein Kampf* and the speeches, writings, doctrines of the Nazis on race superiority.

The American party was the name the Know-Nothings gave their organization. One of their slogans ran "Americans first!" Their leaders met followers in secret and the password letting members in was "I know nothing." They and their works gave Abraham Lincoln a troubled mind and a shaken soul. Our modern one-time flyer in similar cases today would diagnose it "hysteria" and lacking in cool surgical approach. In a letter to Joshua F. Speed, dated August 24, 1855, Lincoln wrote:

"Our progress in degeneracy appears to me to be pretty rapid. As a nation we began by declaring that 'all men are created equal.' We now practically read it 'all men are created equal, except negroes.' When the Know-nothings get control, it will read 'all men are created equal, except negroes and foreigners and Catholics.' When it comes to this, I shall prefer emigrating to some country where they make no pretense of loving liberty—to Russia, for instance, where despotism can be taken pure, and without the base alloy of hypocrisy."

Nowhere in speeches and writings of the one-time flyer do we find any hint of the passion for freedom and equality of opportunity that shook Lincoln at the time of penning these sentences. The flyer's father, however, would have understood it completely. The father, as I noted him in the summer of 1917 speaking outdoors to a thousand farmers in a wheat field just outside the city limits of St. Cloud, Minnesota, had a large mouth, a face with a touch of the Lincolnian, a deep and compelling baritone voice, an Old Testament bitterness over the wrongs suffered by the farmers of the Northwest. The son is something else, and I could go into score-card points. The father had passion where the son has a precise mind and everything under control, the instrument board registering like a mechanical brain without bowels or solar plexus.

Turning to Heywood Broun's book *It Seems to Me—1925-1935,* we find Broun had a touch of hero worship for the father and dark doubts about the respectable son so many years silent on human issues, Broun writing, *"Possibly* the young man was familiar with his [father's] passion for human rights. He *may* have heard him [the father] speaking."

And I am not sure what Heywood Broun, the Nazi-hater, in view of recent performances, might be writing now, if alive. He might be saying there are known cases in history of a high fame turning to ashes of roses, and forget-me-nots going to the alley ash can. Or he might hazard: "I'll take Wrong Way Corrigan."

Mirages over the Russian marshes

July 6, 1941

Old-timers had it there was a king who liked to pitch horseshoes and drink beer with pickled pig's knuckles. Then an idea got fixed deep in his head as though bored in at the end of a gimlet. No matter how many ringers he threw with horseshoes, no matter how cool the beer and sour the pig's knuckles, the idea had him fixed. Near his country was another ten times as big, with an army twice as big as his. And did he want to step in with his army and show the world he could lick the daylights and the living whey out of this other army? He sure did. The idea gimleted deep in his anxious, fretting, furious noodle. So he decided to put on a war to show he could be colossal.

An old uncle said: "Listen, hearken, and lend an ear. Suppose you do win this war hands down and come home with a lot of flags and loot—then what?"

"Then I will have a colossal name and I will settle down to a quiet life and pitch horseshoes and drink beer with pickled pig's knuckles."

"But," offered the uncle, "that's what you've got now, and you don't need the colossal name."

"Forget it," said the king. And he put on the war. In his head he had it won already—on paper. He would show the world he was colossal. Yet the war dragged on and every month became something else again and refused to behave like it had been put down on paper. So many long and lean years did the war run on that the king died before he ever had time for another horseshoe ringer and the beer he got was only soso and such pig's knuckles as he could get hadn't been pickled like he was used to at home. On a granite monument to him they chiseled: "He was colossal and won a war—on paper."

Many guesses will come on the parallel of the Corsican Napoleon Bonaparte and the Austrian Adolf Schicklgruber and the mirages over the marshes of Russia. Napoleon had it won—on paper. And now Adolf figures his Luftwaffe and tanks have more class, for now, than Napoleon's cavalry and artillery in 1812. Adolf thinks so. But he doesn't know. Nobody knows. The famous ex-flyer says, "It is a matter for profound analysis." So it is. Who can analyze, either profoundly or offhand, 180,000,000 people of 182 nationalities and dialects on one-sixth of the land surface of the planet Earth? The conqueror of it who can hold his conquest will for sure be colossal.

Suppose Russia does wage as ruthless a warfare against the Nazis as she did against Napoleon? Would that mean, in the agony of a crisis, that the Reds would sabotage the oil wells of the Caucasus, so that the flowing oil supplies of this year could not be restored in many years, if ever at all? Would that mean the crops of the Ukraine would be set afire this year as coldly and cunningly as the city of Moscow was laid in ashes in 1812? We do not know. Nor does Adolf nor the Gestapo nor the man in the moon.

We do know that the Japanese Luftwaffe took off from Tokyo and took mastery of the air from the Chinese years and years ago. We do know that the Japanese won the war against the Chinese years ago—on paper. We do know that the Chinese are still fighting, that Russia more than any other one country helped them in their fighting, and there is guessing in some quarters that the Chinese will yet win the war against the Japanese Luftwaffe which so long ago took mastery of the air.

A war is won when the people against whom it is waged are ready to quit fighting, even in guerrilla style. If the blitzkrieg should send the Red Army in retreat, back and back to the Ural Mountains and the hiding places of Siberia, would that mean the Russians have a pattern of war like that of the Chinese? We do not know. Neither the plain folks nor the experts know.

It is possible for Hitler and Himmler to police Denmark, Norway, Holland. It is possible for Hitler and Ribbentrop to do tricks with Pétain and the two hundred owning families of France. And what is possible for Hitler, Himmler, and Ribbentrop in the vast lonely human cross-weave of Russia? They themselves do not know. They are gambling. They are led by the grand paperhanger gambler.

From the Munich beer-hall putsch that failed, on through the four-power Munich pact and the invasion of Russia, he has been gambling, mainly on his air power. One surprise met him in British air power. Another surprise met him in the United States Lend-Lease Bill and other affairs. Now he is gambling that having subdued Russia, he can get production out of a Russia he hopes to devastate.

Maybe it will make sense when he gets through with it. Maybe it won't. Russia may as of yore have mirages over her marshes. We will see who is colossal—for sure—or on paper. The decision may be long coming.

New traditions for old

July 13, 1941

A man asked, "What is a trend?" and had the answer, "Something alive, not yet a movement."

All around us these days are trends. Some will trickle off into nothing. Others will channel deeper and spread out and command attention and action.

One trend now says too many of the army and navy heads think in the past, shrink from playing too far with the new ideas of mobile, mechanized warfare, unaware that the ghost of Billy Mitchell walks and must be heard. When as a nation last year we suddenly wished we had the 50,000 planes we didn't have, some of us asked how many thousands of planes we could have bought with the $81,000,000 paid for a battleship we launched in June.

How far will this trend go? Will its pressure get results? My guess is that this trend will go on, will not let up. It is by now nearly a movement, not organized but spontaneous and concerted, believing it has a righteous anxiety about potential waste of life and of national defense resources. This or that high official may pooh-pooh the idea of gliders for tens of thousands of American youth, but the arguments against his official pooh-pooh will go on.

Another trend is much smaller. Back of it is the restless, inventive America of original minds. It hears officials say, "We can't listen to every nut who comes along with a screwy idea," and points to other officials saying: "It will be held against us if we reject an idea or invention that in the future revolutionizes warfare. The main body of naval authority rejected John Ericsson's *Monitor* till the Assistant Secretary of the Navy, Gustavus Vasa Fox, joined President Lincoln in approval of Ericsson, with the result that the navies of the world changed from wooden to iron construction of vessels."

I met a colonel who did a lot of flying and supervised the making of thousands of air photographs in 1917-18.

"When you ride over a city blacked out," he says, "you know at once here is a blackout, here is your target if you are an enemy plane. It looks smoother and darker than the rest of the landscape. It may be that as the war goes on it will be found under given conditions that the opposite of the blackout is an effective Niagara of lights that dazzle the enemy pilots, beams and flashes located outside cities, lights planned to bewilder the enemy as to where population centers, dry docks, arsenals, or airfields are located. Such strategy would consider the fact that when a dive bomber goes for a ship he tries to get between the sun and the aircraft gunners, who have a hard time sighting their target in line with the dazzling ball of the sun."

Nobody foresaw John Ericsson. He was a surprise. Nobody now foresees the fellow who may come along with an idea making a basic transformation in traditional ideas of attack or defense. He will, if and when he arrives, be a surprise, with plenty of us saying, "Why didn't we think of this before?"

There is a minor trend among writers that looks good. The poets

77

Stephen Vincent Benét and Archibald MacLeish, for instance, can be infinitely subtle. They are not sure themselves what some of their poems mean. Now they are stepping out and writing, in the language of the plain people, prose and poetry and radio dramas that carry a punch, that get across to the public.

Benét and MacLeish are specimens of the writer who knows that propaganda can get terrifying results, that always there is a competition among propagandas, that unless you get your own propaganda across to masses of people, then by your silence or lack of clarity you are doing the same thing that helped get the intellectuals of Europe where they are. Where the intellectuals sit back as ineffectuals, the Nazis say their chances are better.

The changing world jigsaw

July 20, 1941

A year ago was deep sorrow. France was gone, Britain next on the Nazi card. Then Hitler failed. He couldn't take Britain as planned. Months later he told high Nazis, top-rank generals, and the wide world, "England will fall." As though this judgment might not be taken at face value, America's famous aviator, no longer flying, repeated it, with personal testimony as to what he had seen that made him sure Britain had lost the war when she declared it. This was the time the President of the United States used the word "dumb" to characterize such a cocksure judgment about a stupendous and incessantly changing world jigsaw.

Then what happens! Then comes the secret decision of the Nazi leader that the fall of Russia must come before the fall of England. Only the men of the Nazi leader's intimate inner circle know of this decision. Do some of them argue against it as a desperate gamble that may in the end lose them all their winnings so far? Probably. It was then perhaps that Rudolf Hess saw red, saw black, saw hell on wheels, and flew to Scotland. It was then too, perhaps, that Hermann Göring shook his massive head and pleaded for a change of plan. Maybe Göring did that. The demands on him would be fearful. His Luftwaffe would have to cover two fronts. He had questions.

Whether he is now running the Luftwaffe as always or whether

78

he is for practical purposes in a lockup, there are chances that he split with Hitler on the same issue as Hess did in those April and May weeks when their leader told them he was going to make the Russian plunge.

The controls of Adolf Schicklgruber as to the Russian invasion don't look so good. His speech as he let loose the blitz was convulsive, more than touched with hysteria, mad with a hate that could not find words. The "New Order" in Europe, the Germany of a thousand years to come, gave way to frothing rage at Russia, her crimes and perfidies. Once more he staged himself as he did before Munich, before Austria, before he invaded the Rhineland, before Hindenburg named him Reichschancellor, telling the world he would save it from Communism. This had won him influence and money from high places, more than any trick in his bag.

Precisely who among his advisers of the inner circle told him it had been used too much and wouldn't work again, may be known later. And those so frank and loyal as to plead that he should not take on Russia till he knocked out England, we may know of them later.

One question back of these other questions is "How is Hitler as to form?" Has he got what he used to have? Or is the pace and strain telling on him? He used to be credited with wonderful timing sense. Has he lost it? Have events and the daily decisions required of him piled higher and heavier from day to day till his nerves and brain cells no longer function and respond as they did in the old days? Has a weariness crept over him that he is able to subdue millions of people with guns and Gestapo while their silent faces more than ever baffle him? Does the map of Europe float unreal before his eyes in moments when it comes over him that beyond the borders are many fine thinking minds that may outthink his?

Maybe it will be written that in the year 1940 the dank and diabolical genius of Adolf Schicklgruber reached its top form and then started to go stale. Running Germany is one thing. It is something else to manage the political, economic, and cultural affairs of the continent of Europe. Madmen trying it go madder.

In a stump speech at Peoria, Illinois, the old-timer Governor Dick Oglesby once had a Corn Belt crowd meeting him more than halfway when he said, "Why, my friends, the Democrats can't run the government—it's all us Republicans can do."

Postscript: Out of a car window near Washington I see nine or ten gliders, sailplanes. They look so birdlike, so gay—more free and easy, their wings more winglike, than motorplanes. May the boogie-woogie find less favor and American youth take to gliders by the thousand!

Godless Russia and godly America

July 27, 1941

Several important citizens not lacking in self-importance have been telling the country lately that Soviet Russia is "godless." We were not surprised to hear Mr. Hoover use the word "godless," for we have heard him on several occasions bring an address to its close with the two final words "Almighty God." Also we have come to regard Mr. Hoover as an essentially solemn man, and when he points to Russia as "godless" we know out of many former utterances from him how he would define and describe the godly man or nation as distinguished from the godless.

And we have Bruddah Bill Bullitt, near to a dancing dervish at the University of Montreal when they hang a kudos, a doctor's hood of honor, on him. Does he fling a mean javelin? He do—he shore do. He too joins those who must now stress the point that Russia is "godless." By direct implication he tells us that our own land, this America of ours, is godly.

We are, of course, a Christian nation in terms of church membership and avowed faiths and denominations. And in a very broad and loose sense, rather than by strict application, we are a godly nation, though God knows we have our shortcomings and anyone who wishes to be instructed as to how our works are not equal to our proclaimed faiths has only to listen to either Monsignor Sheen or Dr. Fosdick or other godly men who have done more studying in this particular field than Bill Bullitt.

The last time I saw Bill was for about two minutes in the Supreme Court Building, and he was in a hurry. I gave him a definition I got from Bugs Baer: "A diplomat is a man who knows just

80

where to put a piece of soap in the bathtub so the next man slips on it." Bill didn't think it was funny, and rushed away.

One little oddity about the United States Constitution is that it nowhere mentions God. This was done on purpose. It came through men well aware of Europe convulsed and blood-drenched in wars over religious issues, over questions ranging around the right and freedom of every man to worship God in his own way.

Occasionally a proposal has come that by act of Congress and the President, the United States should recognize God by name in the Constitution. President Lincoln's Secretary of the Navy, Gideon Welles, wrote briefly in his diary of how Lincoln one day read to the Cabinet such a proposal from some respectable citizens, and of how the Cabinet seemed unanimous that even as a gesture the action would serve no good.

Lincoln shrank from assumptions of personal holiness. One clergyman read the Second Inaugural of March 4, 1865, as having behind it the cry "God be merciful to me a sinner!"

People read again and again those fateful sentences: "Neither party [the North or the South] expected for the war the magnitude or the duration which it has already attained. . . . Each looked for an easier triumph, and a result less fundamental and astounding. Both read the same Bible, and pray to the same God; and each invokes his aid against the other. . . . The prayers of both could not be answered—that of neither has been answered fully. The Almighty has his own purposes."

The Council for Democracy

August 3, 1941

Having years ago elected myself not only president but chairman of the board of the North American Paw Paw Growers Association, I have learned a little about the respect or at least curiosity that people give to a name that sounds like you are organized. You might try to tell some folks, "I am a lone wolf and I don't belong to any club or society and there are times when I enjoy having my own thoughts, so here is my card which reads that I belong to Me, Myself & Company." They would take you for an odd number or a picnic cutup.

However, if you can inform them, "I am the first charter member of the North American Paw Paw Growers Association and at every annual election I have been named president and by authority vested in the president I have been appointed chairman of the board of directors," then you have them guessing. You may be important—they are not sure. You may be a featherweight, a peanut, a leaf in the wind, and yet there is the possibility you have a wad, a treasury, a membership, a lobby, and three or four high-priced lawyers—they don't know till they have you looked up.

Getting down to facts, the Council for Democracy at 285 Madison Avenue, New York City, is not a front nor a phantom. It is a reality. It works. It grows. I have seen it go up from a little acorn to a flourishing oak. They started last year when the big scare hit us and did good to hit us as it did. Their business is propaganda.

Like Goebbels, they run a Department of Public Enlightenment. They aim to show what the word "democracy" means and how it works and where you—and you and you—better be asking yourself where you come in and what you can do. I saw them last year hauling and mauling, ready to try anything once. Propaganda—yes—for democracy—and how to go at it in your own home neighborhood to make it work.

They set programs going on the air waves, national hookups carrying such straight stuff as in that Fourth of July radio play by Stephen Vincent Benét. Maybe more important are their pamphlets, little paper-covered books that get down to cases. They ask questions. What is free speech? How far can you go shooting an uncontrolled personal bazoo without crossing up the rights of others? At what point in a street or a hall meeting should authorities interfere? Supposing you are an authority, at what point are you in danger of overreaching? What would you do, in given cases, if you were an official? Such questions, and others like them, get discussion in a little handbook titled *Freedom of Assembly and Anti-Democratic Groups*.

America's free public schools—there they stand—buildings, rooms, equipment. How in your community you can use it for discussion and enlightenment on democracy is told brightly in one pamphlet. Textbooks, teachers—what to watch and what to bear patiently—this is nicely covered.

The one most important booklet aims to answer the question

82

"What can I do?" It runs eighty-eight pages close packed with common sense. The title: *Defense on Main Street, a Guidebook for Local Activities for Defense and Democracy.* Every public school and library in the country should have several copies. It ought to be on sale at every newsstand and cigar store from coast to coast and from the Great Lakes to the Gulf. I hope to see copies of it read ragged and dirty from being passed along among young workmen who like its plain and practical wisdom for this hour of crisis and danger.

How democracy works, if, as, and when it works, is nicely and patly told in these little publications of the Council for Democracy. The ghosts of Tom Jefferson and Ben Franklin might be saying, "Nice work, boys." The shade of A. Lincoln might be murmuring, "I wish some of my zealots could have had your guidebooks on what to withhold from doing in a time of crisis."

The job of Chief Magistrate

August 10, 1941

A White House visitor last year on leaving the President mentioned how Lincoln once compared his place and job with "being the Head of Hell." There are open enemies, hidden double-crossers, snipers, male gossips, malcontents, honest incompetents who hope they are good, well-meaning blatherskites who like to tell the country where we go from here, silent men who are strong and able, besides say-nothings who know nothing, nincompoops who strut and are well read in regulations, show-offs, genuine heroes ready with the endurance, valor, and humility required in a crisis. A wonderful human menagerie it is the President is supposed to co-ordinate.

The President with a face both droll and solemn speeded his parting guest with this anecdote: Two Negroes at church had heard a sermon on how fierce and hot are the fires of hell, one saying, "If you don't do right, don't live right, you're sure going to hell." The other said, "Yes," and the first one went farther, "If you don't do right, don't live right, you're going to ev-er-last-ing hell," with the stress on "ev-er-last-ing." And this was challenged, "No, no, no, duh human con-sti-tu-tion can't stand ev-er-last-ing hell."

The story should become a White House tradition. It goes with the job and place of Chief Magistrate. In the morning he must think about domestic turmoil from the St. Lawrence Waterway to the Lockheed plane works, in the afternoon about foreign policy from the Panama Canal to the oil wells of Iraq, in the evening about both domestic and foreign affairs, and when he goes to bed he can do some fancy writhing and gentle moaning about what Georges Clemenceau meant by such a phrase as "the grandeur and misery of victory" or by the statement "Rest is not a word of free peoples—rest is a monarchial word."

If he speaks to the country, there are those who are sure he has said just the right thing and others sure that once more he has opened his mouth to no use and avail. If he says nothing, there are those who are sure he will speak in the future at the precise hour when his words will count, while others are sure that either his silence is significant and connects with his ignorance and vacillation or he is holding back and keeping secret important matters he should be telling the country about. If he opens any door of policy, he is sure to hear it should be opened wider, it should be closed entirely, or there should be a new door or a return to the door that was there before or the original intention of the Founding Fathers was that a window is better than a door anyhow.

Twenty years ago on a Chicago streetcar I heard a woman explain to a child, "The President lives in the White House in Washington where he signs bills they bring him and he can do anything he wants to so long as they don't stop him." And high-priced constitutional lawyers can't frame a more accurate description in the same number of words.

Through the White House windows float many voices. In their varieties of crying and laughing they register more faces and wants than there are in all the books of Hawthorne, Henry James, Mark Twain, Petroleum Vesuvius Nasby, John Steinbeck, Hemingway, and Archie MacLeish. Just now out toward the Great Lakes, the Rockies, and the West Coast are hysterias become vocal. Unless this or that is done and done today, the United States will go to hell in a hanging basket, lose its shirt, commit national suicide, sink into death or the innocuous desuetude akin to death. The President may consider, "Is it probable that in a democracy some of these hysterias cancel each other—and as poisons have antidotes so there are hysterias that breed counter-hysterias?"

84

The Fight for Freedom Committee utters its desperate cry that we must now and forthwith declare war on Nazi Germany while the Committee to Defend America says use convoys if need be to land our cargoes in Britain, win the Battle of the Atlantic, and then see what happens. Meantime the America First Committee pushes a furious campaign aimed straight at terrorizing every father, mother, or sweetheart of a drafted boy with a promise that it looks as though the boy is going to be butchered by crazy galoots running the government who just naturally enjoy the bloody shambles of a human slaughterhouse.

Meantime all along the President goes on giving the Nazis a taste of their own war of nerves. We are in the war. We are not. We are making up our minds. We tell the world we favor the Four Freedoms in language making it plain that if we believe in those Four Freedoms we are not going to start in and try to introduce forced feeding of freedom at any point. We declare a national emergency. We order Axis consuls off our premises. We take over Iceland. We freeze assets. We stop oil to Japan. We collect a mountain of aluminum scrap. We freeze silk. We send skilled workmen to Ireland who seem to be building naval bases—or are they? Through our President we seem to Europe as a whole people and a united nation to be standing up and saying we are going to throw in everything we have to smash Hitler. Does this bother and annoy the Nazis? It does. They want the suspense over. They like to calculate. And we are the incalculable.

My neighbor over at Decatur, Michigan, Arba N. Moulton, sends me a late number of his country weekly, the *Decatur Republican*. Therein a humble contributor, Fred W. Green, points to the intrigue and strategy of war, how "certain things cannot be made public so that the enemy can arrange matters to prevent what is contemplated to be done." Green makes himself clear. "Personally I do not agree with the President in everything, but I am with the people who placed him for a third term in the White House. Give him the chance he is entitled to. He may be wrong but don't hound him. He has secrets impossible to give out. It is absurd that he should do so. He should be given every power to conduct this terrible ordeal the country is facing. He should never be harried and abused in the manner he is now. On the contrary, he should be given the support now that was placed in his hands when he was elected."

I like this quaint viewpoint of Citizen Green. He writes the sidewalk talk of some Michigan Republicans. They agree with Bishop Hurley of Florida that hours may come when the President must act on an immediate issue without waiting for Congress to thresh it out in discussions and Nays and Yeas.

The man now in the White House could properly repeat what his predecessor, A. Lincoln, once laughed to a visitor: "I'm like the Irishman, I have to do some things 'unbeknownst to myself.' "

Bill White's kneebones

August 17, 1941

Either in the hush of a back-room huddle or the babble and booing of a national convention where the dark horses are getting neck and neck, Bill White of Emporia, Kansas, is at home and never yet had his straw hat stolen. I have a shelf holding every book he has written, a couple of commencement addresses, and clippings from the *Emporia Gazette*. Some of the books weigh heavier than others. The sum total will be consulted by future historians wishing to get the decisions of an umpire as between a class bewildered by its tall possessions and common men caught in a squeeze play of wages and prices.

A Puritan in Babylon reads like a well-done novel, holds pity and laughter as it gives us the pathetic pilgrimage of Cal Coolidge from nowhere to somewhere. In October of 1939 he gave the country his book *The Changing West,* his say-so on how democracy works. "The more liberties we enjoy the more duties we assume," he writes, as though each of us might well be asking what civilian or military chores we have taken on lately in service for peculiar freedoms not yet lost to us. "Two things made the wilderness blossom as the rose: first, a neighborly faith in the decency of man; second, a never faltering vision of a better world."

Bill White preaches. If he thinks the customers need a sermon, he lets them have it in John Bunyan speech tones. He goes for sentiment, holds that men charged with sentiment of high voltage are the makers of history. He may deal with cases and verge on the

:omic. Widely assorted varieties of Kansas farmers, including cattle-
nen, wheat and sugar-beet growers, dairy farmers, answered the call
of Senator Arthur Capper to confer in Topeka on farm trouble.
The twelve hundred who came wanted different policies for their
different interests. "It was a cat fight. The Tower of Babel was com-
paratively an a cappella choir, singing in perfect harmony beside
the Kansas Senator's farm conference. All day long he sat trying to
soothe the opposing groups, to bring them together. He refused to
take sides. How could he? . . . At last one old Puritan from eastern
Kansas, a barnyard stockman with half a dozen crops on his three
hundred acres, rose up in exasperation and, shaking his finger at the
Senator, cried, 'Oh, Senator, we are all tired of seeing you so damned
wishy-washy!' "

Now Bill White's hot-weather advice to the Republican Congressmen from Kansas runs pointed and abrupt. He sees them on foreign
policy heading for the doghouse again. "Come to your senses. You
have gone as far as you can on the Quisling route. Watch out for
a record vote which you can never explain if this country is in the
war in 1942 and particularly if this country is losing ground in the
war because you have torn our armed forces to pieces when war
was threatened. . . . Take an old man's advice: When the folks
know that you want your jobs worse than you love your country,
you'll lose your jobs."

In the same week that White threw this mental tear gas into the
Jayhawker arena, fifteen Republicans, headed by Frank O. Lowden,
announced themselves opposed to the President's "warlike steps, in
no case sanctioned by Congress." In the fifteen signers was only one
white crow, a Midwest university president who has approved the
main direction of the New Deal. The others properly belonged,
among them two authors, one labor leader, each freely confessing
he has not yet found phrases to adequately report his scorn and
detestation of the President. And to some of us it was news that
Geraldine Farrar's eminent soprano is also an eminent Republican
voice. Till now we had a hazy notion a soprano is neutral or non-
partisan, though perhaps we should pair Miss Farrar with Marian
Anderson. Missing was the Republican-party bannerman of 1940,
Wendell L. Willkie, who indorses the President's "warlike steps,
in no case sanctioned by Congress."

If Bill White is correct, then Willkie, in taking a course opposite to that of the Kansas Congressmen and the fifteen wheel horses, may a year from now be a party spokesman with a following and the dissident wheel horses groping in outer darkness. Time will tell. The matter now is worth this much attention. Bill White before this has served warnings on his party. When his kneebones register stormy weather ahead, it usually comes and for the reasons he names in advance.

"Sure we're neutral—who for?"

August 24, 1941

One of the leading hate-Britain propagandists asks questions. The hate-Nazi propagandists in return ask questions:

If you are for America first and therefore democracy first, why are you silent about Hitler and the Nazis, who openly announce they plan to destroy democracy and replace it with a world "New Order"?

If you favor the republican form of government and the democratic system which is the basis of American political life, why have you managed in seventeen speeches to carefully, scrupulously, evade and avoid any slightest word of disapproval of Hitler, of the Nazi movement and the Nazi plans which aim at conquest of democratic countries?

Does your silence about Nazi Germany mean that you are trying carefully and scrupulously to maintain yourself as an honest neutral?

If so, why have you without care and without scruples gone out of your way again and again to deliver harsh and bitter condemnations of the British Government and the British nation, which like ours is an imperfect democracy?

Why have you carefully and scrupulously so managed your speeches that you have never spoken any similar harsh and bitter words about the German nation and its Nazi government and its leader Adolf Hitler?

If neutrality means carefully and scrupulously not taking sides, not favoring one side as against another, why have you taken the side of the Nazis to the extent that you have repeatedly made the positive declaration in public speeches that Britain had the war lost when she declared it?

Can such a statement, made publicly and responsibly on your part, mean anything else than that it is your judgment that Hitler and the Nazis will take the British Isles and win the war?

Did you deliver this publicly pronounced judgment hoping that it would sway opinion and feeling in America and over the world and to that extent help Hitler and the Nazis take the British Isles and win the war?

Or were you so modest and self-effacing that you didn't for a moment realize that you were doing your best to help Hitler and the Nazis win their war to destroy democracy and set up a world "New Order"?

When the President of the United States employed the word "dumb" to characterize your pronouncement that Britain had the war lost when she declared it, is it your belief that he might more accurately and delicately have used some such phrase as "innocent but honorable"?

If you say that on one occasion you did go so far as to declare that the fall of Britain at the hands of the Nazis would be a quote colossal tragedy unquote, are you not aware that Hitler and the Nazis themselves know it would be a colossal tragedy, and the reason they want to see it come is because the whole world knows it would be a tragedy and a colossal one and as a phrase from you it might mean that like the Nazis you want Britain to go down?

Are you aware that your silence about Hitler and the Nazis, your refusal to say whether you are for them or against them, carries more than a faint implication that you believe the Nazi system may be better than our democratic system, and unless we change and improve ours we will have to take the Nazi system whether we want it or not?

Are you aware that when your mouth opens and you tell an audience of millions of listeners, including army and navy units, that we have a government of "hypocrisy and subterfuge," you are saying the same thing Hitler and the Nazis say about our democratic system?

Are you aware that when you complain that there is powerful propaganda operating against your own propaganda, you invite close examination of your own propaganda against an administration chosen by an American electorate by legal methods and prescribed forms?

Why do you in your propaganda put the emphasis on our hypocrisy and our subterfuge and give out no word or intimation about the infamous hypocrisies and the unspeakable subterfuges of Adolf Hitler and his dripping and bloody stooges?

Where has there been hypocrisy or subterfuge in the leading spokesman of our government telling the wide world that we favor the democratic system, that we hate the Nazi system, that we hate Hitlerism and we hope Hitlerism will be destroyed and crushed to dust?

If it is hypocrisy and subterfuge for an American spokesman to so openly declare himself to the whole world in favor of the democratic system as against the Nazi "New Order," do you believe there is no touch of hypocrisy and no lingering quality of subterfuge in your keeping silence and never saying a word one way or another about the Nazi way of life as distinguished from our way?

Inside a Nazi youth mind

August 31, 1941

Once a foreign statesman arrived at our shores on important international business. Asked what was the most pressing question he hoped to get answered in this country, he replied, "Do fish sleep?" At aquariums he learned that fish do sleep. That was settled. Whether fish think, of course, has been asked. And at any zoo having a hippopotamus or a chimpanzee are onlookers asking, "Does the hippo think? Does the chimp think?" These same onlookers have queried the last year, "Do Nazi flyers think? And if so, what is it the Nazi flyer thinks?"

I began the book *I Was a Nazi Flier* not expecting much. The diary might be authentic and its author seeing nothing, hearing nothing, and writing the same. That happens in most diaries. Here, however, we do get a portrait of a person with sketches of other persons, his comrades of the Luftwaffe.

Do they enjoy bombing London, Coventry, Birmingham? They do. Are they pleased to handle machines that drop explosive eggs on people in houses and on streets? They are. And if that was all, and if their cold efficiency and their Nazi mechanical hearts and their unfailing spoken adoration of Hitler as a superman and a prophet of a New Europe were the gist of the book, we might think it a "plant," one more piece of the Nazi strategy of terror.

As the months pass, however, from May of 1940 to November, the diary entries look more and more like what one of the Luftwaffe set down of things heard, seen, felt. In May he welcomed orders to pilot his bomber over Holland and France. Then and later, after the first flights over England, on return to the home field he would get out of the plane and walk around "to see where she was hit." Comes September and the excitement is worn off, the kick gone. "After every flight we inspect the plane carefully, of course, because we have to make our report. But we simply find out what has happened and don't get particularly excited about it any more. . . . The whole thing [of regular bomber flights over England] has become a habit, just like going to the office in the morning and coming home in the evening."

Comes November—then what? "There really isn't anything wrong with me. I'm just tired when we're on the way back. When we start out everything is fine and when we're in the middle of a battle I feel fresher than ever. But on the way back I suddenly feel all done in. Sometimes I feel as though I won't be able to last until I set her down. It feels as though I'm going to fall asleep at the stick. And then, when we finally taxi to a stop, I'm not tired any more, and I can't go to sleep at all." Another of the crew "always takes sleeping medicine," but the diary-writer is afraid it may bring on a habit. He resents it, too, that at this time a commission is soon to arrive "and we all have to take tests again." He writes: "We passed our tests long ago. And this last year we've really proved that we know our business. Why should they suddenly decide that we aren't good enough?"

Quarrels and insults have run on daily between two crew members, Hesse and Richter. "But yesterday it was worse than ever. It ended with Richter saying that Hesse was a democratic swine and Hesse saying that Richter was a Gestapo agent. Afterwards Richter asked me whether I had any idea how Hesse had found out. I was just speechless. Naturally, I had never dreamed that Hesse meant it seriously—about Richter's being a Gestapo agent, I mean—and I still don't think he really meant it. But Richter really is working for the Gestapo. He admitted it to me right out. He said of course he worked for the Gestapo and what of it? He's quite right. What of it? Richter kept grilling me trying to find out how Hesse could have found out. I promised Richter to feel Hesse out. But I told him right off that I didn't think Hesse really meant it. Still, the whole thing gave me something to think about."

Later we read more of Richter's fury at Hesse. "Richter says Hesse has been infected with the bacillus of democracy [a Goebbels phrase]. He thinks it's because Hesse used to go abroad so much. It's possible that Hesse is really infected with the bacillus of democracy."

Then with the unquestionable loyalty or the safeguard caution of a Nazi-party member come the closing sentences of this diary entry: "I'm not writing this because I think Richter may read my diary. I'm really not worried about that. But it's possible that there's something to what he says. When you think about a thing long enough, you begin to see it in a different light."

In coming months or years Luftwaffe morale will vary. The variations will depend on how the crews of bombers and of fighter planes feel. Some have a mechanical heart that occasionally goes human. They can resent the Gestapo getting too snoopy. Watching the bombs stream down from the plane gets monotonous. Dogfight thrills wore some of them down to where they couldn't sleep. And always they will be thinking about the opposed morale of the R.A.F. and the Russian flyers.

The swaggering, staccato slang of this particular flyer who wrote the diary told me he is a new breed, as our American gangsters were a set we had to learn. Their spoken contempt of death is sometimes pretty good and real. Then again it's just a front. Back of their Nazi-taught phizzogs some of them do wish the war was over.

For us the living

September 7, 1941

The American labor movement is no longer a boy in short pants. It is grown up, has hair on its chest, and eats regular. Therefore questions are in order. What about its mind and conscience? What of its human spirit and the stuff of dreams without which no movement lives, grows, develops? What is it doing with the material gains and the new freedoms it has won?

The foregoing themes and shadows of themes run through the little radio play *For Us the Living,* first put on the air just before the President spoke on Labor Day. The difficulties to be surmounted in such a play at such an hour are enormous and entangling. Bernard A. Schoenfeld made the grade and gave the world a finished production in plain words with momentous implications. The story is there. Only citizens dead from the neck up would think of dialing it out. We wonder what is coming next, what the unfolding will be of the loyalties of a young labor leader to his sweetheart and to the ghost of his father. Jimmy Cagney was never nearer perfect than in his lines as the young labor leader. Edward Arnold ghosting as the father, a labor leader of the previous generation, missed none of the required shadings. I failed to catch the name of the young woman, but I can tell her she has sweet gravity and a touch of doom, enough so that we know she is not the glamour girl of whom Pavlova said, "She will never dance except with her legs."

The free labor of the world is at a crossroads. Over some areas of the continent of Europe they had trade-unions, co-operatives, journals of wide circulation, funds and treasuries competently handled for many human benefits. Then out of the dark came the Unknown. Into power with weapons and authority came the Unknown, wrecking the unions, the co-operatives, the journals, looting the funds and treasuries, handing death, torture, and concentration camps to thousands of the leading figures of the labor movement. Then by the will, desire, and plan of the Unknown, a war began, scaled to world size, announcing its aim that after the continent of Europe the British Isles were next and then the Western Hemisphere, not forgetting the United States of America. To what extent, the question rises, shall free American labor take a hand in fighting the Unknown that seeks eventually to put the same screws of death and repression on this country? Is it possible that unless American free labor throws in and joins up with all others who are out to kill off and bury deep the Unknown, the job will not get done?

These momentous questions are handled in the Schoenfeld radio

93

play *For Us the Living*. It proselytes against Hitler and the Nazis. A hammer of crisis knocks on terrible gongs as the girl leaves the young labor leader after telling him the labor movement now must fight for other causes than wages and hours and collective bargaining rights, and as the ghost of the father says the same thing, saying it solemnly and lovingly.

This play, so deeply human and richly motivated, has the values that make it merit repeated presentations.

Along with several other American citizens who do not hang breathless on the words or pauses of Bill Bullitt speaking, about a year ago I decided the phrase "moral and spiritual values" no longer rings a bell in the minds of listeners. Those using the phrase so often seem to think they are not required to explain it, bound it, compass it. Therefore it may be noticed that nowhere above has there been any reference to "moral and spiritual values."

"Stop his mouth with a corncob"

September 14, 1941

The great Negro biochemist George Washington Carver, who has made the lowly peanut perform with more new human uses than anyone else, spoke at a dinner in the old Theodore Roosevelt home in New York City.

They were honoring him with a medal on account of what he has found the peanut will do for farmers and industry, besides other important findings.

It was a long time since he had washed and ironed enough shirts from week to week to pay his way through a tall-grass college in Iowa.

The first year in college he went in for art and painting, changing his mind and shifting to chemistry, botany, soil culture, and the applied sciences that were to lead him into microscopic detective work on the peanut.

In a little speech of appreciation for the medal he mentioned how much talk we were hearing about free speech and how little it counts for those who let others do their thinking for them and let others tell them what to say.

94

So long as there is free speech there will be argument about precisely what it is, how it should be used, how far it should be allowed to go in this or that direction during a crisis.

There are those who must talk to hear themselves talk—they appreciate the metronomic beat of their own incessant chin music.

Some of us have moments when we understand perfectly the woman who was asked why she talked so much and came back, "How do I know what I think unless I can talk what's going on in my head?"

She would have been interested to hear that scientists in the field of language and thought have a theory it is impossible to think unless you have words with which to think, that words make a framework for the shaping and holding of an idea.

Once during a debate in Illinois, Lincoln explained how useless it was to argue with an opponent who disregarded his own admissions and their implications, and to win against such an opponent the only thing you could do would be "to stop his mouth with a corncob."

Later, as President, he had to deal with such an opponent, an Ohio Congressman, personally sincere, intellectually honest, as those phrases go.

What this agitator said one day tallied with what he said the day before or the day after.

And what he said always and again and again was that the war was wrong, the leadership was false to the people, the leadership was betraying the people, and the President more than anyone else had led the country into the war—and the war, if not stopped, would end in economic ruin and national suicide.

Lincoln would have liked to let this Congressman Vallandigham go on talking, because Vallandigham liked to hear himself talk and cloaked himself as a martyr. But what Vallandigham was saying might be having its effect on soldier boys who, what with marching, toiling, fighting, didn't have time to find out whether Vallandigham was a sincere voice or a well-meaning fool or both, which he was.

In a letter dated June 12, 1863, and given to the country Lincoln made himself clear on whether Vallandigham and others saying the same as Vallandigham should be allowed to have an unlimited right of free speech. Lincoln then wrote:

"Long experience has shown that armies cannot be maintained

95

unless desertion shall be punished by the severe penalty of death.

"The case requires, and the law and the Constitution sanction, this punishment. Must I shoot a simple-minded soldier boy who deserts, while I must not touch a hair of a wily agitator who induces him to desert?

"This is none the less injurious when effected by getting a father, or brother, or friend into a public meeting, and there working upon his feelings till he is persuaded to write the soldier boy that he is fighting in a bad cause, for a wicked administration of a contemptible government, too weak to arrest and punish him if he shall desert.

"I think that, in such a case, to silence the agitator and save the boy is not only constitutional, but withal a great mercy."

Far horizons

September 21, 1941

"We may wish to have nothing to do with Europe," cables Ray Clapper from London, "but Europe affects us in our very vitals and there is no escaping it."

He unbosoms himself, "For a long time I was an isolationist. I wish it were possible for us to be isolated. But I can't see how it is possible. . . . Experience is a stern master and we are learning the hard way."

In other words, he is now a warmonger and has joined what is termed the war party. As fishmongers sell fish and cheesemongers sell cheese so he now sells war and thereby is a warmonger.

Some of us understand exactly and down to fine shadings what Clapper is saying. This is because we say the same thing. And we came to what we are saying by the same road, the same twists and windings.

Often we agree with every point made in an isolationist argument. Then we take up where they leave off.

Air transport, turbines, radio, have shrunk the earth, the oceans, and the continents. If we could unshrink them and go back to the days of George Washington, then again it would be good policy to beware of what he meant by "foreign entanglements." Now, however, on our shrunken earth, we will either find a set of foreign entanglements that work, which will cost high, of course, or we will for years and generations to come dig ourselves in and hide behind impregnable shelters, which will cost higher yet and which will load us so heavy with toil and confusion that we will not have time nor means to work out the economic and cultural developments so many of us dream of.

Paul Douglas of the University of Chicago is sure he underestimates when he says that an isolationist policy will mean that for many years, perhaps a generation or more, the armaments that maintain our isolation will cost us more than $20,000,000,000 a year. What Clapper, the former isolationist, now hopes for is a tie-up with Britain so that British and American might and authority, jointly, can police the world and so throw their force and influence that armaments can be held to a minimum of cost.

"Police the world?" asks Clapper. "Well, it would be cheaper and easier to police the world than to have to go through these periodic frantic rearmament programs at fantastic expense and effort." Like Clapper, we know all the main hazards, obstacles, hurdles, difficulties, challenges. And we ask, "What does the other way offer?" To us it seems to offer spending first one hundred billion and then a second hundred billion of dollars on armament to hold our own against an outside world, with no guarantee nor assurance as to what outside forces and fleets may do to us while inside forces supplied and nourished from the outside will operate on a scale and by methods against which we may be immune—and again we may not. The one most possible civil war, bloody intestinal conflict, that can come to this country is the one that might rise over the question of how far a United States Government could collaborate with the Nazis if and when they and their allies should take over the world outside this country. Other possible civil wars loom, but the foregoing has the highest expectancy.

Two factors mainly have given Hitler his gains—a head start and air power. Our lack of accommodation to Hitler, our way of throwing in this and that against him, our potentials as voiced to the world by our President—it may be written by future historians having hindsight that without these helps, in realities and imponderables, Hitler would by now have won his war. Quite a case can be made out that if we had from the first been strictly neutral in thought and action, and strictly isolationist in viewpoint, on foreign policy, by this time we would be alone against an outside Axis world.

We know deep and sure that only terrific struggle and bloody fighting can now decide that the next world order, including this Western Hemisphere, must not and shall not be dictated by a jungle outfit of ancient medicine men crossed with Machine Age quacks.

Thumbing through *Mein Kampf,* we find they divide mankind not into the good, the bad, and the indifferent. They see only the racially pure and impure, and hope for a world where Nazis manage Nazi puppets, work Nazi slaves, with death for those they term "democratic swine." They have discovered a disease which results from what they call "the bacillus of democracy." They burn books because those books creep and crawl with the bacilli of democracy. Their undercover organizations in this country support journals and speakers who spray the landscape with Nazi bacilli. This spray will increase just about in proportion to Nazi military victories and prestige.

Time will tell us

September 28, 1941

Time is to tell whether this country will have to fight a war—a long, heavy, bloody war—against the whole outside world.

Time is to tell whether we win that war, if or when it comes.

Also time is to let us know whether the outside world trims us to the point where we give them what they want—or whether after prolonged knock-down-and-drag-out affairs, with both sides groggy and punch-drunk, they negotiate a peace wherein each gives the other nothing because nothing represents what they have to give.

Time, for those who wait and listen, always accommodates with information please.

Possibly in 1946 or 1948 the President of the United States elected in 1944 will meet the Chancellor of the German Reich on the Azores Islands (any one of them will do) and work out the celebrated Azores Peace Treaty. The President and the Chancellor sign the treaty because so many planes, ships, cities, and supplies have been destroyed that the people and the soldiers on both sides say the war has gone silly and a little peace won't do any harm.

And because the war settled nothing, except that again war is hell, the peace fails to work out. And as always happens with a stalemate peace, it lasts only till the next war begins. And the next war, like the one preceding, continues till the combatants cease fighting. And by that time everybody will know more than they did before about sea power as compared with air power, about bomb sights and air-borne troops, about gasless Sundays and holidays, about ration cards allowing one ham sandwich a week and lamb stew on Wednesday and you eat it on that day or go without.

It is not considered possible that the war will run to where there is only one man left on the earth, but if that should happen we do know he will be saying, "Where is everybody?"

And according to Jim Poole of the Chicago stockyards, at any moment when there should be exactly two men of the human family left on earth they will find something to fight about and war will be declared to see which of the two is the last man on earth.

Time is to tell us much—those of us earmarked to live on to later hear what time has to tell.

Wendell Willkie is sure the next world capital is either Berlin or Washington. If it proves to be Washington, then Illinois Congressmen will try to know as much about the fortifications at Dakar as they know now about the river improvements at Peoria or East St. Louis.

If Berlin is the next world capital, then Berlin will have the prestige, organization, methods, and inside pressure to tell us what in any big way we can do or not do.

The Nazi propagandas and pressures now operating in this country are only a hint of the heat that will be put on us at any time Hitler should carry through his announced plan to break Russian and British power.

Time is to give us lessons, teaching us for one thing whether a nation of our size and resources can escape a role and a place in world leadership.

In the 1920's we said, like the Hollywood producer, "Include us out." Time is to tell us whether we get by in the years just ahead with being included out.

Time may bring us news worth hearing or it may be the headlines will have us wailing over what we might have done that we didn't do.

Can we go to the great books for light on immediate national policy? For an answer to that we can look at two University of Chicago men of learning. Both of them have read what they pick as the one hundred great books of all time. Both of them have for years been telling the country that if you read these one hundred books, you will know the history of human ideas and the old marvelous bean at the top of the spinal cord maybe will know right from wrong and what to do now and how to do it now.

So what? So one of them is for the Roosevelt foreign policy and the other against. So, as to light on ways and means now, it's no use to read the classics unless what we want is pleasant confirmation of what we already know.

The gist of our lesson is that time will not fail us, time will be sure to tell us what we ought to have done that we didn't do.

Charlie Chaplin owns himself

October 5, 1941

Now or later this country makes its decision whether the Nazi agitation and propaganda organization can pull the tricks here that it got away with in Germany.

When and if the investigation into movie propaganda goes to a finish, it will be found, my information runs, that control of the major picture corporations is held by the Chase National Bank, a Rockefeller concern, the Atlas Corporation, a Morgan subsidiary, and A. P. Giannini, the California banker.

Charlie Chaplin, of course, owns himself, owns his business and owns his sweet immortal soul. I have lately heard him described, by investigators, as "a British subject." To me this is almost as though someone should speak of William Shakespeare as a British subject. I wonder if a man who belongs to the whole human family, who is brother to anything human anywhere, can be stuck into a convenient category designated "a British subject." If I should hear a remark to the effect that Thomas Jefferson or Abraham Lincoln was an American "subject," my ears would feel they were registering to something phony and finicky.

Yes, put Charlie Chaplin on the stand. Ask him, "Sir, was it your intention in your picture *The Great Dictator* to bring Adolf Hitler into ridicule through the character you named Adenoid Hinkel? Sir, were you aware that in thus caricaturing the Chancellor of the German Reich, you were not maintaining a correct neutrality and you were distinctly conducting a propaganda intended to bring Herr Hitler into disrepute?"

And it will be all right with some of us if Charlie answers, "Sir, being on oath and wishing to tell the truth, the whole truth, and nothing but the truth, I must confess that besides giving people merry entertainment, I did have in the making of *The Great Dictator* another distinct motive. I hoped that the portrayal of Adenoid Hinkel alias Adolf Hitler would be so effectively moving that the whole world would be glad to hear of his death and burial."

The bear that walks like a man

October 12, 1941

Ten years ago several travelers coming out of Russia had a long talk about what they should report back in the good old United States of America when asked, "Well, how was things in Russia?"

And after their long talk they decided the best short answer would be "Whatever anybody says about Russia is true."

An eminent New York dramatic critic went to Russia five or six years ago, came home to find quite often someone buttonholed him, asking, "What did you see and hear in Russia?"

No sooner had he got started telling what he believed he had seen and heard in Russia than he was interrupted.

They had not been in Russia, but they wished to correct him as to what he believed he had seen and heard in that country.

They had not been in Russia, but they knew better and had for sure learned otherwise than what he began telling them.

He got tired of this, kept a fishy eye on anyone asking him about Russia, letting his answer be that of the privileged witness, "I stands mute."

His advice to other travelers coming out of Russia was "Write a magazine article or a book, let it go at that, and refuse to talk."

Few travelers or none at all from the outside world have in recent years been shown the works in Russia, though she was among the first to send out photographs showing parachutists with machine guns dropping from the sky—and she took an open pride in her flyers who took off from Moscow and flew over the North Pole to Alaska, finally landing in California.

That she had air-borne baby tanks or that any nation had such novel armament was not known till she insisted on shearing off Bessarabia from Rumania so the Nazis couldn't have it.

Parts of her armament and production Russia showed to the world to give an impression she had what it takes and might be dangerous.

Parts of it she kept hidden, and to what extent spies from the outside got at what she didn't want to show is yet to be learned.

Hitler's information led him to believe Russia would be a walk-over for his blitz—which means lightning you run from in terror.

Others in London and Washington, whose information was about the same as Hitler's, gave it out there was "no reason for optimism," and privately said they hoped otherwise but it looked as though the Nazis would take over what they wanted of Russia, maybe before the end of last July.

Now there are no experts, not even in Russia, who can tell us how long the vast and terrific fighting there is to go on and what will be the shifting zigzags of the monster battle.

Nor can we repeat now what the merry travelers agreed on ten years ago, "Whatever anybody says about Russia is true."

There is a fighting morale in the Russian people and a degree of efficiency and valor in Russia's arms and soldiers that has astonished the world.

The Russian people, the wide-flung variety of types and breeds composing it, we know of them in part from the books of world great writers such as Tolstoy, Turgenev, Dostoevski, Gogol, Push-kin, Chekhov, Gorky, and from Soviet writers and from conflicting observers.

Next winter, next year, is to tell us more.

John Gunther gives us what Winston Churchill told him about the bear that walks like a man.

The Prime Minister of the United Kingdom told the boy from the Chicago stockyards, "Russia is a mystery within a mystery within a mystery."

Hitler cannot conquer Russia

October 19, 1941

A peasant girl on a collective farm in Russia told Maurice Hindus, "In this country learning to shoot is even more important than learning to read." Another girl said, "Even if not all of us can shoot with equal precision, each of us can always hit the head, if not the heart, of a Fascist." And Hindus comments, "I have neither known nor heard, in all my travels in Russia, of a single woman who would take exception to those fiery words."

Young and old sharpshooters in Soviet Russia, trained to hate and to kill with hate, will carry on an endless warfare—in occupied areas—hiding out in swamps, forests, mountains, wilderness—coming out of hiding when the time is right—then fading like our own Marion the Swamp Fox, like Quantrell's band in the Missouri-Kansas civil war, like the Chinese guerrillas whose inferior mechanized equipment has not yet brought their conquest by the highly mechanized Japanese. The Russian people will use not only guns but "treachery and deceit, the knife and the ax, poison and the torch, hunger and disease," Hindus indicates in his book *Hitler Cannot Conquer Russia.*

Born in a Russian village, seeing his father and mother wrangle a scant living from a few acres of land—and later a farm hand in central New York State for four years—going back to Russia many times and talking in cities, villages, and far places with high officials and humble workers—Hindus has much to report. He tells it plainly, often vividly. It pours from him. Deep and unfailing, at moments actually grand, is his love of the Russian people and his faith in how their will and vision in the end is to work out a high destiny. When at a few spots here and there in reading his book I find I am a little skeptical and have my personal reservations, I speak a prayer that he may be right in all his hopes and predictions.

When Hitler swept over Poland in September, 1939, Hindus played a hunch and went off the deep end. He cabled from Helsinki to his publisher in New York suggesting that he write a book to be titled *The Coming War between Russia and Germany.* A few weeks later, in October of 1939, landing in New York, he was interviewed and correctly quoted as saying, "I am convinced that Russia and Germany will go to war . . . the more they co-operate now, the more cause they will have to clash later on."

As a forecaster Hindus's batting average is good. And he has a good and natural right to tell now in 1941 why he was no screwball back in 1939.

He sketches the turmoils of Russia these past ten years, what sacrifice and hope went into the shaping of the Red Army that met this summer and fall the headlong smashes of the colossal Nazi aggregate of troops and mechanized weapons. The book cannot be summarized. It is a manual on morale, on guerrilla warfare—and much more. He italicizes Stalin's historic remarks in 1931: "We are fifty to a hundred years behind the advanced countries. We must cover this distance in ten years. Either we do this or they will crush us."

And now? Back to the Ural Mountains may go the scattered remnants of a beaten Red Army. They will rally. They will carry on. They will come back. The end, across howsoever many years, will not come till the Nazis are driven out. And out of heroic struggles and incalculable sufferings will come a Russia changed to some pattern not now to be seen. So Hindus believes. My prayers go with his for the Russian people. If they are merely "Asiatic hordes," then I am a barrel-house bum. Hindus knows his Russian people and their big mystic dream better than I do—and I will hope as long as he does. Soon I shall give a second reading to his book—it is that close-packed. And his faith, I take note, is not merely in the Slavs, but in all humanity.

Human rather than neutral are the Swedes

October 26, 1941

The caldron of the war seethes. Material resources melt. Hitherto invisible motives of men suddenly come to view and shine. The Swedish nation, for instance, might be silent, shrinking, shivering before its hidden fate. Almost, at moments, Sweden hangs to a precipice by an eyelash. Yet she speaks, unafraid, keeping her soul.

Some fine purple shadows of things a little beyond utterance are there in a speech of Prince William, second son of King Gustav, at Gothenburg this summer, saying that while his country is fond of peace, it does not lack arms, and: "We are resolved to protect our inheritance and to pass it on to our children. Undaunted we face the future, well knowing that it might bring storms. But the flag always did look best in a head wind. If necessary we shall nail it to the mast in the old sailor way rather than strike our colors. If we fail our own people, we abandon our only anchorage in life. But a nation which refuses to sell its soul can never entirely lose it."

The Nazi Embassy staff in Stockholm had been increased from fifty to a hundred and fifty just a few weeks before this speech. Considering the time, the place, the war caldron, the smoke of battle, and the stench of conquest not so far off, the speech is near-heroic. The word "undaunted" and its like did not go unnoticed on the part of the one European power which has figured down to fine fractions what might be the cost of taking over the land of Sweden.

Came September and other Swedish leaders spoke as free men who, because of what had happened, could not hold back from declaring their minds and hearts. Standing and facing a Norwegian flag hung with crape, the delegates of the Swedish Labor Federation listened to an address by their president, August Lindberg, and then honored the memory of the two Norwegian labor-union officers, Viggo Hansteen and Rolf Vickstrom, executed by a German firing squad.

"We wish to voice our solidarity with and our sincere admiration for the Norwegian working class," ran a resolution adopted. "We regret that all avenues seem closed to any free intercourse with the German working class. We refuse to believe that the prevailing use of force which violates the rights of other peoples can find support among the German workers. Germany's Nazi rulers have often stated that a people is not deprived, with impunity, of its honor. Neither can the Norwegian people be subdued by violence or force of arms. Hansteen and Vickstrom have written their names indelibly in the history of the Norwegian people. We honor their memory, which will create a closer bond among the Scandinavian peoples."

Notice the restraint. They don't want to fight. They want to keep out of war. Yet they can't keep silence over a cruel wrong, a monstrous action, by those ruling their next-door neighbor, their sister nation. They had to tell the world where they stood as between the Nazi killers in Norway and the trade-union officers killed by the Nazis.

Came then a protest by Major Quisling's official newspaper, *Fritt Folk* (meaning *Free People*), terming the Swedes' memorial service for the two Nazi-executed Norwegian labor leaders "an unprecedented affront to Germany," voicing a threat not thinly veiled: "The Swedish Government, which did not see fit to stop this outrage, should realize that Germany will not be offended with impunity."

Thus an event has echoes. The echoes become realities with repercussions. The Nazis cry neutrality is gone—and impunity, too. And about all that the Norwegians and Swedes can be sure of is their honor, with *Svenska Dagbladet* of Stockholm, the leading daily newspaper voicing business and industry, saying: "The bullets that felled Hansteen and Vickstrom whizzed closely above the heads of the Labor Congress delegates in Stockholm, ricocheted across the Baltic Sea, and did not miss their mark even in Finland. The Congress voiced not only the agitated feelings among 1,000,000 organized Swedish workers, but also the sympathy of the entire Swedish people for its sister nation, Norway, in its proud sorrow and deep suffering."

So Quisling's Nazis shoot down Hansteen and Vickstrom as though two good men are a couple of mad dogs. So the news of it flies. So Swedes take risks on their neutrality. So there are Hansteens and Vickstroms in every corner of non-German Europe. So crape, seen or unseen, tells of "proud sorrow and deep suffering." So men step out in holiness as martyrs. So there is no telling how far it may go and where it will end. So the flares of heroic action in Norway cross the Atlantic to Kansas and move that Quaker-blooded elder statesman, Senator Arthur Capper, to one of the noblest speeches of his career, a broadcast to Norway, declaring across the Atlantic airways: "Through your own brave and steadfast resistance on the home front and through the help which the outside world, and especially America, is more and more bringing to you, I am convinced that Norway once more will be free and independent, and will again pursue her role as one of the leading civilized nations in this world."

Then Senator Capper repeated solemn lines from a broadcast the week before by the United States Secretary of Agriculture, saying the lines expressed "not only my sentiments, but those of the whole American people." Those breathing lines read: "We are with you in spirit as you carry on in the great tradition of a free people. Your battle is an inspiration to us and to free people all over the world. Long live Norway!"

Invisible motives

November 2, 1941

The kettle of the war, the vast caldron, seethes and boils. Inside this kettle of violence, this caldron fuming and shaking, is what?

Nearly the whole human family, parts of it not yet touched by the heat, other parts burned out—"annihilated" seems to be a favorite word lately.

Yet here is humanity—out of the jungle and the wilderness—sometimes taking aim and killing so they see the killed fall and twist, sometimes watching them starve and beyond help in their starvation.

And humanity here out of science and civilization, man thinking, man in a leather seat high in the clouds pulling a lever and dropping a load of death as easy as ordering a breakfast of ham and eggs, the bomber who never sees, never after knows for sure whether five or fifty women and children lie horizontal with ashes in their mouths, a pile of splintered wood and broken plaster burying them before they are located for later decent burial.

Into the war caldron are swept the material resources of the whole round earth and its land and water—and the secret invisible motives of a great host of mankind who perform with valor or shame, with toil and sacrifice or with a desire for comfort and convenience.

When after a time the heat is gone and the fire cooled and living men take a look at the then quiet caldron, they may say it was material resources that decided what came—or they may say the controlling element was the invisible motives in the hearts of men.

And after the high boiling point, the deciding crisis in the caldron, there may be a long cooling-off, as hard to look at as the time of the fiercest heat.

The Pope, speaking to his family which has its members in all

107

elements of the crazy, boiling caldron, tells the world in fear and sorrow of the harvest of hate to follow whatever end the war may come to.

Maurice Hindus points to the hate harvest now being sown and cultivated. It is nationalist, "not workers but peoples that are chafing with bitterness and hate against Hitler, Nazis, Germans." He quotes a young Polish girl, daughter of a nobleman, "I shall be happy when I can go back to my native land and turn a machine gun on the German swine." The key adjective was not "Hitlerite" nor "Nazi" but "German."

One correspondent after another coming out of Germany reports a feeling among the German people that unless their army wins the war, they will for years and years be a folk and a breed meeting a fury of hate, contempt, revenge. Instead of becoming the *Herrenvolk,* as promised by Der Führer, they will, if their army fails, be the foremost swine and the most unspeakable pigs of the continent of Europe—for years, perhaps generations.

A stalemate war, a negotiated peace, a standstill for breathing and resting and healing while getting ready for more of the same thing? Yes? While Hindus tells us—and he could do another book on the facts and the evidence—that whether or not the German Army takes over all of Europe and puts its Nazi-trained administrators in charge, "As long as eighty million Nazi-led Germans are seeking to subjugate and annihilate three hundred million Slavs, there will be neither peace nor order for Germans or Slavs—there will be only terror and blood without end."

Labor leadership

November 9, 1941

In the beginnings of the labor movement in this country, local trade-unions elected an officer known as the walking delegate. That is, he was delegated to walk from the union office or headquarters to any place where there was trouble to settle or business to arrange for the local union.

Of course, there were some walking delegates who drove a horse and buggy or took a hack, but most of them did really walk. And in those "gay nineties" quite often the walking delegate could carry in a top vest pocket and an inside coat pocket all the main records and documents of the union. A closed shop, in that time, was about as scarce as a John L. Sullivan bartender mustache is now. And a good majority of the union men of that time had been strikers, had suffered and sacrificed personally for what they regarded as the sacred cause of organized labor.

Then the walking delegate vanished. In his place came the business agent. Labor was not a commodity, but wages, hours, production costs, profits, were strictly business matters and the local union's business agent came to be regarded as a practical negotiator and a man of affairs rather than a blatherskite shooting his bazoo about the rights and wrongs of labor.

Here and there was a union business agent whose record for fidelity to the union's rank and file could not be reconciled with his style of living, which changed from plain and simple to fancy and gaudy. Such a business agent was often referred to as a labor skate and later as a racketeer.

This generation of union memberships differed from the preceding generation in one definite condition. A sizable majority of them had never been in a strike, never went to a strike meeting, never knew at first hand the struggle and sacrifice by which the union had been established, never cared much about the union one way or another, seldom went to meetings of the local union—and these union men have got into the habit of feeling it is more comfortable and convenient to stay away from local union meetings, or if they do attend to let the slate offered them go through.

In this period the checkoff system of paying dues developed. Unions arose where the employer, the company, the corporation, paid the dues of each and every member. This eliminates ill will as between dues-paying and non-dues-paying members while it concentrates huge funds and responsibility awesome to contemplate in the hands of the man or men holding leadership and high office.

The next period in American labor history must take account of the rise of a peculiar phenomenon. He might be styled the labor leader magnate or the labor leader tycoon. He is the friend of the horny-handed sons of toil who believes he must not neglect his regular manicure. He began perhaps with a Grand Chief of the Brotherhood of Locomotive Engineers who had his salary raised to $25,000 a year and who would have been worth ten times that yearly salary if he had had the horse sense to stay out of Florida boom investments and bank-management schemes that lost millions of dollars to the men at the throttles in the locomotive cabs.

The $20,000 to $30,000 a year man is now become fairly common in the labor movement. Some of these labor leader magnates still keep in close touch with their rank and file, still hope and pray that democratic processes may go on alive and functioning in their own particular union as well as the labor movement in general, still hope and pray that the words "democracy" and "freedom" may not become a mockery and a travesty in organizations born out of devotion and sacrifice by the rank and file.

Others of these labor leader magnates are making a record not so easy to look at. To what extent, for instance, can a labor leader be sure that in this hour of national defense effort and possible war the issue of the closed shop and the checkoff system is the same thing that it was before the present crisis? To what extent in the present hour of national danger can a mistaken and precipitate use of the strike weapon make harm and ill will and bad feeling with results eventually not good at all for the country or for the labor movement?

Personal considerations, personal feuds and spites, can well be sunk till the harder days to come are better known and may be more clearly read as to the future. Some of us find it not so easy to believe that of one temperamental feudist among top-flight labor leaders it may be written: "While the country and the people brooded over a wild hurricane looming on the horizon he tended the frail orchids of his personal ambitions and nursed his dark dreams of wider personal power."

Hitler and Huey

November 16, 1941

Mein Kampf is a book out of the year 1924. Rudolf Hess took it down as Hitler was serving a jail sentence in a comfortable cell in the fortress at Landsberg on the Lech in Bavaria. That was seventeen years ago. Since then Adolf Hitler has come to be known as the wildest single human tornado that ever tore the map of Europe to pieces, spitting in the wind four ways at once and show-

110

ing the world how to get on a horse and ride in all directions at once. Where he will end, whether the outside world is to get him or whether one of his own crowd will finish him, is anybody's riddle. In the book *Mein Kampf,* however, we get a self-portrait of him. He tells us how he wants us to think he looks inside and out.

Those who would like good company while reading *Mein Kampf* can enjoy Francis Hackett's *What Mein Kampf Means to America.* Hitler is a statesman, a politician, an evangel, a great executive, organizer, and conspirator. Also he is a fraud, a spieler, a charlatan, and a lunatic. Hackett calls the turn. Hackett knows when. He spots the paradoxes, the gyrations, the monkeyshines, the doodle-bug tricks. In case you don't have the time to wade through the thousand pages of Hitler seeing himself as God's pick of God's best race and breed, Hackett's 280-page book will give you the gist of it. Also his book is a pamphlet and an exhortation. An Irish-born American, he says his say for the hour.

I like his Irish eloquence and his American wrath and wit and scorn. He writes: "Of the thousands of sweet-minded Americans who have swarmed to read Mrs. Lindbergh's book, how many have recognized the ideas in it that are derived from *Mein Kampf?* How many see it as the star-eyed child of that ideological father? . . . Wishing to exclude the Hitler process, she imports the Hitler idea. Her whole intention is honorable, well meant, utterly solicitous for America's welfare, but on every page she evidences the extraordinary degree to which she is under Hitler's influence; and only the person who takes the trouble to read *Mein Kampf* can possibly know this. Which then is better: to consume sugared *Mein Kampf* out of the Lindbergh feeding-dropper or to probe for yourself what the Hitler argument is? You are bound, in any event, to be subjected to Hitler's ideas."

Quite likely in reading *Mein Kampf* there are things we miss, that we can never understand unless we should go back and be reborn in Germany and live through the years that saw Hitler rise and go to town. However, in reading *Louisiana Hayride* by Harnett T. Kane, we get the accent and we know the game play by play. Here is the living Huey Long, mocking, irresistible, as he laughs, "Just say I'm sui generis, and let it go at that." He, too, had the stuff of a dictator. "Can you handcuff an eel?" Hackett asked as to Hitler, and it would go for Huey Long. An eel, a liar, a monstrosity

111

of shabby and shameless ambitions, there are many parallels in the ways of Hitler and Huey Long. Hitler went into long explanations of how "the strong man is mightiest alone," reading the dreams of the people for them and then making them into realities.

To Forrest Davis, Huey Long explained he would be President for four terms. When the people saw how well he was doing, nobody would be able to budge him out in less than that. Long's theory of democracy: "A leader gets up a program and then he goes out and explains it, patiently and more patiently, until they get it. He asks for a mandate, and if they give it to him, he goes ahead with the program in spite of hell and high water. He don't tolerate no opposition from the old-gang politicians, the legislatures, the courts, the corporations, or anybody."

And then what? Then I'll take Huey Long as against Hitler. The Vienna paperhanger never has laughed. He is subhuman and clammy. Huey Long, the eel and the liar, the patent-medicine seller, laughed, and his laugh yet lingers. If by wile and circumstance he had become a dictator it would have been on a Mussolini pattern rather than a Hitler one.

Huey Long's assassin, Harnett Kane tells us, was "a quiet, gentle scholar . . . who felt deeply on the subject of dictators and dictatorships. He had done postgraduate work in Vienna when the Social Democratic movement was crumbling, when Dollfuss ordered the destruction of the workers' co-operative apartments. He remembered those days, and he thought bitterly of the days that were now upon Louisiana."

The dying eel and liar, en route to the hospital, moaned, "I wonder why he shot me." That was the poorest wondering Huey Long ever did in his life. Certainly not half the men of Louisiana that he had called "thieves, bugs, and lice" were what he called them. And it is possible he might have lived on and on had he not let his rash, evil mouth speak follies about the ancestry of the father of his assassin's wife.

One-string cello

November 23, 1941

Hans and Jacob Grimm earned the thanks of millions of children when they went among the peasants of Germany and found a lot of nice stories, yarns so good that many a grown-up today likes to peep into the book to see if he remembers correctly just what it was that happened to Rumpelstiltskin.

Now William Saroyan is going to earn thanks. He grew up among Armenians in the San Joaquin Valley of California, and has written fables the old-timers heard before they left Armenia and took up grape-raising at Fresno. The book is printed fancy, almost gawdy, sells for $7.50. This would not be worth mentioning unless for the fact that two and three years ago Saroyan was hollering his head off for books to be published and sold for two bits apiece. Anyhow *Saroyan's Fables,* just off the press, has some noble little tales we are grateful the author has rescued from the shadows of nowhere.

One of these is about a fellow who gets to pawing around a secondhand store and picks up an old cello with one string to it. He takes it home, sits in a corner of the front room, finds a place for one finger to hold down that one string. Then he saws back and forth with a bow. Hours on hours every day his patient wife has to listen to him sawing back and forth on that one string and his finger always on that one place.

Weeks pass, and she notices he never once changes his finger from that one place as he saws and saws back and forth on that one string. Sometimes she went so far as to wish he would drop dead and his one finger be loosed from the one place where he always held it on the string. Other times she hoped and prayed he would suddenly realize what he was doing and stand up and smash the cello and throw away the bow. But this didn't happen. He went on playing.

He had taught her to speak softly or else. So one day she said softly to him that she had watched other players playing the cello. And, she went on, they always had four strings to the cello. And, more than that, they kept changing their fingers from one place to another all the time they were playing. This, she went on, she had particularly seen, they never kept one finger in the same place on one string while playing the cello.

He looked at her a slow moment. He laid down the bow and the cello. He told her: "I might have expected this from you. You are a woman. Your hair is long, your understanding short. Of course, the other cello-players are always moving their fingers from one place to another. They are looking for the right place. I have found it!"

So goes this story which is also a fable. I have varied it slightly in the telling because Saroyan wished me to show how a genuine folk tale is never told the same twice.

As a fable some of us find it timely. It could be titled "The Pigheaded Man Who Liked Himself Very Much." We could name a Michigan Congressman who would hotly deny that the portrait bore any resemblance to him.

So would John L. Lewis deny it held any speaking likeness to him. Yet there he stands. The others are wrong and he is right. The others seek a knowledge of equity in a national emergency. He has found it.

Equity? I remember reporting the threatened rail strike of 1917. And Garretson, one of the best-loved of rail Brotherhood leaders of all time, made the outcry one day when the torment of a general strike loomed: "We are like two cave men fighting to see who will get to gnaw a bone." It hurt him to say it. He writhed saying it. He spoke one day of how he hoped he was "growing in inner grace." I had never before heard anyone mention "inner grace" in such a tone and with such lights on his face that I knew if I could get some of it, the same would be good for whatever ailed me and if nothing ailed me it would be good for that.

National unity

November 30, 1941

Most any traveler nowadays by listening with either right or left ear half-cocked can hear the simple question "What is national unity?" and the likewise simple answer "National unity is when the country is united." Which is like saying water is wet and if it isn't wet it isn't water.

National unity—yes—when have we had it? In peacetimes? Where was the unity under Grover Cleveland as President when the American Railway Union had transportation wrecked forty ways and Federal troops went to Chicago under the protest of Governor Altgeld of Illinois?

Where was national unity when the embattled farmers of the West in the Populist movement had Wall Street terrorized by demands for free silver coinage, government ownership of public utilities? The mere names of Theodore Roosevelt and Robert M. La Follette, Sr., call up the years when there was shouting and crying out loud about America headed for the ash cans.

And national unity in wartime? Take the war George Washington handled. It ran eight years. Some years, it seemed, almost nobody cared. There was selfishness, apathy, no will to do or to fight. Washington assembled enough fragments of unity to get by from year to year.

And Lincoln, in his war, over and again felt national unity had slipped away so far that maybe he was sunk. He was able to summon, negotiate, buy, trade, coax, manipulate, persuade, just enough national unity to get by. When Lincoln came to Philadelphia in the spring of '64 to speak at a Sanitary Fair he dropped a little remark that for historical portent didn't mean a thing except when looked at in the framework of events. The little remark, so widely discussed by friends and enemies of national unity, ran "It is difficult to say a sensible thing nowadays."

Lincoln knew he had once in a while said a sensible thing worth men's thinking about. Then it was picked up and made into something else than he meant or there was the old habitual horselaugh that he never meant what he said.

The last speech of Lincoln before he died was all on national unity. His war had been won. And he was pleading for a unity he saw as possible. It was a difficult speech. He was again saying sensible things that if listened to might have steered the country clear of much of the bloody and useless wrangling of what is termed the Reconstruction Period, when for years national unity was sad to look at.

In any democracy it is always going to be difficult to say sensible things about national unity. When unity gets too smooth and perfect, then there is the danger of too much power being in the hands of those in control of the unity. Yet unless those in control are allowed to have a certain amount of power, the national unity can sink and diminish to the point where things fall to pieces that ought to be holding together.

This is one riddle that a free people always wrestles with. It is a riddle that the editors of the *New Republic,* for instance, have for years tormented themselves and their public about. The right to speak, the right to print and publish, the right to go anywhere and tell 'em what you think, this side of libel or slander—for these rights the *New Republic* has been foremost.

Yet now the *New Republic* editors, in a calm and searching statement, have come out for a declaration of war by the United States against Germany. And one main point they urge is that if and when we go all-out for war, there will be possible a control of the Nazi underground forces now operating in this country.

Does anyone having plain horse sense or ordinary household gumption, and familiar with the Nazi methods of total espionage, suppose that the Gestapo agents and the Berlin propagandists now doing their work in this country are limited to merely millions of dollars? Will the tangled underground story, if ever dug up, show that the payments have run into tens of millions, some of it for purposes that outrun present imaginings?

Take a look through Curt Riess's book *Total Espionage,* published this month. Ask yourself whether it is a cool recital of sinister facts that ought to be known to every American. He analyzes the setup of total espionage by which the Nazis begin war in a country long before there is any shooting.

One reason they took some countries with little or no shooting was that they were able to paralyze them without war before moving in and taking over. These eight Nazi divisions work on total espionage: 1. The Intelligence Service of the War Ministry. 2. The League of Germans Living Abroad. 3. The Foreign Department of the Gestapo. 4. The Foreign Political Office. 5. The Special Service of the Foreign Office. 6. The Foreign Office of the Propaganda Ministry. 7. The Foreign Department of the Ministry of Economics. 8. The Reich Colonial Office. Do we like 'em? Their slogan is "Results count, and let nothing stop you from results."

"Nothing" includes dirty work at the crossroads mentionable and unmentionable, spies, saboteurs, arson, murder, robbery, bribery, torture, collusion, extortion, blackmail, thuggery, and any conceivable device of sex or shame or threatenings of dear ones and next of kin.

There are those who think and say such a kettle of stink-fish can win only small results in so big a country as ours. Others of us don't agree. We favor surgical operations. We have seen the spread of antidemocracy doctrines. We have seen race-hate theories spread. We have seen reports, rumors, concoctions, canards, malicious gossipings, spread with the aim of making confusion, chaos, folly, mistrust, and a feeling of "What's the use?"

Not all of this is a result of Nazi operations. Some of it is the result of an old-fashioned violent American national debate over great issues on which honest men can differ.

Yet every hour the Nazi total espionage organization is working. Their funds are unlimited. Their ways are new to this country. Their job is to throw in wherever there is any chance to help wreck national unity.

They bring fresh meaning to the remark of those who today echo Lincoln's saying in the spring of '64, "It is difficult to say a sensible thing nowadays."

Their aim is to make the national headache so mean and tormenting that there will be a cry for a change from the democratic system—permanently.

Mr. Johnson's book is independent as a hog on ice

December 7, 1941

Not until I visited Baltimore for the first time, some twenty years ago, did I hear it is a saying there, "Baltimore is a city of good oysters and bad women." I did not believe it then. Nor do I now. Nor do they. They say it because it sounds interesting and mischievous.

It is like the bashful and backward Maine farm hand who called on a girl several times and couldn't find anything to say to her. One evening, however, he did break a long silence with asking her, slowly and as though not sure of what he was saying, "Do you want to buy a shirt?"

The girl's reply came fast, "No, are you selling shirts?" And the

117

farm hand crawled into a still longer silence after answering her "No, I was just talking to make talk."

So when you next go to Baltimore you might say it as they say it or see how it goes in reverse to tell them, "Baltimore is a city of bad oysters and good women."

Anyhow, Gerald W. Johnson might be able to tell you about it. He writes editorials for a considerable newspaper in Baltimore. What he doesn't know he looks up in the morgue or frankly says he doesn't know.

Washington is near by and often he runs down to Washington and gives the government a once-over and rides back to Baltimore saying not yet is he sure how the government runs, whether it is a mechanical clock or a biological organism or a little of both.

Now this fall Mr. Johnson launches a book at the American public. He dedicates it like this: "To Every Man Who Cast an Honest Vote for Willkie This Book Is Inscribed with Respect."

The book itself is titled: *Roosevelt: Dictator or Democrat?* So, with that dedication and with that title, you don't know beforehand what the book is going to be like.

The opening sentence of the first chapter is a honey: "Franklin Delano Roosevelt will continue as President of the United States—disregarding unpredictable acts of God or of the common enemy—at least until January 20, 1945."

Nothing like an utterly naked fact, strip-teased of all possibilities of contradiction, for a start of a book. From there on Mr. Johnson gives his readers many similarly utterly naked facts. And in between he offers his personal guesses and surmises as to how and why this happened, with his own personal judgments as to what was bad or not so bad in policy or method.

May I say here that Mr. Johnson, to borrow one of our Chicago expressions, is independent as a hog on ice?

The book grew in him and he had to write it to get it off his mind. Of himself he writes, "It may be worth while to note that the author has never been a candidate for office and never held a political job under either party and hopes, God willing, never to do so."

So the reader may know, Mr. Johnson sets forth: "No one at the White House or even remotely connected with the White House

118

suggested or intimated how any fact should be presented, much less how any sentence should be phrased. The book, in short, does not present the official view; on the contrary, in a number of instances it is distinctly anti-official."

That was the distinct impression I got while reading the book and before I came to this foregoing statement on the inside flap of the dust jacket. Mr. Johnson is nobody's yes-man. Patiently, even crabbedly at times, he writes his personal views and judgments.

I have the feeling that any true friend of Willkie who reads the first chapter slowly and carefully will go through the rest of the chapters and then thank Mr. Johnson for having let himself write the book.

Mr. Johnson's sense of humor has play quite often, but in the main he is sober, judicial, with no flagrancies of either bad oysters or bad women. "The President," he informs us, "was kind enough to talk to me about this book, and good-humored enough to answer frankly any number of questions pointed to the verge of bad manners."

From the above there will be people making the inference I believe this book ought to be read all over the country. I do so believe. I would write the book differently. I would shade many of its graver judgments differently and develop them farther. Yet I salute it for what it pretends to be.

Here is that man in the White House. By fate and circumstance of destiny, he is now in the wild whirls of an incessantly changing international storm, the spokesman of the American people before the world. What in the past of this man can we look at that will give us more light on how he may prove up in hard and terrible days to come?

Mr. Johnson puts that question and hangs to it from start to finish. What is there to show that maybe this man might develop into a dictator? What is there to show that he may have the strength, patience, cunning, sagacity, resilience, to move through awful ordeals, with a later verdict perhaps that no other man could have done better?

In discussing these questions Mr. Johnson never gets absolute, never noisy, never petting himself about pet opinions of his own. He has searched the hearts of men who honestly voted for Willkie and thereby honestly voted against Willkie's opponent. His analysis of the NRA, the pivotal point at which Mr. Johnson finds it cockeyed, this may have been one of the things he questioned the President about "to the verge of bad manners."

Much unusual information, some of it keenly dramatic, is packed in. Those seeking fresh light on American politics of the past three decades may find more than a few essential glints here in Mr. Johnson's book, which I believe future historians will use as one of the indispensable items ranking among what historiographers call "primary sources."

A primary source, to be frank and simple, is one that has gone to the horse's mouth, like Mr. Johnson rambling around the White House, then strolling to Capitol Hill and on through Senate and House cloakrooms, then thinking it over while riding back to Baltimore and its oysters and women, good and bad.

Note: Like many another writer whose piece was written before the news of the Japanese attack on Pearl Harbor, the above was completely lacking in any breath of the excitement of that date.

Amazing Russia

December 14, 1941

The battle that began at dawn of June 22, when the German and Finnish armies opened their attack on the Russians, has now lasted on into the winter month of December, nearly six months in the going and nowhere near an end. It is known as the Battle of Russia, not a campaign, but rather a series of campaigns so swiftly telescoped and jammed together, with action never stopping, that it classes as one vast battle.

The 1940 Battle of France was a small affair, and in the sense that France did not actually stand up and fight as at Verdun in the First World War, it was not really a battle at all. The Red Army and its supporting people of Russia, their will to do and to fight, their refusal to be conquered, their valor and tenacity and strategy, raise many questions as to how and why they have performed as they have.

First of all, the Russians had more to fight with than was expected. Where did such men, women, and armament come from?

120

They had to stop or slow down the mightiest machine for "lightning war"—blitzkrieg—the human family has ever seen. As a sporting event it stands as supercolossal.

In numbers of men, cannon, tanks, planes, supplies, and munitions, the Nazi machine surpassed anything launched for attack at any time in the First World War.

Nothing that allied France, Britain, and the United States met in 1917 and 1918 approaches in size, weight, speed, fury, what the Russians have faced these summer and fall months just passed. Back and back the Russian lines have moved, holding intact, losing cities and plains, losing supplies and resources, always cool and prepared for the next onslaught, over and again when they seemed to be crumbling launching another and another counteroffensive.

Day and night, these summer and fall months just passed, the Nazi and Red High Commands have hurled millions of men at each other. Around their operations each has thrown impenetrable curtains. What they are doing to each other, except as to bare claims and counterclaims as to ground taken or retaken, is kept from the outside world. How many millions of its own are dead, wounded, or lost as prisoners neither side tells. Each fights, suffers, hides its wounds and losses, and goes on, day and night, month on month. About all that outside experts do is to estimate today and next week revise their estimates.

Two surprises have come to the outside world. One relates to Russia's material preparation for the war, the huge and almost unbelievable amount of tanks, planes, guns, shells, bombs, grenades, land mines, concrete pillboxes, tank traps, guerrilla hiding places—and all of these joined up in a grand strategic scheme for meeting exactly what came.

Quite likely Hitler thought Russia would be a pushover. And possibly Hitler had the wrong information, like others outside of Russia. Walter Duranty in his just published book *The Kremlin and the People* reports what Lindbergh saw and where Lindbergh went in the only five days Lindbergh had in Russia, spending part of the time with Soviet flyers "patriotic and utterly hostile to any thought of defeatism."

So, for what it is worth in the record, Duranty writes: "Lindbergh did not get and could not have got his pessimistic story about the Soviet Air Force from the Soviet flyers, any more than he got it

121

from his personal observations. If you wish to know, he got it from the Germans, who doubtless knew better themselves, but wished for their own reasons to have him say what he did."

Not least among certainties is that Hitler would have had Moscow last July could he have dragged down enough Soviet flyers. They still fly, outnumbered, but still flying, with scant though real reinforcement from the British R.A.F. The industrial morale of Soviet Russia before her war came, the huge production required to make any showing against what the Nazi machine brought, this is one of the surprises.

The other surprise is a mystical thing. You can search and probe and never be sure just what it is. A patriot is sometimes defined as one who loves his country and shows it by faith, works, and sacrifice. In that sense Russia has many millions of patriots.

About 1935 in the press, in the movies, in songs, the word "Rodina," meaning "Birth Land," took the place of the old phrase "Socialist Fatherland." This helped. But how would that account for the exiled Russian Whites whose hate of the Reds is now overwhelmed by love of their "Holy Mother Russia"? By thousands they are now seen in this country active in their Russian war-relief work, their contributions, and some of them hoping they will see good old Russia again before they die. This mystical motive operates.

Day and night, in that long two-thousand-mile front in snow and wind and mercury at zero, where the world's most titanic grapple of armed men goes on, a mystical motive operates. One short phrasing of it: "Quit? We'll die first."

Duranty in Washington talked with a high-placed and sad Frenchman about the purge in Russia, thousands shot, millions suspect. "Yes," said the Frenchman, "it must have been awful, like a madness, as you call it. But don't forget, *mon ami*, that in Russia they shot the fifth-columnists, and in France we made them Cabinet Ministers. You see both results today . . . at Vichy, and on the Red war front."

The free world favors Christmas

December 21, 1941

A Scotchman it was who told me about the meanest Scotchman that ever lived. On Christmas Eve he stepped out of the house with a big pistol, shot it off with a loud bang, and came into the house telling the children there would be no presents because Santa Claus had committed suicide.

My Scotch friend who told this fool invention liked to tell it because he himself had a giving and forgiving spirit and he enjoyed, whenever he could afford it, doing things in a Christmas way any day in the year. When he died a few weeks ago, his wife, eight children, and a circle of understanding friends all agreed they would miss an essential Christmas light he carried.

Had he lived, he would have heard the Sabbath-morning news of presents the empire of Japan dropped on Pearl Harbor and the island of Oahu. He would have joined friends in sorrow over the Christmas darkness of the continent of Europe, where the usual millions of lighted Christmas candles must be blacked out.

And yet the Christmas season this year might have been darker than it is. A world that came near crashing still stands and fights. It could have been worse, so easily more tragic than it is. Some of us still hold our breath over the narrow margins of circumstance giving us the chances we now have before us.

There was a free world, very imperfect, heavy with many wrongs, yet a world having definite political and personal freedoms scorned and mocked at by the world's all-time high-record slave masters. Much of this free world is wrecked, humanly torn, bleeding, starving. Yet an immense section of it stands, sees, resists, fights, refuses to accept the Nazi anti-Christmas idea, prays for those in bondage and their eventual release.

The phrase "anti-Christmas" goes well enough for the Nazis. Free-world readers of *Mein Kampf* find it a howling wilderness stony and bare of Christmas feeling. Goodwill to all men gets a high and harsh horselaugh, and the chimes are keyed to a shrill jackass bray. Charity is just a bowl of cherries.

Faith, hope, kindly words and deeds, except as done among folk

123

of the German Reich, except as of direct arithmetical, bookkeeping benefit to Germans, are a snare and a delusion with no pay-off. *Mein Kampf* means *My Fight* though it could have been titled "Me, Myself & Company." Also it might be titled "Me! Me! Me!" or "I! I! I!" and mislead no one.

Vast reeking ego, gone hog-wild and raving, this mainly I find in a recent rereading of *Mein Kampf*. And more of the same, with added arrogance, is seen in the newly issued book from Reynal and Hitchcock, another thousand pages titled *My New Order,* giving the speeches since 1921 of the world's Number one egoist, Adolf Schicklgruber, who wants what he wants when he wants it. The argument is here, with and without ravings, against democracy, against goodwill to all men, for race hate, for breed hate, for national hate, and for the Nazi way of life.

For contrast we may turn to *The Balance Sheet of the Future* woven of speeches by Ernest Bevin, England's Minister of Labor. A rather plain man with much common sense and high hope we meet in Bevin.

"May we not, in the centuries that have gone," he asks, "have developed so much wealth that we have really been struggling to protect it rather than to create new wealth? May it not be that out of the vortex of this terrible struggle, the creative genius of our people will be let loose, and may not there be a great renaissance resulting in a New Britain, freed from the snobbery at one end and the poverty at the other?"

He quotes Disraeli: "There are two nations, that of the rich, and that of the poor," and declares for himself, "I want a Britain that places humanity first." Getting specific, he takes up the eight-point Atlantic Charter of Churchill and Roosevelt, especially the provision that all states, great or small, victor or vanquished, shall have access to the trade and raw materials needed for economic prosperity. "If I could have my way I would introduce to the raw materials of the world the postage-stamp principle. Such things as wheat, rice, rubber, oil, coal, ore, chrome, bauxite, and other similar things I would pool internationally, and make an equal charge for their use to anybody who needed them."

Bevin is a patient and moderate man. We see that he could in this hour rake up plenty of dirt in England's past, knowing it well, yet he sees the course of policy now must be to beat Hitler and then pray and work that part of the blueprints for a better world may come true. He puts it about like that.

There is an air of Christmas about Bevin. The word "mankind" he uses as holy. For the struggling masses of the whole world he has an open heart, barring none. By thousands, men of like vision with his have in Germany got the concentration camp, the firing squad, the headsman's ax. The human climate of Bevin's book has Yuletide in it, lighted candles of hope and goodwill to all men, except those who regularly remember London with bigger and better bombs.

Always waits the unforeseen

December 28, 1941

"How long will the war last?" This we hear often. I meet in one day two sober and informed men, one saying a year, another six to eight years. Both are positive, willing to bet. Neither cares about the factor of fate, the unforeseen event which makes any fixed date for the end of the war just a guess, a blind estimate, picking the winner of a county-fair horse race in heavy mud.

A commander takes a great new battleship out into the open sea. Overhead is a cloud screen. He has good reason, from weather forecasters, to expect it to stay there. It doesn't. It moves away. Then come bombing planes. They sink her. The cloud-screen behavior was fate, the unforeseen event. Likewise, the same week a bomb from the air dropping down a smokestack and leaving that battle wagon not a chance.

A powerful German tank drives full speed toward a Russian objective. Is it not the latest design, the last word in power, armor, guns? Suddenly it is in a mass of hay on fire, so much burning hay and smoke that it is tangled, lost, captured. Hay—they had not thought of tanks being tangled and lost by burning hay. Is that a way to make war? It was fate, the unforeseen.

New Year comes and some of us look back at the calendar of 1941 and see two high-spot dates, blazing and unforgettable. One is June 22, when the Nazis moved into Russia telling the world that in six weeks they would have the Red Army knocked off and take over

125

what they wanted of Soviet Russia. Till then that was the least-predicted major event of the year. Then comes December 7 and the Japs dealing death from the sky over Pearl Harbor, in a savage and undeclared war killing American sailors and soldiers by thousands. And that was the least foreseen event of the year.

Then with almost a touch of miracle came the national unity of the United States. That it could come so fast, so clean and so complete, was beyond anybody's telling beforehand. It had reminders of the dream of the prophet Ezekiel when he saw the dry bones scattered over a valley and how those dry bones joined themselves to each other and stood up and walked.

In their journey of destiny the American people on December 7 came to a Great Divide. And they crossed over. Millions of plans and projects canceled themselves like writing on sand after a storm wave. The Japanese deed at Pearl Harbor could not be undone. The finality of it, beyond any conceivable apology or negotiation, smote home to every American-hearted listener of the news and the tolling bells of doom. They were wanting war. They were asking us to meet them with any and all steel and wit and will we might have for war. Their intentions were beyond any hairline's shadow of doubt. They came dealing death, knowing death would be dealt in return. They came as killers, knowing killers would rise in retaliation.

"The causes of war are profound, the occasions slight," wrote some ancient. And the Scotch say, "Nothing comes fairer to light than what's been long hidden." Old Man Scripps once wrote to his boys, more than fifteen years ago, that a war between Japan and our country some day was sure to come. He had cruised the Pacific and scented the dominant thirst of the Japanese ruling class to control that ocean. They took it as "our sea." Scripps made clear it would be a dirty war. He could wish it was not coming. But he could see it was. He foresaw.

Now the Nazis throw in with the Japs. Now the pure Aryans of Berlin yoke themselves with the pure Mongols of Tokyo. Now it is four-fifths of the Family of Man signed up for a finish fight against the "New Order" in Europe and the Pacific. The "New Order" will lose. It will be outfought and outthought. The war ending when? That depends on unforeseen events. Within possibility too are sev-

126

eral cataclysms, colossal in explosive force and reverberations. Against these the Nazi-Jap alliance has less assurance than the anti-Axis line-up.

Hitler's man-killing job

Some of us forget which battle it was that Napoleon lost because of a seizure of stomach distress that befuddled his brain, a little stomachache not taken care of in the detailed preliminary preparations. Also there came to Napoleon a paunch. And conquerors with paunches don't do so good, losing tempered steel for pig iron.

Something like this is in many minds now with reference to Adolf Hitler. We saw him earn a reputation as a marvel for timing. Now we know he is not so good as he was, even though he has no paunch and eats less and sleeps less than any high commander on earth. For the question is "What has happened to him who originated the war of nerves? And how goes it with his nerves?"

Any time Hitler's health cracks, any day it is known his brain is spent and his nerves shattered so he is taken out of the game—that will be news about equal to hearing that a million German soldiers have quit fighting and ten Japanese battleships are sunk. It is near-fantastic that this can be so. And it is fact as well as fantasy that so many strands of actual and terrible power rest in the hands of a tragic galoot whose mind dwells on the borderline of lunacy.

Every day, every waking hour, they keep coming to Hitler for his Yes or No. Messages arrive by courier, by phone, by radio.

What about this or that? And he can't wait. He must say Yes or No or name someone else who is to say the Yes or No. Key men arrive at his quarters. They tell him this and that can't wait. It must be Yes or No now. And he either says the Yes or No, or he racks his brain for the name of whomsoever he perhaps can trust to say the Yes or No.

How many reports piled in on him of German troops frozen to death by thousands on the Russian front and still other thousands so smitten by merciless 30°-below-zero atmosphere that fingers, toes, ears, legs, arms, required immediate amputation, we do not know. We do know that he knew something must be done, no

127

delay. So there came that peculiar and solemn radio "request" of Goebbels and Hitler saying warm clothes must be sent to the freezing German troops on the Russian front.

Reading that order slowly out loud, you will see that if you were a citizen living in Germany or any of the conquered countries, you would think twice before going out on the street in fur or woolen clothes that looked fine and warm. Wearing a fur coat, a fur cap, or fur gloves, you would expect to start a riot. This was one item not thought of when Hitler began his war on the largest fur-production country in the world.

How many hours a day he must give to Gestapo reports on German morale, on morale in the occupied countries, on morale in Britain, Africa, the United States, and South America, on morale in the private and confidential affairs of his own High Command, we do not know.

How many hours he can spare for the intricate and far-flung Nazi-party organization when he must also say Yes or No on what kind of a permanent winter front to establish in Russia if he can, what should be the next move in Africa, the Mediterranean, the Near East, the Battle of Britain, the Battle of the Atlantic, the undercover operations in South America, the collaboration with Japan, the finespun webs of intrigue around Vichy that may or may not get him the French fleet, the new propaganda tones that must emanate from Berlin, the secret details of the joint action plans formulated by the Allies at Washington, the further secret details of the schemes arrived at in the Stalin-Eden talks at Moscow—we do not know.

We do know that any future biographer trying to report completely the vast spiderweb at whose center stands this weird paper-hanger will often be sick while sunk in the documents, and dead before the job is finished.

So goes history, often. On the microscopic physical facts of health or decay in the little brain paths of this person born Adolf Schicklgruber may depend the further development of whether it will cost the anti-Axis allies one million or five million more lives to wreck and destroy him.

He was born for storm and blood, and likes it. He may last. Yet he may see in preparation, and due for relentless arrival, forces that can outburn and outkill whatever he can scrape together to meet it with.

This language he understands. And he has heard of the will to victory.

And he sees four key men against him that are baffling. He wishes he had more time to study and perhaps solve the different styles of Churchill, Stalin, Chiang Kai-shek, Roosevelt. He may or may not realize they are perfectly armored against his "war of nerves" that used to work, finding that in psychological warfare they have devices he never thought of. His brain cells and nerves may stand the terrific wear and tear of the toils and decisions piling on him. And again they may not.

Maybe Hitler is on the downhill. His percentage of errors now runs high. Perhaps his decisions are due to get worse and worse. Maybe from now on he is the worst leader Germany could have. If we could be sure of this we would know whether to pray he lives on or dies soon and no longer cumbers the earth.

Russia got production

January 11, 1942

Russia got production. Somehow or other she did get that production. One answer to why Russia has been able to stand and not go down under awful punishment is the production she got. The same answer goes for why she has been able to hand out punishment as well as take it—production.

One story, fairly well vouched for, has it that information came to Hitler showing clearly that if the production rate in Russia kept going higher and higher they would before long surpass and outclass the Nazi empire in planes, tanks, munitions, armament. Hitler knew when he struck with all the lightning he had last June 22 that the Russians packed weapons not known to the outside world. How mighty those weapons were he testified in his Sportspalast speech on October 3, when he wished the German people to have the best possible explanation of why he seemed to be losing the world's most far-flung and bloody battle.

Hitler's explanation ran: "We made a mistake about one thing—we did not know how gigantic the preparations of this opponent

129

against Germany had been." He might have said "I made a mistake" instead of "We," for it was his decision. Letting that pass, we notice that before the whole world he credits a people he terms "bestial barbarians" with the toil, skill, ingenuity, patience, and discipline to create "gigantic preparations" for war almost equal to the vast preparations of his own widespread Nazi empire.

The former United States ambassador to Russia, Joseph E. Davies, heard this speech by short wave in New York and wrote in his diary: "The self-proclaimed divinely inspired one admits himself that he has made a mistake. It was the first crack that I have seen in the supreme self-confidence of the paranoiac mentality of Hitler. If the morale cracks at the top, it is apt to spread very rapidly down below."

Britain bothered Hitler. So did America through the voice of Roosevelt. It was Russia, however, that smote him, made him bleed and cry "gigantic preparations." He used to wisecrack. Now he is cracking instead of wisecracking. Yet he is only cracking, not going to pieces. That is not in sight yet. That will depend mainly on this country and how soon we carry through enough "gigantic preparations" to throw in the added weight that will finish Hitler.

Are there lessons in the Soviet Union we can go to? There are. For one thing, through the duration of the war we might pay less honor to some of our national sports and give more stress and a higher spotlight to aviation, flying of all kinds, as a sport. Not so long ago our Secretary of War, for instance, threw his dignified frown on gliding and gliders. A flareback came from many folks more air-minded than he, so he modified the frown into a benevolent smile.

We may quote here from a book by Lucien Zacharoff, an associate editor of Aircraft Publications, telling us: "Virtually all world records for all varieties of parachute jumps are held by Red Army and Navy men or by Soviet civilians. A woman pilot, Olga Klepikova, set the world's long-distance glider mark in 1939 with her flight of 465½ miles. Airman Boris Kimmelman won the world's record for glider flight and return to point of departure with his round trip of 212¾ miles. Last year 1,000,000 civilian enthusiasts made parachute jumps from Soviet aircraft. Over 5,000,000 jumped in 1940 from 600 parachute towers erected throughout the country.

As early as 1935 there were already over 40,000 advanced glider pilots, figures since greatly increased."

Our War Secretary likes horses and is good in the saddle. He inclines toward the Cossack cavalry rather than the civilian gliders and parachutists who have played hell with communications and supplies behind the German lines.

The high army officer of the "yoo-hoo" incident is a golfer, not a glider.

Let them have horses and golf, we say, but let them not cry down flying as a sport. The aircraft and parachutist efficiency of Russia goes back in part to flying as a people's sport praised and lauded by authorities, political and military.

The war may run long. Who knows? And if it should last three years or six years, there will be several momentous decisions resting on whether we have enough or not enough aircraft and parachutist efficiency and numbers. This is not strategy but plain horse sense. Too often now we hear the sorrowing remark "Maybe if they had been a little more air-minded at Pearl Harbor what happened would have been a little different." They are not croaking or chiding—they are sorrowing.

It is good the golf ball is out of bounds and chromium for niblicks is nix. The baseball, the football, the tennis ball, the ping-pong ball, are still with us. And without crying down any other sport, I believe a fine case can be made that while the war lasts flying of all kinds should outrank all other sports. The reason why newspaper sports pages have so little about gliders and parachute jumpers is because there are so few of them compared with the heroes of other sports. Plenty of fans who know who led the big leagues in batting last year have a vague notion a glider is something new for the kitchen.

Postscript: Mission to Moscow by Joseph E. Davies is a documented book of many fascinating pages. He helps toward understanding the Russia that Winston Churchill once called "a riddle wrapped in a mystery inside an enigma." He throws light on how Russia got production.

131

The road to Vitebsk

Several months ago when the Nazi spearheads had taken Vitebsk in Russia, I talked with Fruma Gottschalk about it. She was born and raised in Vitebsk, later taking a husband who knows more about Lafayette and has written more books about Lafayette than any other living man. And Fruma had wonderings about streets of her childhood and how many houses were left standing that she had known in Vitebsk and who was alive or in flight back of the Red Army. She remembered an old story told in Vitebsk for many generations.

A poor peasant rides in his ramshackle two-wheel cart. Once in a while he speaks to his old bone-rack of a horse. And a better-off peasant, almost counted a well-to-do peasant, asks a ride to Vitebsk and gets it.

They come to a hill, a long upgrade for the horse to pull. The driver tells his guest: "You see how it is. Going up this steep haul it will be a strain on the cart which I hope will hold together. But it will be worse on the horse, who is not what he used to be and has not always had the oats he truly deserved. So perhaps you will be so good as to join me in walking up this hill and we will see whether both cart and horse make the grade."

The guest says he understands and he is perfectly willing. So they jog slowly on and up and make the grade. So the riding is on smooth levels a mile or two and they come again to a long upgrade of a hill. And again the peasant driving asks his guest to join him in the pleasure of accommodating the horse by walking up. And again the guest is pleased to walk, so he says. And as they walk up this hill, the last between them and Vitebsk, he speaks to the owner of the horse, saying: "I know why I am going to Vitebsk. And you know why you are going to Vitebsk. But does that horse know why he is going to Vitebsk?"

The story ends there. No people of Vitebsk have been known to carry it farther. We might call it a featherweight mystery tale carrying a somber, insoluble moral edged with a flicker of silver laughter.

Fall came and the green leaves of summer yellow and wind-blown. And Fruma had a letter from a brother in Vitebsk writing in July of 1941. He did not know for sure who would win the war to begin with, though he was sure that the Nazis could not in the end conquer the Russian people. He did not argue about it. He was telling it.

November came, the leaves gone, deep zero air. Then December with the air far below zero, 30° and 40° below around Vitebsk. And a tank pilot and two tank gunners swore at the bitter wind that swept through their ersatz clothes, swore at the gummed and frozen lubrication, stalled in the snowdrifts and blistered their fingers on frozen steel they touched, put a curse on the rocky and rutted road they had to travel, cursed back to other tank pilots who didn't have room to pass and yelled their curses about it, swore at the frozen food rations they had to eat, cried to the high heavens about the vermin in their armpits biting just when they lay in a snowdrift under the tank making repairs, moaned little prayers they would not, like others they had seen, have to go hunting for the tank-battalion surgeons with a hand or a foot or a leg frozen stiff into complete disability. Possibly one of them in the blowing snow of 40° below zero, after trying to pour lubrication oil that refused to pour, after trying to crank a starter that wouldn't start, talked to himself and the tank. "I know where I want to go. And you know where you want to go. But that low-lived, lying imitation of Jesus who calls himself Der Führer—does he know where he wants to go?"

It might have happened just so. On the hills outlying Vitebsk, in a thousand cruel variations, it might have happened.

Churchill sends a mean one at the Nazis in saying they will lose because they have no sense of humor. It is good Roosevelt can wise-crack between his heavy toils and decisions. And in Nazi Germany it is not good for the people that the fine foolishness of the stories gathered from the people by the Grimm brothers is forbidden, verboten, nix, because we must be a *Herrenvolk* ruling the earth.

Morale is where you find it

January 25, 1942

Morale—what is it? Where do you find it? Dolivet stood with the other French at a bridgehead in early June of 1940. Across the river were the Germans. Over the bridge came two Storm Troopers on motorcycles. Two white flags, meaning a truce, meaning don't-shoot-

133

us, flashed over the handlebars. They crossed the bridge. They got off their motorcycles. They shone in the sun, tall, strong men, powerful to look at.

Naked from the waist up, bronzed by the sun, hair on their chests, they had been picked for their looks and then costumed and staged for a little drama of psychological warfare. One of them stood tall, erect, head thrown back, and folding his arms over his hairy chest, spoke the only French words he had learned and practiced: "*La guerre est finie,*" which means "The war is over."

Dolivet didn't like it. He thought it a fake pass. He pointed his automatic at the fellow: "You are my prisoner." The fellow reached toward his machine gun. Dolivet fired, hitting the wrist. At about the same time the other fellow began operating a radio set, signaling the French position to the Germans across the river. They made him prisoner.

Dolivet searched the prisoner, the first fellow, then questioned him. Since he was eleven years old he had been a Nazi. The party had got him when young and he was a finished product of "Strength through Joy," by works and long service a Nazi, sworn and dedicated.

Had he been a guard in a concentration camp? Oh, yes, that was only one of the many responsible posts he had held. And he had killed men? Quite naturally, for it was in the line of duty at any concentration camp. "And in the line of duty have you ever tortured a man?" "Yes, of course, when that was a necessity."

Then the Nazi youth suddenly lost his faint smile of assurance and swagger. His face changed. He had seen Dolivet's face and tone change and he heard slow terrible words from Dolivet: "Very well, you have tortured men. Now I am going to torture you. I am going to put lighted cigarette ends on your eyes till you go blind. Then I am going to make you know pain. You are going to feel exquisite pain in every part of your body where you can know pain."

Then came what Dolivet didn't expect. The face of the Nazi youth began twitching, his lips trembling, knees shaking. He crumpled, fell on his knees, blubbered and cried in shame and tears.

And that was the nearest to torture the French gave him.

A Free Frenchman now in the United States told me the story. He knows Dolivet nearly as well as Dolivet knows himself. He told it when asked about Nazi morale. He rates Nazi morale low. They

134

may be good up to a certain point. Then they crumple. They are hard till something harder softens them and then in a hurry they are blubbering bundles of fear. Thus a viewpoint high-lighted from a single incident.

How Nazi morale will stand against the shapes to come we do not know. Precisely how the Elite Guards, the Gestapo observers and spies, the higher circles of Nazi-party workers, are taught and trained, we do not know in detail. Their schools in the main have been kept secret. In the higher party circles there are bunds within bunds and one bund on occasion purges another bund. We do know they teach conspiracy as an art and their wide-flung fifth columns have praised the double-crosser and given the English language the new word "quisling."

In such outfits loyalties get complex with splits and factions and divided counsels as to what fresh falsehoods should be rehearsed. The extent of such explosive material in the Nazi party may determine whether the war runs long or ends soon.

A Czechoslovak friend tells of morale in the Skoda works. A German army commission, twenty-two officers, on inspection of air bombs to be delivered, happened to walk where they stood under a caldron of boiling-hot lead, swinging out over the molds. The big bucket swung upside down and poured a shower bath of hot metal down, killing fourteen German officers, burning and disfiguring eight.

Old Vacek, the crane operator, dove from his cab and crushed his head on the concrete floor. He was avenging Munich and probably murmuring, "One lives only once, and they asked for it." The Gestapo questioned many, found old Vacek had no accomplices and had merely seized what he thought was the chance of a lifetime to make war on those who had violated the land he loved.

Morale is where you find it.

The rise of the common man

February 1, 1942

What we are now going through, a world struggle between conflicting ideas, has its roots in the past.

Several deep thinkers tell us it started when Gutenberg invented printing so that books, ideas wrapped in written words, the findings of men of thought, began spreading over the world to all who could read. Knowledge, learning, the society and instruction of trained minds or aspiring human spirits, became free to all who could get books and use them.

This little but distinct stream of history widened into a deep river when the demand grew for "universal popular education," public schools, with free speech, a free press, public libraries, and in many American states free schoolbooks and in many cities a figure known as "the truant officer" whose job was to watch the poolrooms and the railroad yards and round up any youths who didn't want education and make 'em take it.

The Machine Age, mass production, carried the trend farther. Books and learning had been made available to those who might hunger for them. Now came machine tools, the assembly line, automatic mechanisms for production, and the chain store, advertising, and high-pressure selling methods for distribution.

So the idea spread far that there was plenty, an abundance of the goods of life for all. By thousands of irresistible devices the masses of the people were told they ought to want more, use more, have more, of the goods of life making for a higher standard of living.

For the first time the human family gazing over the earth could see that no longer was there dignity, justice, reason, or decency in the poverty of millions of human beings. There came a President of the United States, Herbert Hoover, whom no one has ever paused for a moment to designate as "radical," and he spoke of a hope he had: "the abolition of poverty." Now it was possible. Production was solved. So far had it been solved that some economists and engineers agree that an overwhelming plenty of the goods of life could be poured out if the whole production apparatus was set going—and if there should be a few millions of the population refuse to work, they could have prefabricated houses and groceries delivered to them with either pity or laughter and no charge.

To America, to Europe, to Asia, came movements cutting down the power of political absolutists and putting more power in the hands of the people. This deep trend was beyond any man's reading as to how far it might go. It tied in with political democracy resting on the common man free to read and free to vote. And it was further tangled with the economic trend, the roaring laughing machines bringing a production that made poverty of goods look contradictory, irrational, sardonic, ridiculous.

While thousands of voices, in print and the show windows, told the common man he ought to have more of what Herbert Hoover termed "comfort and convenience," he was asking why he didn't have them.

When a king of England walked over the marvelously complete steamship *Queen Mary* for her launching, he asked why the ingenuity of man that could create such a wonder was not equal to doing more for the miner he had talked with who had been on the dole and workless for fourteen years. Year after year a minority stockholder of the United States Steel Corporation, an obstinate Boston visionary, fought against the brutal and dehumanizing twelve-hour workday not finally and completely abolished till the CIO came.

There is this trend. It is terribly human. It has tragic and comic phases. It is a cruel and laughing gargoyle. While the war is being fought it cannot be forgotten. When the peace is made it must be taken care of. Substantially that is indicated by the four key men: Roosevelt, Churchill, Stalin, Chiang Kai-shek.

The common man is the main figure in the fighting and the production. The forces working for him are immense. There are movements and ideas having voices—and power. The saying "It is a people's war" is not empty.

The colossal production achievements of these war years are a rebuke to any who cannot foresee, following this war, an abolition of human poverty in material goods of life, where the birth of another child is truly "a blessed event" instead of more worry about another mouth to feed.

Either the Four Freedoms are going to work over this modern world where each continent listens to the others day and night and man flies across oceans every day—or else the Family of Man over the globe can hope and expect nothing more than one world war for each generation.

So small the earth has become, with Singapore just around the corner and occasional boys on furlough who have flown a bomber across the Atlantic not once but fifteen or twenty times. And they mention it as an interesting stunt and they are going back for more of it. What we have done in transport related to time and space was hinted at by Mother Shipton but never faintly foreseen by George Washington on horseback writing a message to be delivered by a waiting courier also on a horse.

Production boss

February 8, 1942

Donald Nelson, not a West Pointer but a mail-order merchant selling "Gen'l Mdse" from A to Z, now holds the most important high command since Lincoln arranged for Ulysses S. Grant to run the Federal armies from the Potomac to the Rio Grande.

When Paul Bunyan contracted to dig the Great Lakes and excavate the Grand Canyon, he foreshadowed Mr. Nelson's job. In the mistlands of myth no Titan nor Vulcan ever had such hammers and forges handed him with the word "Results is all we want—re-sults."

At a distance any ordinary citizen can be a little dizzy about the size of this job. But Nelson at the controls is cool and practical, tinctured with a love of arms for America. He is impressive now by what he says and the way he hopes. His genius for exact statement has us reading some of his sentences twice. In this he reminds us of General Grant. Like Grant, he will make mistakes. He can't afford to play safe, to take no chances. He is lost unless he risks his neck every day.

We must in advance allow him several, even many, wrong decisions as to what will work. If he gets us the wanted production, we will forget the errors and throw him rose wreaths.

If and when the roses come his way, he will be sure to say he did nothing worth doing alone and those who helped must have equal credit. He is no fool promiser. What he says is conditioned. He knows equations. You can have this only when joined to that. He will move to C and D after A and B are taken care of.

The job will be done if, as, and when enough of us throw in with the best we have.

Those who feel no pull to throw in on the basis of what Nelson says are not alive to what he is saying. They may, of course, one fine day find they are monkeying with a buzz saw. Nelson is dynamic. Not yet a pompous word from him, no affected humility, both plain-spoken and short-spoken.

Responsibility—how often Lincoln lingered over that word. And the word Duty—how Robert E. Lee put it among the highest. Freedom, yes. But we can't have it without chastening periods when we get our shoulders under heavy loads of responsibility and duty.

"Free as a bird" is a nice antique phrase we have heard from many a pint-sized poet parroting previous pint-sized practitioners of verse. Unless a bird has at least as much discipline as freedom, he goes crash. Each wing has its specific assigned duty, and the bones and feathers of the fuselage are responsible for balances, weights, and adjustments related to the wings.

Those who fly pay a price. Not yet does either bird or man in the wink of an eye wish himself from one place to another. Bombers cost. Pursuits and fighters cost. Tanks, guns, ships, cost. Priorities cost. Tires, rubber, aluminum, nickel, cost. Mr. Nelson tells us this. Wishes won't wash dishes.

Lincoln sometimes gave the country fine lines about freedom and government of, by, and for the people. Then again he put the accent on plain, hard work, saying, "There is nothing to do but just keep pegging away." There were cartoons and editorials around those four words of his—"Just keep pegging away."

Patience—American knowhow—and no letup—and no cry-baby acts—for these Mr. Nelson asks. The millions of Americans to whom he has sold little rattraps and large parlor organs, snowshoes in the winter and fly-swatters in the summer, know his language, for he knows theirs.

Ralph Waldo Emerson liked to tell about the New England farmer who asked a minister to pray over his stony acres for better crops. The minister walked over the farm and said, "What this land needs is not prayer but manure." And Mr. Nelson has complete license to be telling us, "Your prayers will help, but don't forget the manure."

Planes come first

February 15, 1942

The hard-learned lessons of air power now come home. As some-one put it, "The sky is dark with chickens coming home to roost." An air force of 2,000,000 men, no less, says the Secretary of War. The infantry, the tank battalions, the cavalry, horse and mecha-nized, are to have their paths blazed by planes. So it should—or must—be. Millions of high-school boys making miniature planes, as proposed by the Secretary of the Navy, this shows we are going to be air-minded.

And why not? Battleships and tanks count. The planes count for more. If either Britain or the United States had bought bombing and fighter planes with the money spent for five or six superdread-naught battle wagons of the sea, then the news bulletins from day to day would be easier to take. Singapore, Russia, Libya, brave and battling MacArthur in the Philippines—each would be a different story if but a small part of the money thrown in one direction had gone in another, into planes.

In three weeks on the West coast I learn they are more air-minded here than on the Atlantic seaboard or in the Midwest. In a score of colleges and universities you can find from 20 to 40 per cent of the student body is flying, has licenses to fly. I have talked with gals as handsome as any on the magazine covers and they are flyers. One at Whitman College in Walla Walla, Washington, says matter-of-fact, and as though she is only one of many, "Sure, I had my thirty-five solo hours and I got my license."

One-third of the student body at Whitman flies. Over Walla Walla and Pendleton, Oregon, near by, the four-engine bombers roar and the students know them without reading the letter and number.

Let us hope the army and navy heads go on learning. An emi-nent plane-designer recently argued that planes must lead the offen-sives, blaze the way. Yet an army representative stubbornly held in reply that tanks and infantry must move in and clinch the ground won. Sure—what the army representative had to say seemed true and correct enough. What was disheartening, rather bitter to see and hear, was the army officer's lack of enthusiasm about planes; he seemed jealous of planes, as though they might grab off from some other service branch a little credit or glory. By his silence and omissions and hesitations he said just about the equivalent of that.

Of course, we know other army officers don't go along with this particular spokesman who shies away afraid he might overrate the air service. Part of this connects with each service having its own pride, its own traditions and character. No one would deny a Marine his pride in the Marines. And the record of the regulars, infantry and cavalry, is pretty enough for any man of them to be proud he belongs. Such pride helps rank-and-file morale. When, however, officers of high authority, like the removed army and navy commanders at Pearl Harbor, let themselves drift to where they get careless about co-operation with other departments, then comes the lack of co-ordination that brings disaster.

Toplofty generals and admirals, playing petty politics and jealous of encroachments on their own authority, temperamental as any peevish operatic prima donna, spiteful as any village gossip—do we have them? We do. In what proportion? We do not know. Can they play havoc with morale? They can. Without their bickerings and fears we would now be a long way farther toward the planes needed now.

And we will have to put up with the worst of them till time and events show them as useless or worse than useless and they are given the gate of removal.

Of course we're going to have 100,000 planes next year and 185,000 soon after, with pilots, crews, mechanics, altogether composing a service of men who will fly, bomb, shoot, first of all, leading the way, over the battle areas of the next few years. The decision as to this has come slow and hard. Why bring it up now? Because we are not going far wrong to remind ourselves that army and navy heads, in the main, are slow to take up with new ideas. Quite likely as the war moves on into new phases, original men will come into view with projects and devices not heard of before this war. And usually, not always, what they have to offer will be scoffed at, rejected, lost in the discard.

On this point I heard an industrialist notable for national innovations in his own field the last twenty years, after conferences on production in which he could make no headway with army authorities, comment patiently and quietly, "The military mind is not flexible." He meant the McClellan or Braxton Bragg type, not

Grant, Sherman, Lee. He meant the naval board that threw out John Ericsson's designs for the *Monitor,* so that Ericsson had to get higher authorities to indorse him.

He meant the temperaments that could find it important to personally feud with Billy Mitchell, getting so sore at the way Mitchell kicked their dignity in the slats that they couldn't hear what he was saying about this war that we, the living, are now fighting.

"Give us this day our daily croak"

February 22, 1942

Stormy weather now—and the worst is yet to come. Any one of us may now report that this is a correct one-sentence summary of the latest dispatches.

On three continents and three oceans and seven seas men are fighting a world war with more styles of weapons and strategies, longer hauls and bigger mauls, than any war seen before this one.

And this war is young yet.

And the man has not come into view who can read its secrets and tell us its ultimate drift—now—beforehand.

We have with us, however, the chronic croaker.

Plenty of Congressmen, Senators, newspaper columnists, editorial writers, politicians national and local, possibly about half of them as it seems, have been croaking and giving us nothing else but.

There is nothing in particular can be done about them, and I verily am not trying to reform them or change their personal habits—I am merely countercroaking and writing my calm contemplations.

They do let their croaking become a habit and they like it and call it good, and we can almost see them getting out of bed in the morning murmuring their paraphrase from the Lord's prayer, "Give us this day our daily croak."

Each day brings its fresh wild winds of passion, hate, jealousy, greed, pet peeves, and they let their tongues cut loose with the latest savory morsels of spite, folly, or malice, forgetting if they ever knew the ancient verse "Be not rash with thy mouth."

There is a healthy minority, a saving remnant, toiling, heaving, hauling, spending the limit of their wit and will every day toward

142

finishing specific blueprinted jobs marked "Immediate" or "Rush."

These have full license and perfect rights to the few rare and occasional croaks heard from them.

When out of the noise and fog of his particular production job William L. Batt rises to let out a croak I have found myself croaking with him and praying that the whole country might croak in unison.

Batt croaks that even though we be strong and tough we can lose this war. It is more than a croak. It is a cry of alarm and a forecast related to hazards we face. He speaks in vest and shirt sleeves, yet he may be wearing the mantle of a Jeremiah foreseeing doom unless we step up morale into a national effort not now in sight. History may so write. It is in the range of possibility.

The end of the war may come sooner, and the peace nearer to what we want, entirely in relation to more Americans who are now dry bones of inaction becoming clothed with the flesh and spirit of struggle, hope, vision. That sounds like preaching. It might sound like reporting fresh information to say that plenty of our well-to-do and comfortable people know less of the need of this hour than did one little finger of Colin P. Kelly.

"Hard, adverse war for many months ahead," says the British Prime Minister in a warning no one can call a croak. "More costly and longer" than the ordeal of the summer and fall of 1940 will be many months ahead, with "remorseless, gnawing anxiety." Stormy weather—and the worst is yet to come.

In traveling the past month from New York to San Francisco, from Los Angeles to Billings and Minneapolis, I saw much of youth and of the elders. I'll take the youth. I found plenty of croakers among the elders, few among the youth who are to know smoke and steel.

In the main, these youths say we might as well quit trying to be a nation and invite outsiders to come in and run our country as not to fight now—the Japs at Pearl Harbor and the Nazis at Berlin and with submarines in the Atlantic have given us no choice but a war to the finish. Some in the army, others soon to go in, hope for a peace that will last many generations—they would like that for their effort.

The air arm as partner

Of course it sounds like croaking to say that of the $400,000,000 spent to fortify Singapore one-fourth spent for airplanes with air-minded generals and admirals could have held Singapore till reinforcements arrived.

Such a point can be brought up with decency around the further point that we have generals and admirals now in command of operations who have their fingers crossed as to planes. To some of them an air force is still merely an "adjunct" not yet of equal importance with the other services.

Some of them do not yet see that the grand strategy of this war will be shaped and determined by whether we are able first of all to tear down our enemies from the sky. We have learned that sea and land operations require planes to locate the enemy and then to protect the fleet or the army from enemy planes. We have learned at high cost that planes can wreck forts and compel battleships to hug their bases. Because this has been learned and nearly everybody knows it now, we have set a goal—an air force of 2,000,000 and 185,000 planes—soon—by the end of next year, we hope.

"We have the most air-minded navy in the world," said Clark Howell Woodward, Rear Admiral, United States Navy, then Commandant of the Brooklyn Navy Yard, in an address to the Academy of Political Science at the Hotel Astor, New York, November 13, 1940.

And how did Rear Admiral Woodward mean it? In saying he and the navy were air-minded, what was in his mind? It came out in a discussion after his address. The Admiral spoke as a prophet and a forecaster. He spoke with unqualified assurance that the future was going to be the same as the past. He was so sure of what was going to happen that he forgot even the element of chance that Grant meant in saying "Battles are often won by accidents." The report of the proceedings of the Academy has Rear Admiral Woodward pronouncing these judgments in November of 1940:

"As far as the aircraft are concerned, they have done no severe damage to battleships or armored cruisers. They have sunk a few torpedo boats and done some damage to the upper works." And this, of course, was strictly the fact then in 1940. The Admiral proceeded, "But the decks of battleships are constructed to resist 16-inch armor-piercing shells and therefore are automatically protected against any bomb that is used today, or that will be used in the near future."

That was where a sea dog went off the deep end. Since then much has happened, at Pearl Harbor and elsewhere. And Singapore might still be holding out had not Japanese bombers done what the Admiral said couldn't be done. And Colin P. Kelly shattered some prophecies.

Rear Admiral Woodward proceeded: "So the battleships are not worried." That was November, 1940. Now in February of 1942 they are worried. Or at least we hope so. They should be worrying. They have seen two grand British battleships, the last word in modern construction, sunk off Singapore because they lacked the planes to fight off the enemy bombers that now have those superdreadnaughts sunk, scrapped, rusting and unworried in Davy Jones's locker.

"Do not misunderstand me," pleaded the Admiral. "We do think that the air arm is a very efficient and very necessary adjunct, but it is only an adjunct to the navy, and it can be nothing else." Until this patronizing and toplofty tone as to the air arm fades away among high men of the army and the navy we shall make slow work of this war. It is a jealousy that borders on criminal ignorance. The air arm is more than an "adjunct," and outside of prejudiced army and navy circles is almost universally so regarded.

"Airships can never win a war," continued Rear Admiral Woodward. "They can never win a battle." Which was more prophecy, more loose statement like any country-store cracker-box commentator. In his address was the statement: "Our westernmost stronghold—base at Pearl Harbor—is being made into the most formidable and impregnable bulwark of American defense in the Pacific area." So what? So we pause and don't say what.

At this same meeting of the Academy of Political Science, however, Robert C. Candee, then Chief of the Intelligence Division of the War Department Air Corps, said: "It is unfortunate that air power has been regarded by some as the enemy or competitor of sea and land power when in reality it is the complement and partner of the elder forces of military might."

Sure—that's all we're asking. It is a complement and a partner, not an "adjunct."

Candee quoted Secretary Stimson as saying in August of 1940: "Air power today has decided the fate of nations. Germany with her powerful air armada has vanquished one people after another." And as to the air arm for defense, it was no adjunct of which Winston Churchill spoke when he said of the Royal Air Force in 1940: "Never in the field of human conflict was so much owed by so many to so few."

As the grand strategy of the war unfolds through events now unknown, the greatest probability is that every main offensive action will see the air arm leading the way, "making interference" for battleships or landing forces carrying the ball.

New styles in war and training

March 8, 1942

In San Francisco I met a United States soldier from the Midwest Corn Belt. I first met him years back when his diet was milk only and he grew on it and liked it. Later I used to pick him up and throw him toward the ceiling and catch him coming down. I was one of his first drill sergeants when he wore skirts, learning how to walk before he could talk.

Now I look at him and see a trooper in khaki. Now he can talk, but he couldn't tell me where he was going from San Francisco. Now he knows a lot of words, though his next journey and destination is a secret kept from him. And he likes this, because he gets one surprise after another. He guesses where he is going and the High Command outguesses him. So there is no monotony for either him or the High Command.

He asked me where he was going, as though I might have run into some grapevine lead. So I gave it to him straight that before he gets his honorable discharge he will find out why the Pacific is the biggest ocean there is and how you can't help meeting archipelagoes in it.

When he asked if there were any man-eating archipelagoes I told him they would be marked on the maps given him. This satisfied him.

He grinned. He looked overweight and a little greasy with good health, so I asked him how was the army life. He said it was hard,

146

ery hard, and the food was poor, very poor, and he had gained only thirty-two pounds since he enlisted.

At the time he was drafted his practice in his profession was coming along nicely. And he didn't like being drafted. He wasn't interested. Now the new life suits him. Now he is interested. He had begun to like it before the Pearl Harbor incident. Now he feels he is on a great adventure, sharing history and danger with other men, his life having surprises and unknown meanings.

I could see definitely in his case and others I have met that there has been a personal development all to the good. The General Staff of the United States Army seems to be doing a fine piece of work in its theory and policy, holding that the soldier in a mechanized war should have his originality, initiative, personality, and drive interfered with as little as possible. "Let him have his own head—if he's got one" seems to be the gist of it. As I have met this theory in practice it is working out nicely.

Down in the Los Angeles area an American Legion officer gave me his slant at this theory as compared with 1918. He was sore, saying: "The fine discipline we had in 1918 is gone. The officers ask the men, request 'em to do this or that, instead of ordering. It won't do. The men would be tougher if the officers were tougher with 'em."

Well, this complaint doesn't worry me. An English colonel wrote the same thing about General Robert E. Lee's rank and file at a time in 1863 when that army was swift, terrible, and co-ordinating.

They saved their dumb, unquestioning obedience for the hours of crisis. When some of Sherman's crack fighters were court-martialed for getting drunk and misbehaving, Sherman said he couldn't punish these men for anything short of treason, so well had they performed in action when they gave everything called for and more besides. We are sure that MacArthur has some of this breed. They probably originated the anecdote of the sergeant bawling to the rookie, "Watch your head—here comes a woodpecker."

The war is "mobile," meaning movement, change, drive, requiring men who can think fast because the machines and weapons operate fast. The rank and file of foot troops going through "right shoulder, humps" and hiking along to their horselaugh chant, "hayfoot, strawfoot, bellyful o' bean soup"—they are not what they used to be.

147

The rifle and machine-gun squads, their co-ordination with planes and tanks, their problems of transport, assembly, repair these are more involved than in previous wars. An out-of-order precision instrument gets back into service by some other way than an old-fashioned, hard-boiled sergeant, lieutenant, or captain hollering, "Fix it—go ahead and fix it—that's orders."

It was the Czech poet and dramatist, Karel Capek, who invented robots for his play *R. U. R.*, meaning Rossum's highly recommended workmen, who were patented, manufactured, and sold—not born of woman. And Kapek died soon after the war began. He was a dreamer who loved freedom. He saw his country and people lost to the Nazis. Whatever the medical term for what he died of, one contributing factor was heartbreak.

Complacency too is where you find it

March 15, 1942

Four years ago a world-eminent photographer closed his New York studio and retired to the quiet of his two-hundred-and-forty-acre Connecticut farm. There he produced the tallest giant and shortest dwarf delphiniums ever put on show in the Modern Museum of Art.

The war came, and he plowed under one of the nicest plant-breeding fields worth looking at in the United States of America. Delphiniums class as luxury. They are out. He considered cabbages. Then he changed his mind about cabbages.

Now at sixty-two he is wearing the uniform of a lieutenant commander in the navy. Now his experience on the battle lines in France in 1918 comes into use. Then he commanded a thousand men who regularly photographed, from the air, the enemy front at the American sector, developed their prints in tent darkrooms, and laid before the High Command their picture of the front.

Now the navy will send this man of service, one of the supreme technicians, where he seems most needed. He wants to give the one best thing he has to give to America's war effort.

This is one case, the opposite of what is called complacency. I can name six cases where the young soldier was asked whether his more or less "influential" father should make inquiries as to the chances for service in some of the less dangerous branches of the army. And in each case the lad said he would leave it to the military authorities—he would go where they put him, he wanted no special favors.

Riding out of Buffalo on a Lackawanna train, a brakeman told me of a case he had heard about. A father used his political pull to have his boy eased out of the draft, so the story ran, without asking the boy about it. The father liked the boy and thought this the best thing for himself, the mother, the home, the boy.

Then came December 7 and Pearl Harbor. And two days later the boy walked in to dinner to tell his fond father and mother: 'I've passed the exams for the air corps. I'll be saying good-by tonight and the next time you see me I'll have Jap scalps in my belt." And he laughed a fond tra-la-loo that night.

Or take my bookseller friend in Chicago. He has his own shop with a nice line of customers who respect his judgment on Civil War books because he has read most of them, new or old. He has a good home, a wife, and two children he loves to prank with, enjoys books and reading. However, as a reserve officer, an R.O.T.C., he goes for examination, is rejected on the score of bad eyesight.

So there he was. Now he could sit back and consult his ease. But he had been living with Grant and Sherman, Lee and Forrest, with stubborn and stormy men who never shrank from struggles and ordeals. Then too he loves the United States of America, loathes Hitler and all Nazi notions, and believes democracy ought to have every chance across the future world.

So he takes another exam and is one of fifty picked out of four thousand for special study in war production under the direction of army officers and technicians. He changes his schedule as a businessman, a storekeeper. Now he gets to the shop at six o'clock in the morning. By ten-thirty he has answered the mail, made the main decisions for the day, goes to his classes. Each hour in the day he calls the clerk in charge of the store and gives his advice as to what might be doing.

Before long his studies, his classwork, will be over and he will go into some branch of war production. And the store—the shelves of new and old and scarce books he had been handling these past ten years? "Oh, I can put them somewhere. They won't rot. After the

war we'll see what we'll see. Meantime my wife says I don't hav
the kind of war blues I used to have."

Then there is the tall blond Swede boy near our home, writing
poetry ten years ago, hitchhiking to San Francisco, shipping as a
deck hand to Buenos Aires and back, ending after a while at $10,000
a year in charge of radio advertising with a New York agency. Now
he quits that job. Now he's in the navy, his pay amounting to board
and clothes, so to speak. But he likes it. His face had a shine telling
about it.

Another neighbor is a flyer who lived through service with the
Lafayette Escadrille in France, 1917-18. A year ago he would have
been with the Royal Air Force except for the age limit. Months
ago he was wondering whether maybe he wouldn't be some use at
air-training camps where he could answer a thousand different questions about combat in the sky. He's a quiet-spoken daredevil who
has what it takes without being loud about it. If the army or the
navy calls him, he'll step into it.

He carries scars he never mentions and has cool deviltry. He
would leave his home, family, and comfort if called. He would
make a first-rate instructor in morale, though he would laugh at
such a title.

In an Eastern city I talked with a fellow rated as having one of
the best legal minds in the large city where he had practiced. He
ranks now as an army private not yet First Class. In a laundry, day
on day, he checks items and piles 'em, so many shirts, socks, under-
wear suits, washed and ready. He laughs about it. In the end it
will come out all right.

Complacency, like morale, is where you find it.

"We cannot hallow this ground"

March 22, 1942

There is no desire here to drag in anecdotes by the scruff of the
neck. But there does come to mind now the case of the little faded,
shrinking woman at protracted revival meetings in one corner of
Missouri. One by one those who heard the revivalist had come forward to the mourners' bench. And on the last night of the meetings
the exhorter went to her and asked why she was holding back.

"All but you," he told her, "have come to the throne of grace. Why do you withhold yourself?"

In a half-stifled moan came her answer, "Cause I ain't fitten."

"Why ain't you fitten?"

"Cause I ain't fit to be fitten."

She would have had understanding from the somber American poet Edwin Arlington Robinson, who saw many seekers in his country as "bewildered children in a kindergarten, all trying to spell God with the same blocks."

In a time of great danger, either national or personal, there is often bewilderment around the sudden immediate question "What can I do now, today, that tomorrow will look like the best thing I could have done today, now, this hour?"

After the Battle of Gettysburg men of military science studied 27,000 muzzle-loading muskets picked up on the battlefield.

Of these, 24,000 were loaded, one-half had two loads, many had ten loads. Experts couldn't see it any other way than that in the bloody work and the crying-out-loud that day many soldiers lost their heads, loaded, forgot to fire, and then, forgetting the musket was already loaded, they loaded it again. Also they figured it out that each soldier in battle fired away about his own weight in lead before he killed one of the enemy.

One of the useless bullets had been well aimed at the pegleg Confederate General Richard S. Ewell, who chirped merrily to General John B. Gordon, "It don't hurt a bit to be shot in a wooden leg."

So there was the lad of our own hour who chirped his little report to the navy chiefs, "Sighted sub, sank same." By his speech tone we know there was no bewilderment there. He had the advantage of an immediate, unmistakable target before his eyes, threatening him with death or disaster.

And quite likely there are plenty of good American citizens in this hour with hearts and minds ready for such service or duty as might be assigned them by their government authorities. They want specific targets. They might be termed "practical" patriots as distinguished from the "holy."

We have seen and heard those who make a show of their patriotic "holiness" till it loses any solemn effect it may have and borders on

151

the comic. They confuse plain patriotic folk who sort of feel they "ain't fit to be fitten" or prefer to say, "Let's get down to cases."

Lincoln shrank from this assumption of holiness. The Gettysburg Speech confesses that the brave men, living and dead, who struggled there had consecrated the ground beyond any words he could say. "We cannot hallow this ground." And the Second Inaugural has no follies of proud talk.

At a recent round table the four men taking part agreed that maybe once a day, for a brief moment, a man might have and feel and know "the thrill of patriotism." And even then he must be on guard and shrink in humility before what may be happening in his innermost heart and its involuted secrets. The show-off and the reality are different.

A Protestant religious weekly reports a Catholic priest telling a student for the priesthood he had gone too far in his showing of holiness at communion. The sensation of holiness, he instructed the youth, was undependable and unworthy, saying: "That's the way the Protestants act. They think they are holy when they feel holy. Protestants don't go to church from a sense of duty owed to God. When they feel like staying at home they stay at home.

"The only excuse they need to give is that they have a headache, or they didn't sleep well last night. . . . What credit is it to go to church when you want to go? Next Sunday you may want to go somewhere else, then what? No, the religious life is not measured by the ease with which we perform its duties. Suspect your emotions. On the very days when you feel most holy you may be most remote from God. Your feelings may be nothing more than the result of a good digestion. . . . It is when it is hard to pray, when you feel that God has deserted you, that you have your opportunity."

This quote, with more, the Reverend Harmon M. Gehr read to his congregation of the Universalist Church of the Restoration in Philadelphia, with the comment: "That is the best analysis of what is wrong with our Protestant churches that I have met." He could then have properly preached a sermon from the motto of the State of Kansas, "To the stars by hard ways."

The new rank and file

April 19, 1942

Once I had a friend who used to say, "If you feel stupid, be thankful. It's just old Mother Nature making you take a rest you need."

Now we hear a Yale professor quoted, "These days only children and morons sleep well." And some of us like it that a businessman hot under the collar tells Donald M. Nelson in about so many words that Nelson is a fraud and a deceiver and Nelson politely ushers the man out of the office and comes back to his desk: "I nearly lost my temper that time."

When Vice-President Wallace gave out his pointed comment on the latest gyrations of Congressman Dies, I thought it had courtesy and poise, though not as reserved as the Congressman whose constituent went beyond words in what he had to say, with the result that the Congressman, as it is told, replied earnestly, though not wrathfully: "Sir, you have called me a liar and a scoundrel, you have spit in my face, you have struck me twice. I hope you will not rouse the sleeping lion in my breast, for if you should, I cannot tell what may be the consequences."

This may sound like fooling in a tone of undue levity in an hour when for the first time in history American youth is in a shooting war on all the shores of the seven seas around the globe. So I would offer the reporter Walter Davenport down in the Panama jungle. He gives us Izzy Gishmick of Manhattan saying, "Me, I couldn't slug my way out of a soap bubble." That was when he was drafted weighing a hundred and thirty-four pounds, "all of it vanilla." Now he tips a hundred and sixty-two, "all of it dumb muscle," and he can think of two cops at Eighth Avenue and Fiftieth Street he would now like to take on. A comic—and a hero—both at once. Davenport prefers 'em that way.

An old-timer from Alabama, who helped dig the Panama Canal and has stayed there since, tells Davenport: "Gits you down the way these soldiers come in here lookin' downright sickly, no eyes for the jungle, and the next thing you know these lady-white boys from the city are whistling like the birds is their steady company, totin' big snakes up to camp and tryin' to put dog collars on jungle cats. By the time they know enough of the jungle to be skeered of it it's too late—too late for the jungle."

A movie usher from San Francisco did bring in a panther cub, but taming it was no go. A Chicago boy who didn't like to quit a theatrical agency for the army, up on a mountain cliff where he helped the Panama Coast Artillery drag heavy guns, searchlights, an eight-hundred-pound electric refrigerator, tells Davenport: "This is the first time in my life I've ever known what privacy was. Up here it's too big for noise. It smells quiet. You can think if you want to. Private!"

There will be many of them on the shores of the seven seas knowing weary monotony. Still others will get acquainted with hardship and suffering. And still others, like the ones Davenport met, will find surprises, and for the first time take their measure as tested men. Davenport sat alone a while, "thought a lot of foolish things" —war contractors, priority whiners, pensions for Congressmen, politicians on the hunt, tax howlers—and wished they could be up there on that jungle mountain. "Listen, these kids don't have to be exhorted to fight, to make sacrifices."

In Des Moines, Iowa, on Army Day I thought I saw something like that. An artillery battalion from Fort Leonard Wood in Missouri moved in on a downtown street and along eight blocks showed thousands of civilians the workings of their weapons and transport. They had slept in their clothes the night before, so they didn't look dress-paradish. They looked like the jeeps they rode in and, like the jeeps, ready for wear and tear, asking: "What next? We're ready for it."

They set up mortars, machine guns, antiaircraft, light and heavy howitzers, explained cranks and swivels, purpose and range. They took apart the Browning rifle and the Garand. They answered civilians asking questions about shells for loading and how far this or that gun would shoot and what special action it was best in. On one corner the two trucks of a field kitchen parked, throwing a mess tent between them. The troops lined up with their mess kits and we saw ham, peas, potatoes, bread, cake, and coffee, apples if wanted, rationed to each man. They stood or sat on the curbstones and ate like they were at home in Des Moines and would be in Australia or Ireland or Iran. Then they lined up and one by one

154

dipped their used mess kits in a kettle of hot water, brushing them clean and moving on.

Of course they were on their good behavior. And I don't know why they should impress me. I felt they had good order and discipline—and initiative and intelligence. They handled their guns as though they knew every niche and click of them. They answered questions in a cool, quiet, simple way. They seemed to be picked men who had gone to school and had training and learned how to throw in with all they've got. There was a variety of phizzogs and accents: Irish, Jews, hillbillies, mixed with Scandinavians, Germans, Poles, Yanks, and native-born hybrids.

Maybe I was sentimental. I felt good about them. It came over me that the soldier of mechanized warfare, in general, is more of a free man on his own, and necessarily so, than the soldier of former wars. The will to win and the endurance to hold out still count, as in the old wars, but the initiative of noncoms and privates counts for more now. They have weapons and transport that can't be effective without each man being more strictly on his own. They looked to me as though they liked skull practice and were ready to use it in the timing and teamwork of modern war.

Saying good-by to the commanding officer, a West Pointer of 1931, I told him I would probably be a brigadier, maybe a major general now, if I hadn't been dumb in arithmetic long ago as a candidate at West Point. He laughed. I told him I saw General Bonesteel in Chicago last summer and the General invited me to be sure and see him at Camp Custer in Michigan, where he was in charge. Then I hear Bonesteel takes over in Iceland and it won't be so easy now for me to look him up. Then last of all I told the commanding officer maybe before long I'll hear of him in Australia or Ireland or Iran. And where he said he would prefer to be is a military secret of no importance except as indicating where he would rather do his fighting in this global war which is crazy and had its origin in lunatic foreign minds, aided and abetted by sleepers and drifters who called it impolite to ask "What's cooking?"

The press and the reading public

April 26, 1942

Archibald MacLeish, the Librarian of Congress, is a farmer. Those who have seen him on his two hundred and forty acres of Scotch highlands in Massachusetts are well aware that if there were no emergency and no call of country, he would be rotating crops rather than civil-service sheets. He bought his farm out of earnings as a journalist.

As a magazine writer, MacLeish went to Japan for three months and came back and wrote 75,000 words about what he saw, heard, and found, filling an entire number of *Fortune,* and throwing new light on what the Japanese authorities term "thought control." The idea back of that phrase is "We tell you what to think. We protect you from dangerous thoughts."

As a journalist and an independent artist it was proper MacLeish should speak to the American Society of Newspaper Editors. The men and the occasion drew from the Librarian of Congress a curious speech. He read them a paper close-packed, hard-woven. On a third reading I find it a cool, balanced statement, a case and an appeal presented with great respect and fine gravity, but no one can point here or there in it and say "Here is the gist of it." It hangs together with every part essential, like the testimony of a solemn witness hoping to God he's telling the truth, the whole truth, and nothing but the truth.

Equally solemn and portentous before the editors' society was Byron Price, the Associated Press man now Director of Censorship. He too speaks as a troubled man. He too raises the question whether the freedom of a free press can be misused by a minority to the point where the present voluntary censorship must be followed by a compulsory censorship. "An unhappy day for all of us," says Byron Price, that would be.

Beyond those who own or edit newspapers are the readers, the public that buys the papers, and part of it, like MacLeish and Price, troubled and hunting the answer. "The distinction between democratic criticism and defeatist propaganda is difficult to draw," notes MacLeish, adding that "the press must be vigilant to defend the right of criticism everywhere in order that it may be curtailed nowhere."

Among the millions of readers of the 12,000 newspapers in the United States, 2,000 dailies and 10,000 weeklies, are many who realize that the peacetime responsibilities of a newspaper owner, editor, editorial writer, are more than doubled in wartime. There are crime stories and details of crime stories that in peacetime some newspapers welcome and spread big while others go slow or don't touch at all such stories and details. Readers understand this, and buy what they like to read, buying according to their ideas and prejudices and habits.

Then comes war, and to many readers come new anxieties, hopes, fears, duties. Where in peacetime they just quit reading the paper they don't like because of what it is saying, they now take it on themselves to ask how long this or that sheet ought to be allowed to print and sell its papers.

These readers believe they know "the distinction between democratic criticism and defeatist propaganda."

You may have noticed among your friends and acquaintances some who in peacetime never let themselves be bothered about this or that newspaper. They could take it or leave it. But now they are anxious. Now they want to know why and how come.

There is a minority, not a large one, of newspapers definitely going beyond the line of "democratic criticism" over into "defeatist propaganda." Where there are open violations of law, government will crack down, said MacLeish, "but the most poisonous and pervasive defeatism is not practiced by those who violate the statutes of their country openly. It is practiced by those who take scrupulous care to stay within the law."

More gently, Byron Price pleaded with the editors for the rights of those who buy the product of a free press under voluntary censorship: "You are doing your readers and your country a great disservice if you permit your columns to be used for rumormongering and inaccurate drivel, whether it comes from one of your reporters or from a writer hundreds of miles away."

Vice-President Wallace has used the phrase "malicious use of isolated facts." Given a couple of isolated facts, you can, if you have the requisite cunning and malice, so relate the facts as to raise hell and soften the will to win the war now far from won. There is a reader awareness about this. And that awareness will deepen as the war moves into new phases of action.

157

How to read a newspaper

May 3, 1942

The newspaper goes everywhere. Like rain it falls on the just and the unjust. Like history it begins and ends anywhere and leaves much to be expected. The more terrible its headlines, the more welcome it is and the more copies go to anxious readers.

In schools and colleges there should be class discussions of the question "What is the best way to read a newspaper?" so that the young might learn there are many different ways.

How to read the classics of literature has long been taught in the schools and universities. How to know good books from bad, how to use books for laughter and entertainment or spiritual light or practical help, of this there has been much teaching.

But the great universal classic of the common people's reading—the newspaper—has been neglected.

Some ten years ago I was asked if I would care to conduct a university course and meet a class once a week on any subject I chose. I answered I wouldn't be able to find the time, but if I could the subject would be "How to Read a Newspaper."

Now I have before me a textbook published by Scott, Foresman and Company of Chicago, written by Edgar Dale of Ohio State University, and the title *How to Read a Newspaper*.

I would like to see this book go far. It should be handled in bookstores for the general public. It deserves a place in all public libraries. And there should be talk about it, up, down, and across.

What is news? Who says what is news and what isn't? Where do local reporters get the news they write? How do foreign correspondents get the news they cable, wireless, or telephone across the oceans? How can you guide yourself on what to believe or not believe in the headlines and news accounts?

Those are live questions to every serious newspaper reader who reads hoping to learn something about the immense events of history in the making, now.

Between the reader and the news are several strategic points. At each of these the news can get slanted, angled, even mangled or deleted and lost. Before reaching the reader's eyes the news has been handled by the reporter on the spot, by the censor, by the home-office editors, by the headline-writer, and each of these, deleting the censor, somewhat directly responsible to the owner or publisher who originates and shapes what is termed "the policy" of the paper.

Then there is the time element. Mistakes creep in because time waits for no man and the trucks wait in the alley to rush today's paper out today.

Class exercise: Find a news story you think strictly factual and well written. Find another news story you think distorted, explain why you think it distorted, and tell how you would write it better.

Bring in examples of perfect headlines indicating what the reader may expect. Bring in examples of misleading headlines where the headline writer was either careless and well meaning or intentionally was editorializing in line with the policy of the paper. Pick a lead paragraph you feel lacks color and see whether you can brighten it in rewriting.

Will Irwin, biographer of Herbert Hoover and a newsman many of us respect, once wrote: "More than twenty years ago I sat at luncheon with a group of American publishers, talking shop. Conversation turned to the decline of the editorial as a social and political force. 'My front page is my editorial,' said one of the company. 'The headlines are mine,' said another."

In Dale's book we are given cases of the misleading headline that has its purpose. We could paraphrase "I care not who makes the laws of a nation if I may write its songs" to "I care not who writes the news story if I may shape the headline that gives it the slant I want."

The human oddities, the endless marvels of fun and preposterous pomposity, these too are in Dale's book. A country weekly in Iowa once told its readers: "We were the first in the state to announce, on the 11th instance, the news of the destruction in Des Moines, by fire, of the mammoth paint establishment of Jenkins & Bros. We are now the first to inform our readers that the report was absolutely without foundation."

We are asked to scrutinize news stories with ten questions, the last two: "Has prejudice entered into the writing or editing of the news dispatch? Is the reporter likely to have such a deep personal interest in some possible outcome of a question that he cannot, even though he tries, write accurately about it?"

Then there is the quote from that war horse of the *Toledo*

Blade, Grove Patterson: "I am less disturbed about freedom of the press in the United States than I am with the disposition of too many newspaper editors not to do anything with the freedom that is theirs."

Anyhow and ennyhoo, I would submit, news services and newspapers now are a grand improvement on one and two generations ago. Those who know how to read, inquire, and think get more information and entertainment for their pennies and nickels than they did in the days of Horace Greeley, James Gordon Bennett, and Abraham Lincoln who would not have been President if Greeley or Bennett had had the say-so.

Why do men fight?

May 10, 1942

An English deep thinker, philosopher, and mathematician in the last war went to jail on account of his conscience wouldn't let him fight and kill for the sake of old England. Peace came, and he gave the public a book titled *Why Men Fight,* and failed to tell what a fighting man is or why he fights.

Now in our latest war this same Englishman is all for the war and his conscience tells him every fighting man of the United Nations is on the side of right and freedom. If he should now write a book on why men fight, he would come nearer the answer than in his first one.

Years ago I went through a long list of books that promised light on why men fight. Most of them I found useless. I could have got as much or more from the next corner cop or any police magistrate.

There are natural-born fighters who are good at it and like to mix in it because they know they are good. Other good fighters have to get mad at something first—they need targets to hate and shoot at. Still other good fighters like to have a cause, something to them sacred and for them worth dying for. Sometimes the combination of all three may be found in one man.

When Douglas MacArthur arrived at his formal reception in Australia and told them, "I bring to you the unbreakable faith of a free man," he was using simple speech of vast meaning, saying there are faiths that cannot be broken by weapons, hunger, or torture, and there are a thousand lousy, indescribable deaths a free man would prefer rather than have his faith in freedom broken.

The Bishop of Norway, caged in a barbed-wire enclosure with Nazi guards seeing that he doesn't get loose, is denied joining his people in freedom of worship. He is taking punishment and seems ready to welcome death rather than give up this dream, this hope, this holy belief, in the right of men to freedom of worship.

"Freedom" is a dream word. There have been plenty of good men who didn't like fighting for the sake of fighting who got lit up about some dream word like "freedom," and they were unbreakable fighters.

The two words slowly and solemnly pronounced over and over again by responsible spokesmen and mouthpieces in Sweden are "freedom" and "independence." Whatever outside power might try to come into Sweden and take away what the Swedes mean by these two words would find the Swedes saying what Tom Corwin would have the people of an invaded country crying—"We will welcome you with bloody hands to hospitable graves." Stockholm is saying she will die first rather than be run by Berlin.

When Hong Kong went down and when Singapore cracked, like something false and flimsy, neither before nor afterward was anything much heard of the Atlantic Charter, the Four Freedoms, nor "the unbreakable faith of a free man."

I wish I was hearing more about the Four Freedoms, not so much from Asia as from Europe, and especially in this our own country.

"Freedom is all right, but how about some ham and eggs?" This is covered in the one of the four which says "freedom from want" ought to be everywhere.

Nowhere does this psalm of democracy say that we are going to force these Four Freedoms on the rest of the world, "everywhere." You might think so from various references in editorials and speeches. What is said distinctly is that it is our wish, prayer, and dream that sometime, maybe soon, but anyhow sometime, over the whole earth the Family of Man will understand and put into reality the Four Freedoms.

Dreaming bones

May 17, 1942

A poet is a poor fish who buttons when he fumbles, fumbles when he buttons, and thinks, if ever he thinks at all, that a zipper is a synonym for the same as a zither.

A little on the loony side, a poet raves about roses, monkeys with meter, slips on slow and mellow syllables in the moonlight, and don't know the way to the post office.

Like Jojo the dog-faced boy who came with the old-time circus side show, he was "born forty miles from land and forty miles from sea."

Yes? And why not? And what else is to be taken as meant by the word "poet" as slung around by loose mouths nowadays?

A poet is a moon-faced incompetent without evil enough to be a so-and-so—and he ain't regular people—he is something you forget to bring in when it rains and he stays out not knowing enough to come in.

Sure—let him have it—give him the razzberry—pickle him in the amber of comic vinegar.

One cartoonist shows Archibald MacLeish with a book under his right arm titled *Sonnets.* Long ago MacLeish forgot about sonnets. And his long Pulitzer prize-winning poem *Conquistador* has what it takes, and I know two sports writers who read it for style and punch.

In 1939 came MacLeish's *America Was Promises,* a solemn song, a prophecy and a warning as to this hour we now live and see, putting to music the great hopes and prayers of this country, with lines running smooth and winding as the footwork and weaving of the old Yale halfback who wrote them.

And this here Archie MacLeish, who was up front with the artillery in the last war, he can take it if we've got to where the word "poet" means you're sorry for how they get that way—if the country can take it and its deeper faiths not suffer.

To the extent that any society rots in culture and faith, it extends the custom of handing any poet, good or bad, the open horselaugh or the covert and polite snicker.

And that doesn't mean a thing to the Congressmen, cartoonists, editorial and political carbuncles, who use the word "poet" with an inflection as significant as a coarse and unstudied hiccup.

Poetry is where your bones dream and you take a number and make it dance with other numbers. Poetry is a packsack of invisible keepsakes.

For me lately there has been poetry in the numbers "one thousand, two thousand, three thousand." As a parachute trooper tumbles out of the plane and falls headfirst or feetfirst into empty air of blue sky, he says, "One thousand, two thousand, three thousand," which takes exactly three seconds and tells him when to pull the ripcord and start floating.

Mr. William L. Batt, Jr., better known as young Bill Batt, comes back from London, having asked one of the poor people in a bombed slum how ever they had got along, hearing: "The poor always takes care of each other. We ain't got nothin', but we shares it with each other."

That, we might agree, is a specimen of the poem that life writes, and whoever hears it and tells it again is a poet.

The *Washington Post* printed fourteen lines by John Russell McCarthy, ending with these three:

> "No gold ever gleamed like the human spirit hoping,
> No steel ever leaped like the human spirit springing,
> No granite will ever guard like a man's faith."

For me that holds poetry, and for a long time will come alive with music and a wisdom for free peoples at war.

Those who can mock or be light-minded about the human frames and lights from which such lines flow—let them be—they have their keepsakes, as we have ours.

Education's new and different

May 24, 1942

Three things soldiers talk about more than anything else. So a corporal, a University of Texas graduate, tells me. After training hours, when they are free to talk about whatever they like, first it's food they tell each other about as to what is good or bad; second, it's weapons and how their guns and ammunition are behaving;

and third, gambling and what games and plays they have been winning or losing at or whether they have quit lady luck and why.

Booze, sex, women, girls, home, politics—these came after the above-named three topics of conversation.

"They want to fight or go home," said my corporal friend, who for nearly a year had watched them and helped train them in Ohio and Indiana camps. "They like their weapons, the variety of new death-dealing machines we've got in this war. There is great pride about our marksmanship. The boys think our gunnery is the best on earth. And they want to try out their skill. That's why I say they want to fight or go home."

Among the new flyers, I am reliably informed, when training is over and they get insignia wings to wear over the heart, they would like to serve in fighter planes rather than the bomber. Action fast and wild where cool headwork and quick thinking count—it seems this is what they prefer, and the army and navy commands can't accommodate the many who are asking for it.

In the fighter planes they hunt and kill alone—they crash and die alone—they weave and hit and get away and come back for more—alone.

The fighter pilot hears only the song of his roaring engine and in a dogfight commands himself and obeys the orders of his own head. Alone he reads his instrument board—and alone climbs or dives or zigzags. By himself he says Yes or No or Maybe in the whirls of speed and the spitz of fire when he takes his chances, when he tries to pick the right split second for the next six things to do in that split second.

A lot of people are getting different kinds of education in this war, which is not entirely ignorance on parade. Transport and communication are going to be something else round the world before this show is over. Now many millions of soldiers are trained artisans and graduate mechanics, with the emphasis on initiative and the advice "If you can learn a little more than you know now, that won't set you back in this army. And if you think fast in a pinch, maybe you'll be here to tell about it tomorrow."

Who can put down in cold figures what the new education is doing in the Detroit area? Who knows what is happening inside those original minds of owners, managers, and workers of the automobile industry? Who knows what daring plans for new and unheard-of cars and planes are on the way either for war or for peace after the war? Who would have predicted, before war came, that industrial production in China would leap in 1941 to five times what it was the year before, with those once "backward" Asiatics now manufacturing chemicals, gas engines, steam turbines, oil burners, auto parts, precision instruments, electrical appliances, rifles, machine guns, tanks, mortars, antiaircraft guns, heavy artillery, shells, and explosives?

In proportion as we send them factories and plants, with one hand they will fight Japan and with the other produce war material.

On the continent of Europe has been a variety of new educations for old. Michael, Cardinal von Faulhaber, reports to the Vatican ten commandments given out to the Catholics in churches over Germany. In the long shadows of the portentous words of these commandments we can see the hard writhing and hear the low moaning of good men and women tried by dark ordeals. "Neither spread false rumors nor be misled by empty claims of authority," says one of the commandments, "instead, speak the truth and promote its realization."

In the harsh desolations of war there are sensitive human minds reaching for answers. They ask whether life has any meaning, order, sanity. For them and all others there is value in a reading and study of these strange commandments, born of wisdom and patience amid tragedy:

"Do not unleash anger, but conquer your vexations, so that your conscience shall not become deadened by quiescence before injustice, or your spiritual powers consume themselves in discontent and discord.

"Rejuvenate your soul in keeping with the best examples of our culture, so that peace may possess you more thoroughly than war has done.

"Collaborate in the creation of a society that will afford to all men of goodwill an honest opportunity to live in justice, freedom, and truth.

"Do not dissociate yourself from the sufferings of mankind, but instead love men with a warm heart and adjudge your enemy in justice. Praise light, even in darkness, for light ever remains light."

165

History—take a chance

The historian James Harvey Robinson strolled over his farm with a friend who asked, "Could you give in a few words the essence of the thousands of books on ancient and modern history that you have read?"

"Possibly," said Robinson without batting an eye.

"And what words of counsel would you say give the gist of your vast historical learning?"

"I have it now in three words," said the historian, not at all bothered or bored, and even mildly interested.

"And what might those three words be that are so important to us pilgrims and wayfarers of the human ordeal and journey?"

"Don't expect anything," came the three words.

And as though they were worth repeating in case they were not heard the first time: "Don't expect anything."

Following this, and in contrast, we have the eminent biographer Lloyd Lewis walking his acres near Libertyville, Illinois, being asked the same questions and saying he could put the main lesson of many books of history and biography into a capsule of two words: "Expect anything."

Such anecdotes have led to a standard joke among historians to the effect that what we learn from history is that we learn nothing from history, and the books portraying the past merely bring us into a closer understanding of the auk, the bird who flies backwards so as to see where he's been.

"The future is rushing toward us like the wind," I once heard the preacher Charles Clayton Morrison declare, and "The prophet is the spokesman of the unpredictable."

So immense and complicated is the present world scene that beyond expecting victory for the United Nations, in a war that may be long or short, you are safe in following the advice "Don't expect anything." The pattern of the last war is already lost, and the same goes for the peace signed at Versailles. Don't expect that to be repeated. You can imagine a better peace or a worse one, but don't expect the same. It will be different.

Then, too, as the war goes on you have a right to advise yourself "Expect anything." Few there were in the last war who expected it to go grinding and smashing on till three of the most powerful families, ruling dynasties whose fall had seemed unthinkable, should topple like Jericho at the ram's-horn blast—the once highly esteemed Hohenzollerns, Hapsburgs, Romanovs, losing their shirts, their homes, their heads. Who and what will be ground to dust and blown away on the wind as this war goes on writing its dooms not now foreseen? "Heads will roll," cried the Nazi leader a few years ago, unaware that one of his own headsmen may possibly have to execute sentence on him in a high howling yet to come.

Expect anything. You may even go so far as to expect that in more than half of Henry Wallace's recent speech he is "a spokesman of the unpredictable." The Midwest prairie and the Russian steppes met when Wallace said, half fooling and half serious, to Madame Litvinov, "The object of this war is to make sure that everybody in the world has the privilege of drinking a quart of milk a day," hearing Madame reply, "Yes, even a pint."

Before this war began the productive capacity of man had become something marvelous to see. Now, in the war, it is marvelous and heroic. Is there anything wrong about hoping, fighting, working for a peace equally creditable to the wit and will of man at his best?

When someone started debunking our Civil War for Oliver Wendell Holmes, the just judge, he said, as one friend reported it: "Oh, please don't take that war away from me. That was one war that was worth fighting!"

Herrenvolk

June 7, 1942

In a way of talking and a manner of speaking you might say that this war points up around the race question more than any other. Or if "race" is not the word it surely is "blood" or "breed."

The Jap slogan is "Asia for the Asiatics" and the Nazi term for the German race after it has conquered the world and begun its domination of the earth is *"Herrenvolk,"* the lordly people, the folk made to rule.

And the opposition—which is us of the United Nations—says to the Japs and the Nazis: "You can't do that to us. We haven't

167

learned how to take what you would like to hand us. So, for a while, wherever we can get at you, we're letting you have it with compliments and incendiary bombs, best regards and lead in your guts."

As the bombers drop their loads over Berlin or Tokyo, Hamburg or Yokohama, they might be saying, "Sorry, *Herrenvolk,* and excuse us, Son of Heaven, but you asked for it."

That's the negative. That tells what we're against. And what is it that we're for?

On paper, in the national documents, in the solemn covenants that root us as a nation, we are for all races, breeds, and folk, bar none.

And considering the size of our country and the variety of breeds and crossbreds, hybrids and incalculable polyglots, we haven't done so bad. Wicked faults we have, but it might be worse.

Already the war has brought forward Negroes decorated for conspicuous bravery—and when Negro troops of proven hardihood and valor return from the Canal Zone, Alaska, Europe, Asia, and Australia after the war, they may have a changed status as voters. When in 1919 I reported the Chicago race riots I found one factor in the unrest and the readiness to kill was the refusal of jobs to Negroes. Overseas service, even distinguished medals, didn't count. Yet year by year the classifications of jobs open to Negroes have increased. In the present war emergency, I am sure, the record will show they have made gains.

The Irish, of course, don't worry. It is a long time since the Lincoln generation when there were occasional factory signs "No Irish need apply."

The Nazi propaganda poison aimed at wiping the Jews off the earth isn't going as good as it did last year and the year before. Last year this country went through an ordeal, a test of how it would stand up under the Nazi needling of race hate. And we have made healthy progress because of the test and the showing the American people made in critical hours.

The corn-fed Vice-President, Henry A. Wallace of Iowa, at a quiet dinner in Washington last week, was asked: "What about you? Winston Churchill is Jewish-controlled. President Roosevelt is of Dutch-Jewish ancestors. Doesn't the Berlin short-wave broadcast honor you somewhere among its swine enemies?"

"Oh, yes," said the Vice-President. "If you listen you will learn that I am a Polish Jew and before we changed it the family name was Walski."

Harvest of hate

June 14, 1942

After the war is over there will, of course, be more killings. In every one of the Nazi-conquered countries are the lists of those whose heads must roll. The main Quisling and several minor quislings in Norway, for instance, will have to leave Norway or take what comes. And if they should choose to leave, the question would be "Whither?" meaning "Where on the face of the earth can they go and not be found and stood up to face merciless judges and poker-faced firing squads?"

The extent of this violence of revenge, retribution, pay-off, cannot be known in advance. There will be arguments as to who should be killed and who not. Disputes will go on as to who belongs on the list. Whatever forces, factions, or parties for the time control an area will name the traitors or criminals to be "liquidated."

In some areas it will happen that first one faction and then another is in control and having the say-so as to whether this or that man of the opposition shall be rubbed out.

The hate harvest of the last great war, while it progressed and when it ended, had little to compare with the war now on. The overwhelming weight of opinion then was against hanging the Kaiser as the author of the war. His guilt was too complicated with the guilt of others.

And now in this war the case is different. The overwhelming decision seems to have been made already that the war will not be really and surely over till Hitler lies cold and stiff in the rigor of death with assurance that his breath and tongue no longer pollute human air—and alongside of him his henchmen Göring, Goebbels, Himmler.

Violence will in the aftermath of the war have its day. There may be new ways of saying what was heard in one interval of the

French revolution: "If death did not now exist it should be invented for use in this hour of doom."

Those in the Nazi-conquered countries who have suffered, hungered, waited, and taken anguish and shame while they waited, to the extent that they believe a reorganized world of the Four Freedoms is worth study, hope, and action, to that extent the human tragedy may be less violent in the terrors and conspiracies and kangaroo courts after the war. Such beliefs shine out from dark places sometimes.

What man can imagine man can make—is that so? It has happened. There are cases.

In a letter smuggled out of Norway not long ago we find endurance, belief, affirmation. Having served three and one-half months in prison, the writer, just let out, sent these lines to a former cell mate:

"I wish you could see us today—outwardly gray, poor, stripped to the skin, so it seems. But it is only a seeming, only on the outside. Never has the life behind and inside us been less gray, never has the blood been more red. He's trying to kid himself, you say. Well, just consider yourself, when you were here. Even though it was strenuous, you nevertheless lived, felt the pulse of life even in the grayest of the gray which you lived through the final months. You expressed this yourself the last time I talked with you. And today it is still more clear. . . . Seen from the outside it may appear grayer than ever, marked with hunger and distress, loss and suffering. But inwardly life presses forward, irresistibly."

It sounds like one of the unbreakable characters in an Ibsen drama.

Quart of milk

June 21, 1942

Not for a long time will we hear the last about that speech of Vice-President Wallace wherein he stepped up front and went on record willy-nilly in favor of a quart of milk a day for any inhabitant of the globe who daily might be wanting such a quart. It was plain that something would happen to that quart before the shouting and shooting was over. In the very next speech of Wallace he came down to a pint of milk. That would be two glasses.

I hope he makes his stand there and refuses further concessions and reductions. Also I hope he gets tangled in no disputes as to whether it should be cow's milk or goat's. While we happen to be a cow country, the peoples of Europe and Asia favor the goat, which in some places is referred to as "the poor man's cow" and which sustains far larger populations than the cow. And there are nomad tribes in the wilds of Russia who subsist mainly on mare's milk and the members there would like Mr. Wallace to ration them more than a pint or a quart. The American engineer Littlepage in his book *Soviet Gold,* reporting his twelve years at gold production in Siberia, tells of what an elaborate evening party can be gathered in fellowship around a huge bowl of mare's milk soured, whipped, flavored, tricked up with bittersweet.

Snipers have been after Wallace. They don't like the tone and drift of his speech. It packs unknown dynamite. How so? And what kind of dynamite? Well, take that one sentence: "Modern science, which is a by-product and an essential part of the people's revolution, has made it technologically possible to see that all of the people of the world get enough to eat."

What's this? What is our Vice-President saying here? Nothing particularly new. Herbert Hoover had the same picture in mind when he used the phrase "the abolition of poverty" and later forgot to repeat it over and over. Wilson of General Electric has said it in forty ways of warning his fellow industrialists that when the war ends, the whole works of the free-enterprise system will be threatened unless production is set going with a distribution that reaches the common man with a just and decent plenty of the goods of life.

Bill Batt, the Philadelphia industrialist, has spoken anxious and eloquent warnings to the business and financial leaders of the country that they cannot expect the same world after this war, that an open mind on what to do next will be no harm, that the machines of man can be of service toward universal plenty. Eugene Meyer in his *Washington Post* printed the Wallace speech in full and supplied reprints to schools for use in class study, which ought to be a fairly good certificate that Wallace is not shooting at the moon.

Some critics of Wallace go so far as to misrepresent what he said through their allegations sounding as though Wallace proposes forced feeding of milk and those who prefer a pint to a quart will nevertheless have to swallow a quart and such persons as naturally would rather have beer or wine will take milk because the decision has been made that milk is best for them.

The fact is, of course, that Wallace just sort of accidentally first brought up the idea of milk for the whole human family. Quoting from his speech: "Half in fun and half seriously, I said the other day to Madame Litvinov: 'The object of this war is to make sure that everybody in the world has the privilege of drinking a quart of milk a day.' She replied, 'Yes, even a pint.'"

So there we are. And we may recall, if we choose, Artemus Ward, the droll humorist, announcing the subject of his lecture would be "Milk," standing and talking an hour and a half at a table whereon stood a big pitcher of milk and not once in his talk making the slightest reference to milk, not even the milk of human kindness.

Weep not for me—

June 28, 1942

Though I am a wreck at the bottom of the sea
    shed no tears for me.

I am remembered by a photograph showing one
    of my last great moments.

Down to the waters of the sea, sliding down ropes,
    you see the men of my crew.

Down they slide to the open sea where waiting
    boats pick them up.

On the floor of the sea I rest now, the *U.S.S.*
    Lexington, an aircraft carrier.

I shall be remembered for punishment I gave the
    enemy, I and my crewmen.

Maybe you heard how the men of the ship acted
    before they left me.

Maybe you heard how they took their shoes and lined
    them in nice, neat rows on the flight deck—

And the admiral saying in Chicago later sure they
    did exactly that, "Nothing surprising, sailors are orderly
    people."

Tell that Chicago boy John Kmetek I am sorry about him
    and I know his heartache.

I saw him swimming quite a while before he was picked up.

And I believe his telling the home folks he couldn't
     take another last look at me.

A good cook and a mighty nice musician, John Kmetek,
     if you ask me—

Shaking a mean pan of eggs and in the cool of the evening
     handy with the accordion—

Not satisfied till he had a $1,000 accordion—his best
     pal that accordion—

Swimming in the open sea just before I sank out of sight
     for all time

Kmetek couldn't take another last look and Kmetek
     came near crying—

Two things he had loved were fading from him—a ship
     and an accordion.

Weep not for me, the *U.S.S. Lexington,* nor the shoes of
     the crew in nice rows on the flight deck—

Nor John Kmetek nor his $1,000 accordion now soaking in
     sea salt water.

The same sweet crew shall have another ship and they
     will line new shoes in nice rows.

And if and when Kmetek plays sad music on his new
     accordion they will know he is remembering his old loves.

   Of course the above and foregoing is not a poem nor a ballad nor
a ballade. Any good accordion-player, however, knows what it
means and could improvise an accompaniment to be played to
someone reading it aloud.

And if I happened to be good on the accordion I am not sure just what sort of variations I would play to indicate the crewmen of the *Lexington* lining up their shoes in nice rows on the famous flight deck a few minutes before they all slid to the open sea saying good-by to their much-loved ship.

And if you were good on the accordion how would you play it where the admiral says, "Nothing surprising, sailors are orderly people"?

We are returning you now to our studios—with the suggestion that NBC, CBS, Mutual or some independents put John Kmetek on the air with a new accordion, so we can hear what he used to play on the grand old *Lexington*.

When the *Chicago Times* told its readers that it would certainly be right and fair for John Kmetek to have a new accordion, as good as the old one that sank with the *Lexington*, in a few days enough money had come in. Navy men at Chicago put on a broadcast answered by John Kmetek at San Diego playing "Indian Love Call" and other pieces to show he liked his new accordion, which was sailing with him the next day. The $1,000 accordion that went down with the *Lexington* was presented to him under unusual circumstances. His father saw service in the First World War, and there were government benefit payments made to next of kin when the father died. John, however, was not yet born at the time of the father's death, therefore under the law not entitled to any part of the benefit payments. So when John grew up, the next of kin went out and bought him the doggonedest, grandest accordion his heart could wish for.

Lidice

July 5, 1942

From a source that may be considered unimpeachable I learn that microfilm has gone from this country in rather large quantity during the past two years to Britain, the Low Countries, Norway, and more recently, to Alaska. The special purpose of this microfilm was to make a photographic record of documents of property ownership and of the properties themselves.

In a small handbag or briefcase, or even one roomy hip pocket, you could carry the evidence of ownership in buildings, plants, equipments, worth many millions of dollars before they crashed under demolition bombs or burned away from incendiary bombs. The idea is that in some areas they believe it expedient to have matters so arranged that if they lose the property they will at least have their microfilm of it. At the postwar settlements claimants may come forward showing that where now is nothing but rubble, rubbish, and ashes, there used to be something and there was title to it and neither Nazi nor Jap was given a quitclaim deed.

The women and children of Lidice (Leed-eat-say) may show up with claims, with no microfilm but with photographs. There she lay, ten miles to the west out of Prague, a village of Czech miners, woodworkers, farmers, some 525 people in about ninety cottages, overlooked by the tall flowing spire of the Catholic Church of St. Margaret. That was June 9 in the year of Our Lord 1942. In the morning, at noon, through the afternoon, the village of Lidice, humanly, was there. A village, being made up of its population, its inhabitants, is still there so long as it has its people. And in that sense we may say that the village of Lidice (Leed-eat-say) still stood and had a name, an existence and a personality across the morning, noon, and afternoon of June 9, anno Domini 1942.

Yet the next morning that village was gone. Humanly, Lidice (Leed-eat-say) vanished. The population was rubbed out, the inhabitants erased. The word "obliterated" may apply. Any word will do that means nothing took the place of something alive, laughing, hoping. The Prague radio, speaking for those authorities who erased and obliterated Lidice, broadcast: "All men of the village have been shot. The women have been deported to a concentration camp and the children sent to appropriate centers of education."

Many details of the operation are yet to come to make the scene slide together as a whole. After curfew the village found itself surrounded, its streets filled with troops, and at each house those inside were told to pile out and be quick about it. Something like two hundred men, all males over seventeen years of age, were lined up for shooting. Whether they were shot here and there by ones and twos as they came out of the houses, we do not know.

Whether they were lined up in platoons of ten and twenty and given the works by a special slaughtering squad, we do not know. Whether there was any slight degree of resistance, so that possibly one Nazi butcher got a death bullet or a knife or a stone, we do not know. Whether the marksmen didn't like the looks of some of the targets and first shot off a right ear and then a left ear before aiming at the heart, we do not know. Whether the targets were ordered to dig their graves before falling into them, whether they shouted defiant cries or made the sign of the cross and passed out in calm prayers, we have not yet heard. We do know that the men and boys, good and bad, sick or well, Catholic, Protestant, or unbeliever, touched mystic hands in a dark fellowship of death. The Nazi decree was that all males over seventeen, with no exceptions, were to be done to death. Some of the names we know—Josef Bartunek the tailor, Vaclav Karnik the wheelmaker, Jan Sid the shoemaker, Frantisek Kotmel the blacksmith, Ladislav Liska the millowner, Vaclav Cermak the farmer. How they died, their last words, which ones plunged forward unafraid of death or their killers, we do not know.

Considering the night of death in Lidice, the day of fire that followed was not so hard to look at. Said the Prague radio, "All buildings of the village were leveled to the ground and the name of the village immediately abolished." They burned it. With method, by a system, they burned in 1942 a village that dated from 1309.

Sometimes terror works. Again it doesn't. "He created a solitude and called it peace" was written of an ancient conqueror that time mocks at.

"It was like many an American village," says Jan Masaryk. "One street was named for Woodrow Wilson. Wherever free men fight they will remember the name and learn to say Leed-eat-say."

Air power keeps changing

July 12, 1942

I listen to a coast-to-coast hookup where a United States Army general, a good and proven fighting man and a gruff and likable human being, tells the country that civilians are running the war and these same civilians have been doped with mistaken arguments and are running around telling each other that the war can be won by air power alone, that when, as, and if the United Nations can tear the Luftwaffe and all the Jap planes out of the skies, the war is just about over.

It was plain to see that the general trails along with those who years ago thought Billy Mitchell to be fantastic and wrongheaded—and they think much the same of Major Alexander P. De Seversky, whose book *Victory through Air Power* opens with a portrait and a dedication "in gratitude to the memory of my superior, my colleague, my friend General William Mitchell."

Seversky was on this hookup and did the best he could at giving the gist of his 352-page book in six minutes. Seversky could have quoted from his book:

"Only 100 per cent airmen can conceive and carry through a 100 per cent aerial strategy. . . . Only those with the creative imagination to keep them a few long steps ahead of the immediate technological-tactical picture can match the world we are living in.

"Even men trained in aviation have difficulty in visualizing the air power of tomorrow; how helpless, therefore, are those trained in totally different fields, who psychologically are incapable of considering the air as a separate tactical sphere! . . . air power, the newest, the fastest-growing, and most revolutionary military force. A new military art, such as is inherent in aviation, must not be restrained by subservience to old military leadership."

This kind of prophecy, to the old-line army or navy man, duly graduated from West Point or Annapolis before flying and a lot of modern technology became part of the course of study, doesn't sound so good. For it sounds as though Glenn Martin or Henry Ford or the industrialist originators at Boeing, Vultee, Bell, Curtiss-Wright, are maybe experts in military science and what they do and think and produce may count as much toward victory as what the regular professional military or naval man does, thinks, and produces. Who is the more likely to know what the air weapons and the air transport of next year or the year after will be? The aviation industry or the army General Staff? Or if the General Staff does help, will it not be to the extent that it is air-minded?

Boxcars in the air, long freight-train cargoes hauled by multimotored planes—will we see those before the year is out? Maybe soon—because tactics, strategy, logistics, may demand them. They, and what they carry to where brave men are crying for what they carry, may give powerful decisions.

Of course time is going to tell us a few things. The future is going to back up and justify Seversky on the one hand or General Henry Reilly on the other or neither, but not both of them. Thus far Seversky has been winning. And his prophecies may have as much to them as the earlier prophecies of Billy Mitchell. The passing weeks and months will let us know.

As I write comes news of Red Army flyers bombing pontoon bridges over the Don River "as fast as the Germans can lay them." For that operation the Red Army seems at the moment to have enough planes. For the additional operation of tearing the enemy air force from the skies at all points the Red Army does not have the required planes. Here and elsewhere decisions as to victory or stalemate, advance or retreat, rest on the question of who gets there first with the most air power.

Who are the air-minded? You can peg some nice ones in *Youth Must Fly,* a book by an explorer, navigator, scientist, manufacturer, Eugene F. McDonald. Gliders, sailplanes, for peace or war, answers to many questions we hadn't thought of asking, including respects to Admiral William A. Moffett, early an air-minded naval officer.

Let the boys fly, and the sooner and younger, the better for our air corps, says McDonald, citing General Ernst Udet, the great German flyer, as saying that his best combat pilots come from a pool of 250,000 to 300,000 boy gliders. "They found that the glider-trained pilot who had mastered soaring made much more rapid progress in power training than the boy who had never flown, and that soaring experience made him a better power pilot."

Pigeons, silence, and spies

July 19, 1942

"All we know is what we write in the papers!" confesses Tom Ferril, Colorado's most careless and free-going poet and columnist. "Here it is, press time, nothing written and we wish the *Rocky Mountain Herald* was in hell! People who write editorials never know what they're going to write till they write the first sentence. Then it snowballs."

If he could only cook up a little personal and private indignation about some public issue, Tom could get started writing, him being a Republican and his paper the oldest Republican paper in Denver. But this week he was feeling serene, as poets go, and was quoting from one of the poets now engaged in the upper brackets of the Office of Price Administration, Maury Maverick, who when last heard from was saying he plays no favorites and "I ain't mad at nobody but Hitler."

179

By way of firing up his indignation Mr. Ferril came near getting started on his weekly piece by concentrating like sixty on "the fellow who got into the Intelligence Service because he could speak eight languages, so they put him to work feeding homing pigeons." Yet the more he thought about it, the more certain Mr. Ferril became that this was poetic justice if it was fixed up and understood that while feeding the pigeons he would not be required to make a strict and literal translation to be duly written out and immediately forwarded to the Office of War Information.

It reminded me of last February in San Francisco seeing a hard-boiled regular army sergeant giving a cage of pigeons an outing and an airing in a park. A tough baby and a trooper not to be fooled with, this sergeant. So he looked. But the pigeons did fool with him. They perch on his right and left shoulders. He holds out his right arm and four of them fly up there. Likewise when his left arm makes a perch four more flap their wings, circle, and light on his left arm. A centerpiece is needed, so still another pigeon who loves and obeys the soft-hearted and sentimental sergeant perches on his head.

Maybe he wasn't a hard-boiled regular army sergeant after all. Maybe he was Tom's linguist who knows eight languages. Maybe unbeknownst to us he was translating for the Office of Facts and Figures.

Anyhow and ennyhoo, Mr. Thomas Ferril, the Colorado poet who is published by the Yale University Press, had a good quote from Alexandre Dumas which I had not heard in a long time: "Nothing is more interesting than a wall behind which something is happening."

Does that remind one and all of the trial of the eight Nazi spies behind closed doors in Washington, D.C.? It does. And in that connection this observer hazards his opinion that this may be a case where you can't have too much secrecy, like the sea captain who told his crew when he wanted everybody to say nothing. "All I want from you is silence, and damned little of that!"

Maybe those eight spies should have been kept hid and given the works for a longer time, in the hope of what further possible revelations might have come from them as to how many more might have landed elsewhere and be now on the job of wrecking, burning, spoiling, interfering with our war production.

Maybe there has been actually too much publicity in this affair, so far. Valuable information, valuable property, lives beyond evaluation, hung by slender threads these honorable reptiles sought to cut.

So delicate, subtle, involved, and precious are the strands and issues that range out from this particular Nazi web that I join with those who give the authorities concerned and responsible the widest leeway they ask for. The time for assessing the efficiency and intelligence of those authorities in capturing and removing spies and saboteurs before such bribe rats, propaganda snakes, firebugs, and explosion experts can get going—that time must come later.

Nevertheless I must here and now file a mild demurrer to questions asked me by an FBI man in the case of a citizen applying for a Federal position. On my saying that the citizen in question is so mentally alive that I could not guarantee what might be his thinking tomorrow or next year, the query came as though it is a standard FBI query: "Is he intellectually restless?"

The way this query came I am sure that it will be held against the man that I answered: "Sure he's intellectually restless. He's got thousands of questions and night and day he's hunting the answers. This would be a hell of a country if you leave out the intellectually restless. From Ben Franklin and Tom Jefferson on through Abe Lincoln to Edison and the Wright brothers, what we've got that's worth having came from restless minds. Any new military secrets that help us win this war, any new machines, processes, methods, will come from men who couldn't sleep nights on account of ideas that fired their restless brains."

Take a letter to Dmitri Shostakovich

July 26, 1942

All over America last Sunday afternoon goes your Symphony No. 7,
millions listening to your music portrait of Russia in blood and
shadows.

You sit there in Moscow last summer a year ago writing music—and
into the time of the falling leaves and the blowing snow writing
music.

Sometimes as a fire warden you run to the streets and help put out
a fire set by Nazi Luftwaffe bombs—then you walk home and
write more music.

When the Moscow radio tells the world what is news it reports the
Prime Minister Stalin, Marshal Timoshenko—and the composer
Shostakovich.

On a long battle front sagging toward Moscow the Red Army fights
against the greatest war machine that ever marched into any
country.

Dive bombers howl down like desperate steel hawks forbidden to
ever sing any song unless it says death, death, death.

The flack, the ack-ack, the antiaircraft guns, send a rain of steel
upward into the sky swifter than downward ever fell snow or
rain in wild wind.

The tanks come roaring like elephants and land whales with hides
of steel and a poison spit of lead meant to kill and kill.

Against these killers the Red Army sets its traps and sends out its
own tanks, artillery, and antitank rifles meant to cut down
Nazis and feed them death on death.

The outside world looks on and holds its breath and the American
general Douglas MacArthur far over in Bataan radios Stalin:
"Magnificent! Matchless!"

And we hear about you, Dmitri Shostakovich—we hear you sit there
day after day doing a music that will tell the story.

182

These people, your people, named by the Nazi leader as "bestial barbarians," with no culture, no higher lights—your music is to speak for them?

So we see a people, near the awful trial of losing their capital city, telling the world they have a composer who writes music while the bombs fall.

In Berlin no new symphonies, in Paris, Brussels, Amsterdam, Copenhagen, Oslo, Prague, Warsaw, wherever the Nazis have mopped up and made new laws, no new symphonies.

And in Moscow you, Mr. Shostakovich, thirty-six years old, having written six symphonies, go to work on No. 7.

The spring sun of 1942 melts the last of the snows and frost oozes out of the ground and the battle of Russia flares and cries again in the wrangling of steel and blood.

Summer comes and you, Dmitri Shostakovich, see your music writing, your script, put on microfilm, a symphony held in a tomato can.

From Moscow across old Persia to still older Egypt, from Cairo round and roundabout to New York goes this little can of film.

Then what? Then a Maestro Toscanini tells the NBC ninety-two-piece orchestra what to do with it and they put it on the air for the listening millions.

And how does it go and what do our ears make of it and what is it saying across the oceans and the convoys, the subs and planes?

Well, nothing like a fat man's race at a summer picnic, nothing like what a sugar daddy buys at a night club nor any certificate that guarantees comfort and convenience.

It begins calm with the good earth and with plains and valleys naked for the toil of man seeking crops and bread.

It goes on with touches like people in peacetime having a chance to hunt for themselves their personal birds of happiness to listen to.

Then come drums and guns and evermore drums and guns and the war is on and the test of a nation and a people—and an ordeal for the whole Family of Man.

The music marches and fights, it struggles and kills, it stands up and says there are a thousand terrible deaths it is better to die than to let the Nazis take over your homeland and tell you how you must live.

What you say sometimes, Dmitri Shostakovich, is the same as the
message MacArthur sent by radio to Stalin: "Magnificent!
Matchless!"
The people of Russia may fall back and lose and lose and the years
go by and the time be long, yet in the end they will win.
They know when to be silent and suffer, when to fight and how to
sing while fighting, and how to say in the ashes and blood loss:
"*Nietchevo*—it is nothing, what of it? It is for our Holy Mother
Russia!"
So some of us listened to what came in the tomato can from Moscow
to Cairo to Manhattan, we salute you and speak thanks, Mr.
Dmitri Shostakovich.
Your song tells us of a great singing people beyond defeat or con-
quest who across years to come shall pay their share and con-
tribution to the meanings of human freedom and discipline.

Race issues and the color line

August 2, 1942

This month one of the big leagues is going to try out Negro ball-
players. Anyhow, so the management of the Pittsburgh Pirates tell
us. If on the tryouts the Negroes prove up, then contracts will be
signed and the long-observed tradition of the color line will be
gone.

Certainly there was what we might call a sporting equality on
the Tam O'Shanter golf course near Chicago last week when the
national Tam O'Shanter tournament, a distinguished annual event,
with stakes of $2,500, was played. Thirteen Negroes entered. Four
of these Negro players lasted through the finals in a field of eighty.

As this war goes on we are going to hear more and more—and
definitely not less and less—about race issues and the color line. One
of the few countries which is going to have no internal trouble at
all as to race and color measures is Soviet Russia. We in the United
States of America are going to make decisions, for instance, as to
whether the Negro soldier who has borne hardships and wounds in
the service of his country shall be stopped from voting as a freeman
and a citizen on the ground that he has not paid a poll tax now
required from him in various Southern states. We are going to make

decisions whether it is possible and practicable to open new lines of office, factory, shop, and mill jobs to Negroes in recognition of service and sacrifice they gave to the war.

Backing the claims of the Negroes will be that now peculiarly powerful and obstinate outfit known as the Congress of Industrial Organizations. Their little pamphlet titled *The CIO and the Negro* has nothing in it about social equality. But there is plenty about how foolish it is for white and black industrial workers to allow anyone to throw them into strife against each other, and hate of each other, at the instigation of white men who have their own reasons for wishing strife and hate between black labor and white labor.

In her latest book, Pearl Buck writes about the color line, whether we should speak of ourselves as white superiors of the yellow Chinese folk and the dark-skinned people of India, Burma, Java, Malay, Iran, and points east. The Chinese have manners, culture, family and ancestor loyalties, Miss Buck learned when a girl. She heard her Christian missionary father warn one of the Chinese that unless he accepted the Christian faith he would go to hell along with all other Chinese unbelievers. And the Chinese answered that he would be disloyal to his beloved forefathers who had given him life if he wished to stay away from where they were spending eternity—and besides, why shouldn't he prefer the company of Chinese in hell to that of the whites in their very superior and exclusive heaven?

Also we are told of a city in Texas where one year two college teams, one white, one colored, won state championships. Authorities took a stand against any deciding game between the two. Yet the members of the two teams on the quiet one morning, without spectators, all on their own, did play a deciding game—and it was a tie. Authorities asked questions and got the nice sporting answer "We wanted to find out which was the better team."

Swedes who cannot be silent

August 9, 1942

A Nazi organization in Sweden now finds hard going. Using this summer its well-known methods of agitation and propaganda aimed

185

at "softening up" the country, it has met a counteroffensive and is stopped in its tracks. In Helsingborg on the night of July 14 a Nazi group tried to hold a street meeting. The speakers' platform was circled with a crowd of listeners who refused to listen. They hooted. They booed. They sounded threatening to those who wished to present a case for Hitler and the "New Order." Finally the police had to interfere and stop the meeting so as to be sure no Nazi heads were broken. The crowd sang the national anthem and cheered Sweden.

In the same week again Nazi speakers appealed to the police in two towns in the province of East Skaane, where crowds were near rioting. At Landskrona the police hustled a Nazi agitator to headquarters to ensure his personal safety while outside a crowd of Swedes howled and burned Nazi pamphlets. In the town of Umea feeling ran so high that the local authorities told the Nazis it would be a mistake for them to hold a meeting and a permit could not be granted.

Neutrality is not what it was in Sweden. The country refuses to be "softened up." It is well aware of Hitler's saying that before his troops move in he has seen to it that the hard fibers have become slack and the will to fight is mixed up with promises of peace and comfort under a "New Order."

"Indescribable horrors" is the word for what the peoples of German-occupied countries are suffering, says the *Oestergötlands Folkblad*. "Their fate is unprecedented, and any comparable example during the war of 1914-18 is lacking."

The opinion is offered that blame is not so much to be laid on the civilian populations of these countries "being more ungovernable or impudent," but rather the horrors are to be explained by "the sadism of the occupying power."

Long before the war there was fear in some of these countries that they would be Nazified. Now in Norway, Czechoslovakia, Holland, and Poland, these fears have come true "in the most brutal fashion through the introduction of a compulsory internal political order which is hated by a majority of the population." This editorial ends: "It is possible to load a people with chains, but it is impossible to rob it of its free soul. It is possible to gain a temporary external power, but it is impossible to win a people over against its will."

Now when the *Dagens Nyheter* (*Daily News*) of Stockholm, the most widely circulated Swedish daily, picks up the foregoing editorial from a small-town newspaper and reprints it, what are we to make of its added comment? It says on its own: "These people will remain the unforgiving enemies of the usurpers for generations if necessary. That is our opinion, as it is the opinion of other Swedes. We would all react in the same way."

Such words can hardly mean anything else than that these Swedes in thought and feeling hold a deep human fellowship with the German-occupied countries, and if attacked by Nazi forces Sweden will be an enemy and an unforgiving one "for generations if necessary."

For many months Swedish organs of opinion gave Nazi methods the silent treatment. Now the stench of mass death and the pity of throng hunger has become too terrible for silence. And the organ of the Labor party, *Social Demokraten,* carries a front-page article quoting Gunnar Sandberg, an authority on international law, on the German police decree that in occupied France if a saboteur escapes, all relatives must be punished.

It goes against all international law, says Sandberg, and "can only be founded on the ancient and long-abandoned practice of blood revenge." Nowhere in history does he find the equivalents of such mass executions of hostages and civilians as the Germans have handed the occupied countries.

On this same Nazi decree *Dagens Nyheter* speaks out as though it would prefer silence but there are things that must be cried aloud. "Many shameful documents have appeared during the present war, but one may ask whether in its cold perfection, methodical and absolutely unrestrained pursuance of terror tactics, this doesn't surpass all else? It is terrifying to think of the reaction in the minds of the people to this decree. Any regime resorting to such monstrous means to sustain itself simultaneously admits the ground is tottering beneath it. Measures of extreme violence are the surest evidence that the day will come when today's law dictator will be incapable of protecting himself from the consequences he has evoked. Measures of this kind—not arrived at unthinkingly, but systematically planned—shake the foundations of our civilization and put its breath of life in danger."

So run words trying to speak for the speechless. Thus we see

187

wrath that doesn't get the half of it told. Thus we may note acceptance of awful days of judgment and counterterror to come over the lands of Europe.

Scandinavian scenes

August 16, 1942

Ten thousand Swedes and Norwegians on a hot afternoon in a joint picnic and mass meeting in Minnehaha Park midway between St. Paul and Minneapolis was worth going to see and hear. More than half of them had no seats. They stood. For three and a quarter hours they stood. And while standing they listened. And while listening they heard. I know, because from a platform seat I watched their faces, many of them the inscrutable Scandinavian face that half-says, "Don't try to read my thoughts—and if you do let me know, for I am not always sure what I think."

A flyer from Camp Little Norway near Toronto, Lieutenant "Andreas," was speaking. And it seemed to me they were interested and following every word. But I couldn't be sure. He was telling them how in the late winter of 1941 he started from his home near the Swedish border in eastern Norway and how he made the ten-day trip to the seacoast alone. "I took food, skis, and a sleeping bag. I traveled in the night, keeping away from towns and settlements, troubling no one that the Gestapo might come to with questions." He mentioned "sleeping in the snow" as though so many others had done it that it was merely routine, even in zero weather. At the coast he had to wait for a boat to England. The boat's hiding place was alongside rocks, and winds had risen that drove the boat against the rocks and broke it to pieces. He could not start for England till they had another boat.

Then he tells his audience, "We stole a boat from the Nazis and we stole enough gas for the trip from the Nazis." And it was there that the bronzed faces out front unfroze and broke into smiles and laughter, hands clapping an applause at the idea of any Norwegian stealing from the Nazis who have stolen Norway.

His story went on. "On the streets of the cities and towns of Norway, the Norwegians do not get out of the way for Germans they meet." On the faces of the audience as they smiled grimly and

188

applauded I thought I saw the kind of people who would be slow about giving the right of way to strangers who hoped to take away their homeland and run it from Berlin or rather from the headquarters of Der Führer.

The question of who has the right of way on the streets, in schools, churches, shops, mines, harbors, is involved, peculiar, so unnatural that it affects the minds of some of the German soldiers in Norway. "The Germans sometimes go crazy. I have seen them lose their minds so they had to be taken back to Germany for treatment."

And this was revealing: "The Germans in Norway do not all think the same. When I talked with two of them, they both said the same about what they think. But when I talked with each of those two alone I learned they do not think the same. I am sure that in any occupied country there is wide difference of opinion among the Germans. We do not know how many would rather be home. But it is many.

"We hid in a house while waiting to start for England. I do not know whether the man who let us hide in his house is alive now. He was taken to a concentration camp in Germany and since then he has not been heard from.

"Most of the Norwegians sent to concentration camps in Germany have not come back and there is no word about where they are or whether they are living. A few have come back and they have little to say. Some of them were tortured, at first alone, to make them talk. Then they were tortured with their relatives present. The Gestapo expects a wife, a sister or brother, or the mother or father, to cry out something like 'Tell them what you know and stop this suffering.' "

After September of 1941, when the Norwegians had made it clear they would not submit to Nazi rule nor co-operate in the "New Order," the food restrictions became strict and the terror was tightened. "You could see faces change. They became hard, thin, drawn with lines of trouble—that happened to many. We could see the faces of another Norway. The underground began organizing. I lied to my father and mother about where I was going nights. I told them I was going to the mountains to ski when in fact I was going to the forest to make a radio broadcast for a Free Norway.

"If they had been told by me where I was and what I was doing, it would be terrible for them to hide the truth from the Gestapo. They could tell the Gestapo truthfully that they did not know of my underground activity. Yes, in Norway now it is a saying that everybody lies. And it is possibly correct that in all of the occupied countries now everybody lies."

The meeting worked out truly as "a rally." The words "freedom" and "independence" took on new meanings. One speaker quoted an exiled Norwegian professor, Frederick Paascho, saying in Stockholm: "Don't pity the Norwegian people. We have gained something in these last long years—deeper faith and deeper love. The country they wanted to take from us is ours more than ever."

Also was quoted the Swedish Minister of Justice, Karl G. Westman, as to his country on the alert every moment: "It is a mistake to think that the present situation is stable. Nothing is more certain than that it will change."

The Man with the Broken Fingers

August 23, 1942

The Man with the Broken Fingers throws a shadow.
Down from the spruce and evergreen mountain timbers of Norway—
And across Europe and the Mediterranean to the oasis palms of
    Libya—
He lives and speaks a sign language of lost fingers.
From a son of Norway who slipped the Gestapo nets, the Nazi
    patrols,
The story comes as told among those now in Norway.

Shrines in their hearts they have for this nameless man
Who refused to remember names names names the Gestapo wanted.
"Tell us these names. Who are they? Talk! We want those names!"
And the man faced them, looked them in the eye, and hours passed
        and no names came—hours on hours and no names for the
        Gestapo.
They told him they would break him as they had broken others.
The rubber hose slammed around face and neck,
The truncheon handing pain with no telltale marks,
Or the distinction of the firing squad and death in a split second—
The Gestapo considered these and decided for him something else
        again.
"Tell us those names. Who were they? Talk! Names now—or else!"
And no names came—over and over and no names.

So they broke the little finger of the left hand.
Three fingers came next and the left thumb bent till it broke.
Still no names and there was a day and night for rest and thinking
        it over.
Then again the demand for names and he gave them the same
        silence.

And the little finger of the right hand felt itself twisted,
Back and back twisted till it hung loose from a bleeding socket.
Then three more fingers crashed and splintered one by one
And the right thumb back and back into shattered bone.

Did he think about violins or accordions he would never touch
     again?
Did he think of baby or woman hair he would never again play
     with?
Or of hammers or pencils no good to him any more?
Or of gloves and mittens that would always be misfits?
He may have laughed half a moment over a Gestapo job
So now for a while he would handle neither knife nor fork
Nor lift to his lips any drinking-cup handle
Nor sign his name with a pen between thumb and fingers.

And all this was halfway—there was more to come.
The Gestapo wit and craft had an aim.
They wanted it known in Norway the Gestapo can be terrible.
They wanted a wide whispering of fear
Of how the Nazis handle those who won't talk or tell names.
"We give you one more chance to co-operate."
Yet he had no names for them.
His locked tongue, his Norwegian will pitted against Nazi will,
His pride and faith in a free man's way,
His welcoming death rather than do what they wanted—
They brought against this their last act of fury,
Breaking the left arm at the elbow,
Breaking it again at the shoulder socket—
And when he came to in a flicker of opening eyes
They broke the right arm first at the elbow, then the shoulder.
By now of course he had lost all memory of names, even his own.
And there are those like you and me and many many others
Who can never forget the Man with the Broken Fingers.
His will, his pride as a free man, shall go on.
His shadow moves and his sacred fingers speak.
He tells men there are a thousand writhing shattering deaths
Better to die one by one than to say yes yes yes

192

When the answer is no no no and death is welcome and death
    comes soon
And death is a quiet step into a sweet clean midnight.

The son of the Man with the Broken Fingers

September 27, 1942

The piece titled "The Man with the Broken Fingers," in this
column four weeks ago, was read on a Treasury Hour program,
has been put on transcriptions for the use of radio stations, has been
short-waved to various parts of Europe, has been published in
Swedish, Danish, Norwegian, and Russian, having now reached
many millions of listeners and readers. Therefore it is correct to
present here a letter addressed to the present writer by Chauncey
Giles Hubbell of 12 Commonwealth Avenue, Boston, Massachusetts,
the body of it reading:

"Dear Sir: Your startling and heart-rending blank verse poem in
last Sunday's *Globe* raises the question—which others are probably
asking—are the statements there made regarding the torture inflicted
on 'The Man with the Broken Fingers' actual facts, reliable and
authenticated? Or can our Nazi enemies declare, again, that those
statements are only false and mere propaganda? A brief reply will
greatly oblige. Your very truly . . ."

We can be quite sure that Mr. Hubbell is one of those citizens
anxious that the war propaganda of his country shall be kept clean
of false stresses, needless exaggerations, indecent distortions that in
the end work for bad morale rather than good. Atrocity stories
based on imagination instead of fact eventually end in a recoil not
so good.

Yet it does happen sometimes that incidents of horror and torture take place with agony piled on anguish, with one calculated
cruel surprise following another. Unless care is used in the telling
of what then happens, people may say it is too horrible to listen to
even if it sounds probable. Or they may say it is so cruel it could
not have happened and they refuse to have any part in believing it.

When a few months ago some of us heard on Berlin short-wave
that Stalin had issued a secret circular with instructions on how
to prepare a nutritious sausage from the bodies of Russian and

German soldiers fallen in battle, we laughed. It was too smart, too cheap, and sounded entirely fabricated, make-believe, one more Nazi lie.

I first heard of the Man with the Broken Fingers at a mass meeting of ten thousand Swedes and Norwegians in Minnehaha Park, Minneapolis, on a Sunday afternoon in mid-August. The audience listened to a Norwegian flyer from Camp Little Norway near Toronto, Lieutenant "Andreas," his assumed name printed within quotes on the program because his real name, if it became known to the Nazis, would endanger relatives in Norway. He told of families punished, broken, scattered to concentration camps and to foreign labor service, because the Nazis had learned of boys from those families escaping Norway to serve with the United Nations.

He told of teachers by the hundreds who refused to co-operate with the Nazis, taken from their schools and sent to forced labor, of non-co-operating clergymen having their church doors closed and services forbidden, of bishops threatened and one bishop put under guard and "held in protective custody," of labor leaders at Oslo shot to death by Nazi firing squads, of German soldiers whose minds began to crack under the strain of the inhuman acts required of them by their superiors, such soldiers being returned to Germany as "mental cases" needing treatment, of an entire village of some sixty persons near Bergen, where two flyers of the Norwegian Royal Air Force had been sheltered, being wiped out as Lidice near Prague was destroyed.

He was reciting a bill of wrongs, of conditions so cruelly repressive, so befouling of human dignity, that every man and woman with any degree of blood, pride, and decency left was joining the underground movement to fight back at the Nazis. And he mentioned "one man who had his fingers broken one by one because he would not tell names the Gestapo asked."

So I talked afterward with Lieutenant "Andreas," a quiet-spoken and heroic figure whose story when someday written will show him to be a man of no exaggerations, not the kind to be peddling false or distorted atrocity stories. He had further details, given him by the son of the Man with the Broken Fingers. This son trained at Little Norway in Canada and is now a pilot in overseas service.

This son saw his mother and seven brothers and sisters killed in a bombing raid, another small brother shot in the arms of his father, and the father sent to a concentration camp. The father later was released, the Gestapo probably aware that if they let him go he would at once begin work in the underground organization helping boys to escape to Britain or America, and when later arrested they could use their torture methods to make him tell all the names of those in the organization. And that was what happened.

Again the father was in a concentration camp—and a fellow prisoner later released told the son of how his father had fingers broken one by one, then arms at elbow and shoulder, then death—and no names, not a name, for the Gestapo.

I believe the incident took place substantially as related and as he had it from the son of the Man with the Broken Fingers. I believe it is a procedure occasionally employed by the Gestapo when they are trying to break the will and loosen the tongue and memory of some key man in an organization who knows the names of those who belong.

When some night not far off the bombing squadrons of the United Nations drop their eggs of death over Berlin, I am sure if the son of the Man with the Broken Fingers is piloting one of the bombers he will be cool and keen and his conscience will be the least of his troubles.

And who writes the editorials?

August 30, 1942

The classic prayer of the editorial writer goes: "O Lord, give me this day my daily opinion and forgive me the one I had yesterday."

There was one on a Detroit paper, years back, who had his own variant of this. As his eyes opened and first met the morning light, he would murmur: "O Lord, deliver me from any of the dire dooms that may await me today, for I understand and realize that I am conscious again!"

I like the first one for its candor and its contrite spirit. The second one is noble in its admission that in the hours when you are sleeping, perhaps dreaming but not writing the dreams, perhaps scared by sudden nightmares but not writing them down, you are in no danger of fooling the public by a conniving and malicious editorial. It is when you are full awake, "conscious again," that you are liable to sit up to the typewriter and spill the beans so in sixes and sevens that a day or two afterward you are asking, "Who wrote that?" Anyhow, such has happened.

The human mind is a divine and wonderful piece of apparatus. I have known a few men who seemed to detach it, the mind, and then walk around it and watch it analyze—or sit in a chair and listen to it tick as though it might be a time bomb and when a new idea came it would explode.

And once I had a pleasant interview with an editorial writer who was a traction expert. I had become lost in a labyrinth of Chicago streetcar statistics, and he led me out of the wilderness without looking up reports by other experts. He sat at ease wearing carpet slippers. Arriving at his office of a morning, his first little duty was to get into those carpet slippers. Then he would sit up to his typewriter and straighten the traction tangle for that day, whether it was a demand for more rush-hour cars or a consideration of the iniquities of the new seven-cent fare. On a few occasions his slippers were missing. He would misplace them or laughing reporters would shift their location. On such a day there would be no traction editorial. The customary discussion of the newly pending streetcar ordinance would be lacking. His mind, out of long habit, simply wouldn't function on city transit facilities unless his feet were taken care of.

Once I heard an eminent newspaper publisher say that no department of his newspaper gave him so much concern and care as the editorials. Many of his readers could have told him why. He wanted the substance of his own ideas, prejudices, and crochets mirrored daily—and the editorial writer who could even in degree accomplish that fact need not be particular as to style or human appeal. I know another publisher who manages to get his own slant and viewpoint into the editorials of his newspaper—and yet those editorials are rather marvelous in their quality of style, their simple human appeal, always using some of the latest lingo of the man in the street.

Once I saw a bright reporter open a first edition, and after a while of skirmishing among the editorials, he read a few sentences aloud, stupidly conventional sentences that didn't mean a thing, cracking, "Ain't editorial writers wonderful?" Being one myself at the time, I agreed with him. The author of the particular editorial read aloud was still asleep. He had come awake in the morning without being "conscious again."

In these days of chaos and winds of propaganda there are more editorial writers than in the quieter times praying: "O Lord, give me this day my daily opinion and forgive me the one I had yesterday."

The tribe includes some of the best men that ever shoved a pencil or wished well to the Family of Man.

Washington is like that

September 6, 1942

Been reading *Washington Is Like That*. It's a book. Not so short either. And I read it all. Every page. W. M. Kiplinger wrote it. He writes crisp. Smooth. But crisp. Imagine he's a good talker. Talks long if he isn't stopped. But he breaks it up. Washington is like that.

Good book still and all. Takes in a lot of territory. Covers more ground than you'd think. Better than a trip to Washington—if you've never been in Washington. Better than living in Washington—if you live there and don't know what's going on. Washington is like that.

Forty-one chapters, a library of little books on Washington. Kiplinger had thirty-one men and women helping him dig up the facts. They pitchforked the facts on him, nigh smothered him. But he came up and through. He shows off and shows up the national capital. He mocks at it and loves it. The city is human, the government human. Alive! Alive! Watch it. It breathes! It speaks!

Only one long sentence in the book. Goes like this: "Here in this capital city originate the public statements, the ringing speeches which sound the clarion call, which summon all right-minded citizens to battle for the righteous cause, to defy with indomitable will those unspeakable forces which would undermine the unchallengeable rights of the people to work out their inalienable destiny in the light as given by Almighty God—the speech written by a $60-a-week publicity man."

"I passed five years trying to get someone else to write this book," Kiplinger tells us. He was busy. "And besides, I didn't know enough." Says he's just a reporter. Says he's not trying "to sell any particular point of view." And that from Washington. As though Washington is like that.

A good book still and all. He had to cut loose with it. Deserves no credit. Couldn't help writing it. Like the boy in church. "I didn't sneeze, Mamma—the sneeze sneezed me."

Information, history, science, the story of the American government with the American people the last twenty years. More especially the wild, whirling, hair-trigger, jigsaw, kaleidoscopic, colossal years of the Roosevelt administration.

Quite possible publishers suggested title "Kiplinger Tells All." Also possible Kiplinger considered "The Unvarnished Truth about Our Varnished Washington."

Mischievous, but not malicious. No smear. A few mistakes here and there. Not in fact, but mainly in positive, sharpshooting judgments. Says something for sure when he could better say maybe. History and Washington is like that.

Important point. Kiplinger has no ax to grind, no special interest to serve except something that took hold of the artist, the recorder, the lighted observer, in him.

As a reporter Kiplinger leans heavy to what business and industry want answered. He favors free enterprise wherever it will work. When government-planned economy steps in and eases out free enterprise Kiplinger tries to tell how, why, and what were the particular concrete circumstances. Fine, close-packed statement of what the American farmer has plowed up and under in the last twenty years in Kiplinger's twelve-page chapter, "Farmers Go to Town."

"If you want to see a revolution, here it is," he begins this chapter. "The revolutionists are the farmers. They have organized their empire and put the strings of control in Washington."

He sees a second phase to this revolution. It will be for consumers, "national recognition of the right of all the people to have plenty to eat—of the right kind of food."

Having covered parity payments, the ever-normal granary, commodity surpluses, the squeezing of middlemen, science working for the farmer, the farm bloc in Congress, and the big five farmer organizations with offices and lobbies in Washington, he concludes that the New Deal would like what has happened to agriculture to happen to all other major industries, "marriage with government, partnership, joint supervision, in the hope of getting greater production, wider distribution, larger consumption, more things for more people." Then the comment: "That would be fine. The farmer now gets paid well for not doing what he goldurn pleases. Next on the list come the manufacturers. It may pay them. Will it pay the consumers? It may, but that also remains to be seen."

In a chapter "Meet Fifty-Five Big Men" Kiplinger sketches briefly the principal men running the government now during war. Only six did not go to college—Jesse Jones, Steve Early, Lowell Mellett, Milo Perkins, William Knudsen, and Sidney Hillman. Of forty-nine who went to college, thirteen went to Harvard. Four are naturalized citizens—Knudsen, Hillman, Lauchlin Currie, Felix Frankfurter. A "tireless hater" and "earthy, witty phrasemaker" is Harold Ickes, but it is news to some of us that he is "proud of his prose style." Frank Knox can study whether he is "more doer than deep thinker" and "given to hyperbole in oratory." Archibald MacLeish comes off lucky as "Staunch pleader for rights of man. Great personal charm; quiet. Long face with quick boyish grin. Looks younger than age."

James M. Landis has quickie biography ending "Competent legal technician. Realistic New Dealer. Very solemn and earnest, high-tensioned. Kindly. Slender, blond, long-jawed." Landis only one of fifty-five marked "kindly." Superlative on two counts is Thurman Wesley Arnold, being "most vigorous trust-buster of all time" and "breeziest Washington official" besides "mixture of roistering practical joker, serious thinker. Restless. Impetuous. Deliberately picturesque. Dress disheveled. Garrulous, argumentative, loud voice, talks rapidly, leaving sentences unfinished. Vocabulary colorful, Rabelaisian. Puckish wit. Large, paunchy, yellowish complexion, dark mustache."

Okay, Kiplinger. Take it away. No, wait a second. We can see Marriner Stoddard Eccles, chairman of the board of governors of the Federal Reserve System, being "dry, tense, evangelical in speech." And we can picture him "small, spare, beetle-browed" with "alert, dark, bright eyes" but we don't quite visualize the "wan, fleeting smile" you give him. Of course if a smile is wan it's fleeting. Adjective "fleeting" is surplus commodity. Washington is like that.

Thanks, Kiplinger. You seen your duty and done it. Your book stands a good chance of rating as the best biography and portrait ever written of an American big city. And being as how that big city is now a great world capital, it will not be your fault if ignorance of it holds sway over the country even among those who constantly wear the pretense that they are informed and thoroughly aware what Washington is doing. Should they read your book they will be baffled by your simple and humble statement that you didn't want to write the book because, as you put it, "I didn't know enough."

Getting tough

September 13, 1942

"I'm going to get tough." Where have we heard that before? Who lately in government, labor, and industry hasn't either hinted or plainly spoken out that he is going to get tough? And the troops, planes, tanks being trained and made to be branded *"tough"*—have we not heard of them too?

One of the tough columnists—and nearly all of them either are tough or think they are—has taken a crystal ball and peered deep into it and come out with the flat-footed prediction that Franklin D. Roosevelt is so tough and all the time getting tougher that it looks now as though in 1944 political and military necessity will dictate that he must have a fourth term as President, no one else equally tough being on the horizon or in the offing.

This particular tough columnist, who hates Roosevelt politically and loves him militarily, may mean exactly what he says. He may have been reading that curious book *Roosevelt—Dictator or Democrat?* by Gerald Johnson, a Baltimore newspaper writer and historian. The book takes the President across many years and makes out a case that the man is a born fighter and that if you call the roll on those who have set out to destroy him only to find themselves destroyed or ineffective, the list is surprising and Hitler would not feel so good about it if he could understand it.

Tough—we may recall the vaudeville hoodlum who used to thrust his jaw out with "I lives in Tough Alley—see? De fadder up de alley you goes de tougher dey gets and I lives in de last house."

Or the case of the ancient Viking whose men were taking a hard hammering from the enemy, whose chief sent a message, "Will you surrender?" and had the answer, "Oh, yes—sure—I will surrender—when hair grows in the palm of my right hand."

Nearer to us and our time is the instance of Mrs. Ulysses Simpson Grant when she was interviewed by a *New York Herald* correspondent in 1864 who asked whether her husband would succeed in taking himself and his army to Richmond. Her reply: "I have no doubt Mr. Grant will succeed, for he is a very obstinate man." Many over the country liked it that she should refer to the head of all the Union armies as "Mr. Grant," Lincoln occasionally speaking of "Mr. Grant, as Mrs. Grant calls him."

Obstinate—that was her word. And we may yet hear in this war of some official's wife being asked whether her husband is tough or going to get tough, rejoining, "I can testify he is obstinate, if that is what you mean."

On the evening of the first day of the Battle of Shiloh a quartermaster half expected that the next day the Union army would be defeated and shoved off into the Tennessee River. He came to Grant with information for the General that there would not be the transportation to carry the defeated army across the river. Grant asked how many troops he could handle. "Ten thousand," said the quartermaster. "Well," said General Grant, "if we are defeated you will be able to carry all the men that are left."

That, we might say, was getting tough. Or obstinate.

And Grant had his critics, devastating and malicious critics. Letters in the White House mail and frequent callers advised Lincoln he must get rid of Grant.

They made out a case against Grant as malignant in tone as that of Murat Halstead, editor of the *Cincinnati Gazette,* in a letter to Salmon P. Chase, Secretary of the Treasury, writing: "How is it that Grant, who was behind at Fort Henry, drunk at Donelson, surprised and whipped at Shiloh, and driven back from Oxford, Mississippi, is still in command? Governor Chase, these things are true. Our noble army of the Mississippi is being wasted by the foolish, drunken, stupid Grant. He cannot organize or control or fight an army. I have no personal feeling about it, but I know he is an ass. There is not among the whole list of retired major generals a man who is not Grant's superior."

And this letter Secretary Chase passed on to President Lincoln with the indorsement: "Reports concerning General Grant similar to the statements made by Mr. Halstead are too common to be safely or even prudently disregarded."

So Halstead, the editor, got tough with Grant. And likewise Chase, the Treasury head, got tough. And when the Philadelphia editor Alexander K. McClure laid before Lincoln what he believed an impressive indictment from many respectable sources seeking Grant's dismissal, Lincoln groaned rather than spoke the words "I can't spare this man—he fights!"

Halstead, too, it was who printed and spread the report that General William Tecumseh Sherman was losing his mind, was not in his right mind, so that in some quarters it was considered proper to refer to "Crazy" Sherman.

I am not sure but it would be correct to put up some sort of a fantastic gargoylish statue of this Murat Halstead, the distinguished editor who during a great war successfully peddled the notion in many quarters that U. S. Grant was a bungling boozefighter and W. T. Sherman was a lunatic.

"Do you want to live forever?"

September 20, 1942

Met Alvin York the other night, the sergeant, the man-killer. And the twinkle of his eyes, the warm kindliness of his face as he looked down on me and shook hands, made me feel like I had known him a long time. I slid my hand around up his back and patted him on the right shoulder, sort of like you pat a horse that has run the best he has in him. I have done that but three or four times in my life. It came so natural, and nobody minded at all.

York loves people. He made a record as a man-killer when it was saving lives for him to be out there killing.

The record of that handsome Russian girl now visiting this country, she having killed more than three hundred German soldiers, sort of tops everything in its class. How did she feel when aiming a gun at living men and mowing them down to their deaths? She answers that to her each of these Nazi killers was a snake who didn't belong in her country, so why not kill and kill?

That American boy who so located himself in Dieppe that the

sniping was good, so he killed twenty Germans before he called it a day, he was performing in line of duty. Maybe he just considers himself a fighter and doesn't think about the man-killing angle, like General U. S. Grant, who never liked to look at the dead on the field of battle, always asking with a keen interest after a battle, "How many prisoners?" and always preferring there should be few dead and many prisoners.

General Robert E. Lee at Fredericksburg sat his horse overlooking ground where he had won a battle, where the dead and wounded were piled around pitifully, and made a remark to another general that it was a good thing war was so terrible or "we" might grow too fond of it. And the Indiana Congressman Daniel W. Voorhees, the "Tall Sycamore of the Wabash," told of calling at the White House and talking with the Commander in Chief of the Federal armies and hearing President Lincoln, with a pathetic look of anxious pain, make the inquiry, "Voorhees, doesn't it seem strange that I should be here—I, a man who couldn't cut a chicken's head off—with blood running all around me?"

Just what am I getting at or getting into here? I am not sure. Perhaps I am leading toward the point that the best fighters more often get their work done as soldiers with as little talk as possible about how tough they are. The deadliest gunners and the keenest sharpshooters are quiet men, cool men. Who can be sure but it may be written in the course of time that the German Army and its General Staff would have done better in the art and science of war if it hadn't been for the Leader and his habit of ranting and raving, his ignorant custom of telling it around that one German could lick ten Russians any day in the week.

Of course, time will never stale the story of the noncom leading his men into a hail of bullets with the cry "Come on, you so-and-sos, do you want to live forever?" In the last war it was most often credited to a sergeant of Marines at Belleau Wood. In the early 1890's Rossiter Johnson in a historical work published this little story as having happened in the 1860's in our War of the Brothers. Now comes Thomas Hornsby Ferril of Denver testifying he finds this incident "in a book of Civil War anecdotes published in 1868, credited to the colonel of a Confederate regiment at the Battle of Murfreesboro." Going farther, Mr. Ferril finds the same anecdote "again in an old collection of extracts from Thomas Carlyle, who hung it on Frederick the Great at Rossbach, who couldn't have been the first to think of it."

We may be sure the Greeks had a word for it and that among spearsmen at Babylon, Chaldea, and Troy there were commissioned officers, noncoms, and high privates in the rear rank who shouted their scorn of living forever and echoed in some primitive style the lines of the gay ragtime song, "Sticks and stones may break my bones, I'm going to live anyhow until I die."

If the foregoing items are not timely to the issues of the hour, suppose we take a look at some lines from a speech of Abraham Lincoln in Congress as far back as 1848, when he sized up the political layout in New York as follows:

"I have heard some things from New York; and if they are true, one might well say of your party there, as a drunken fellow once said when he heard the reading of an indictment for hog-stealing. The clerk read on till he got to and through the words 'did steal, take, and carry away ten boars, ten sows, ten shoats, and ten pigs,' at which he exclaimed, 'Well, by golly, that is the most equally divided gang of hogs I ever did hear of!' If there is any other gang of hogs more equally divided than the Democrats of New York are about this time, I have not heard of it."

Negro opportunity

October 4, 1942

The human dignity of the American Negro becomes easier to look at now than at any time since white men bought, stole, and kidnapped the first black folk brought from Africa to this country.

And it might be asked, without getting unfair or indecent with anybody, whether the dignity of the white man ever sunk lower than it did when for a century and a half he took his sailing ships to African shores, loading them with naked Negroes fitted by the hundreds in "spoon fashion" so no cargo space would be wasted, shipping this human livestock across tropic seas at a high death rate, with a sanitation so vile and odors of such reek that sailors said when the wind was right you could smell a slave ship five miles away.

And when a man begins talking along this line there is a certain minority of American citizens North and South—a minority growing smaller as time goes by—and they have a standard question they ask as though you are floored and out of breath with nothing to say when this question hits you in the face.

This question—and there are those who think it is an unanswerable looloo—runs like this: "Would you want to marry a nigger? Would you like to have one of your daughters marry a nigger?"

This is supposed to choke off any discussion you might want to start around the question of whether the Negro soldier in this war has as much a right as the white soldier to any or all of the Four Freedoms.

I remember when a Chicago newspaper in 1919 sent me to the Negro district, having then a population above 150,000, and I wrote a series of stories about living conditions there, of slums, of families in single rooms with bad plumbing and leaky ceilings, of scampering rats interfering with human sleep, of high rents and protected gamblers and workless soldiers just back from overseas service—and a couple of times I got phone calls from shrill-voiced birds asking "Do you call yourself a white man?" and warning "Look out or you'll get your trimmings one of these nights!"

So I learned that you must be careful how you bring up any question concerning the Negro, even grave community questions such as "Where does the Negro hoodlum, stick-up, rapist, come from? Is it possible there would be fewer of these if more Negro youth had better chances at living clean, at getting jobs that are not dead-end, at living just a little more free from discrimination and hate?"

The slums get their revenge, always somehow or other their retribution can be figured in any community, whether the slums are Negro ratholes such as those presented in *Native Son* by the Negro novelist Richard Wright, or slums of Polish white folk over the Northwest Side of Chicago, with an unforgettable and reeking house of vice, as reported in the novel *Never Come Morning* by the Scandinavian Nelson Allgren.

No slum is separate from its community. Thousands of mean and sinister secrets stretch out in definite bonds from the slum to the outside world.

Why should some of us find it deeply moving that an eminent spokesman, Bishop Bernard J. Sheil, founder-director of the Cath-

205

olic Youth Organization, spoke last week his fear and anxiety as to the "Christian ghettos" of the Negro race and of how "in the case of these twelve million Americans . . . a disproportionate number have translated a deep inner frustration into an external attitude that is completely antisocial"?

The bishop sees danger signals. Working with Catholic youth of all sorts and conditions, it has come clear to him that again because of hate and discrimination handed the Negro there may be grapes of wrath trampled in a vintage not so good to look at. "These people are no longer satisfied with weasel words and insincere promises. Their demands are most reasonable. The opportunity to progress, to better themselves economically, to share in the industrial, social, political, and cultural life of America—these are the things that the American Negro seeks—and he can no longer be denied them. If the Negro is worthy to die with the white man, then he is worthy to live with him on terms of honest, objective equality."

What are the demands? And what the realities the Negro hopes to fight for? "Liberty to speak, think, and worship as their conscience dictates, economic security free from the specter of unemployment and enforced poverty, the opportunity for education, for the normal fulfillment of those normal human desires which spell human happiness."

Bishop Sheil knows about Christ's poor and how "too much respect for the local banker, industrialist, or politician has caused them to be silent when the teachings of Christ should have been literally shouted from the housetops."

Men of influence "giving lip service to democratic principles"— what of them? "The power of those men, out of all proportion to their numbers, must be broken for the good of America. It is the common man everywhere, whether he be Russian, English, Chinese, or American, who is fighting the battle for freedom in the world today."

The Church, when taking her rightful place, proposes literally to "renovate the face of the earth, to satisfy all the urges and desires of the whole human personality."

This kind of preaching is worth study. What holiness there is here touches many streets, people, and hungry hearts. It may go far. A glint of the priceless shines in Bishop Sheil's declaration: "Jim Crowism in the Mystical Body of Christ is a disgraceful anomaly."

Washington is hell

Washington, our national capital, as someone said of Boston in earlier days, is a state of mind rather than a city. Possibly, too, Malcolm Cowley in reviewing W. M. Kiplinger's book was correct in the title he gave his piece: "Washington Is Hell." In this Cowley is antedated many years by General William Tecumseh Sherman, who in the spring of 1865 wrote, "Washington is as corrupt as Hell, made so by the looseness and extravagance of the war. I will avoid it as a pest house."

Not so long ago J. B. Priestley, the worthy English author who wrote *Out of the People,* had the comment that a democratic people operate like "a noisy family." And in this country the heads of the family are mostly in Washington, and the clashing, cacophonic noises we hear from that city are what we will have to learn to endure if not enjoy while the democratic system advances and develops.

The noise that is Washington quite likely will not grow less nor take on a rich and rare clarity in the days of test and endurance to come when our war machine, not yet geared into high, gets going. And this is not the moment for asking the imagination to play on what the noise that is Washington will sound like when hostilities cease and the war ends and there ensues the period of demobilization, reorganization, peace.

Where the man now President of this country will be when that period arrives is a matter on which we might consult experts who compute what is called "life expectancy." Such experts would not have much to go on in their figuring as to whether he will be alive and if alive whether he will be a functioning and efficient executive person.

Since 1860 we have had two major wars. The man who served as President in the first of these major wars—an intestinal conflict rather correctly termed a civil war—was worn to a shadow and far

207

underweight as it came to an end, when he lost his life by an assassin's bullet.

The next man to serve this country during a major war managed to keep alive and to hold what seemed to be a fair condition of health and strength through the end of the war and the writing of a peace. Then came a collapse, a breakdown hard to witness, filled to the depths with fate and pity. So he died.

In our third major war, we are witnesses of our first President who has been fated to head a government and a people in round-the-earth war. The conflict is vast, ramified, so stupendous with forces, motives, causes, that no one human mind can grasp, write, tell—and any fairly well informed imagination hesitates, gropes, and knows itself helpless in any attempt to compass the present world scene as a whole, seeing with such certainty that five or ten years from now such an imagination can be credited with foresight. Hindsighters will have a heyday ten years from now.

Any war is tentative. You try this. You try that. You waste and waste knowing that wars are won by those having the most to waste and knowing best how, when, and where to waste.

Now we are in our first truly mechanized war and its area is the planet Earth. Theaters of operations include sea bottom and stratosphere, the floor of the ocean and the top of the sky.

We can't compare it with any other war of the human family, because never before has there been a war shared by all mankind from the two poles to the tropics and back. It is grand—and it is coocoo. It is heroic—and crazy. Often when sublime it is so in the sense of the old Nantucket sailor talk of weather where "it takes two men to hold one man's hair on."

Here the man in the White House decides. Every hour he says Yes or No or Perhaps or Not-yet or "We can't see that far." Every day as to this or that colossal venture he must say how, when, where. No escape for him.

If in times of no war at all it was said of the job that it is "man-killing," what of now?

Is it possible for anyone outside of that job to know what it is like inside? Who can be so easy and cavalier as to laugh at the invisible burdens, the unmentionable thongs and pressures, not to be recorded till long after when creatures of clay concerned are nder the grassroots with hard-won names for toil, endurance, alor?

Those who have gladly heard that the springs of life are bitter and evil rather than sweet and good can understand why there is advantage in a journalist following a maxim: "Praise no man till ae is dead."

Yet merit also attaches to the studious apothegm from William H. Davis of the War Labor Board claiming that a St. Bernard dog is entitled to more fleas than a cocker spaniel, a poodle, a Pomeranian, or the hairless Chihuahua.

Lest some hipperdooper deem the foregoing to be cryptic we herewith, in closing, offer the suggestion that Herbert Hoover had something on the ball when, under merciless and unjust criticism, he declared that each President of the United States should be entitled to hang the one liar he hated worst—and no explanations.

The hot-potato questions

October 18, 1942

There are persons who suppose that after a while some of the hot-potato questions about the war will be answered.

They suppose and they hope, for instance, that sometime the evidence will be collected and published which will tell straight and simple, Yes or No, whether this summer and early fall we have been losing the war—or whether Hitler could have invaded and conquered Britain in the summer of 1940 even if President Roosevelt had taken the chance of throwing the United States fleet into that conflict—or whether Timoshenko is the greatest military commander of all time, bar none.

Sure, these questions will be argued back and forth, up and down, with nobody winning the argument, just as no one has ever won the argument whether Grant or Sherman is the greater general, whether Grant or Lee is the greater commander, whether Washington did more with what he had to do with than Lincoln, whether Grant should have ordered the frontal assault at Cold Harbor, whether Sherman would have taken Atlanta if cautious and Fabian Joe Johnston had been kept in command of the Confederate forces instead of being replaced by the impetuous and overly eager John B. Hood.

One of the ifs standing out bigger than any other if in the past year will at a later time come in for many hot-potato debates. This big if goes like this: "If Japan had gone to Hong Kong, Singapore and the Netherlands East Indies without any attack on Pearl Harbor and the Philippines, leaving Hawaii and Bataan and Mac Arthur alone, could the United States have mustered a national unity with anything like the strength she is now throwing into the war? If the Japs had let us alone or if they had waited another year or two, how much longer would the war have run on account of our having the handicaps and disunity there were before Pearl Harbor?"

Many a good citizen has fallen back on this question for consolation in recent months. A good argument can be made that since Pearl Harbor the only question is how long the war will run; that the United Nations in the end will win whether it takes two years or ten.

The Assistant Secretary of the Navy tells the world that we are losing the war, talking so fast that we fail to get any picture of what he means by our losing the war. Did he mean in this September just passed that if we lose the war the Axis wins and from then on the Nazis and the Japs arrange a "New Order" of political government and economic domination over the United Nations? When speakers and writers tell us we are losing the war, do they not most often mean that this country loses if we fail of victory?

And if we fail of victory, are there not a thousand varieties of stalemate where neither side wins and only in that sense do both sides lose? If that was the kind of losing which was meant, why not say so? Or if the official meant that until we have won the war we are losing it, why not say so? Perhaps he was trying to say that unless we get action on all fronts, including production, we will be a long time winning the war.

Maybe he was trying to throw a scare into us so that we would move faster in production, transport, fighting. But if in the army camps and the naval barracks and a thousand assembly lines the men and women should join in a chorus—"We're losing the war! We're losing the war!"—what good would come of that?

If the official had been a plain ordinary Mister of no particular place or rank and if he had been just one more Chicago citizen taking the air, instead of having the title of Assistant Secretary of the Navy, his speech wouldn't have been printed. I read the speech twice. The first time I liked it as rich blunt utterance colored with fine passion. On the second reading I said, "He got hot under the collar and had to explode and it don't mean a thing except he should have found some other way to cool off."

One of the leading script-writers in the government Radio Division in Washington finds that it helps to take his shoes off. Even out into the hallways he goes sometimes, pondering, laying out story and dialogue, his head down, his shoes off. His fellow workers expect and like it.

One of the coolest persons in the Washington turmoils last week wrote a column of shining and singing prose for a respectable newspaper. She told of the Department of Agriculture basement where her typewriter looks out on a cement court and rows of office windows and no sky—and how a basement like that helps you concentrate. And this Alice in a wonderland basement writes: "The boss is a dull one and doesn't like it when I take my shoes off, even though it is fine for concentration. He always wears his shoes, which are so big I wouldn't take them off, too."

They watch the sky

October 25, 1942

In a one-room shack on one of the tallest, loneliest peaks overlooking the California coast line, two old friends of mine share a twenty-four-hour aircraft warning service. Six miles from water, fifteen miles from the nearest highway, they write me: "It's no place to keep goats, as lions prowl by us nightly. A crazy upsidedown life with the kerosene lamp burning all night and the nights long. Quiet deeper than silence. We love it."

By name Mr. and Mrs. Harry Dick Ross they are. She watches till 2:30 A.M. Then he takes over. Prosperity of the late 1920's sent them from San Francisco to Paris. Depression chased them from Paris to the Mojave Desert. War puts them now above clouds on a lonesome mountain, on sworn duty to watch that sky day and night for whosoever cometh.

Mrs. Ross—Lillian Bos Ross—in San Francisco days looked like the actress Jeanne Eagels, a child of Polish and Irish immigrants, blonde, willowy, a clothes-shop model. When she loved a short poem she could learn the lines and say them as though it was a way of talking about life, death, and humble dust. These poems would flow from her tongue cool and quiet, easy as pouring water from a jug in a harvest field.

She married Harry Dick Ross, alias Pocatello Pete, the shy buckaroo from Idaho who clerked in Paul Elder's bookstore and read most of the books he sold, because give Harry a knife and the right wood and he would say a living poem into that dumb wood.

So there they are now, away up where the moon comes over the mountain and you can pick a handful of stars to keep and cherish—if you know how. Sky-watchers in a war fought in high air—the loneliness don't hurt them a minute. They have a saying out of years gone: "We was taught some pride and to take death quiet."

Lillian Bos Ross never planned it she would have a novel published this month by a solid New York firm. She never meant to be an author. Nobody heard that from her. She was bashful about her grammar and diction. And yet pulp magazines began printing things—pieces she expected to come back. She found she could put down one word after another and lo and behold! it made sense. Like a magnificent dope with a deep secret she commenced writing a novel and never let on to her friends. Then word arrived it would come out like a regular book and she was An Author. "I felt peaceful as a basket of chips."

A cattle rancher in the Big Sur Hills of California in 1870 tells off his life in his own lingo, with shifts of the ugly and the lovely, mean as blood on a rawhide whip, frail as fingers of blue light fluttering from long barn cracks. Some readers will linger over the earthy and Biblical speech. "Nobody ever called me a soft man. Here in the hills of the Big Sur men don't come soft. Them that has a vein of it peters out and ere ever you'd call 'em a man, if they're soft, they've drifted out to the valleys and the flatlands. I'm not soft."

Ignorant, prejudiced, arrogant, heroic, this fierce man-child talks his way through the book. The strengths and the poisons that make

America are here. "Them as has gits," whether it is land or a woman. So goes the theory, not always working out.

From a woman, "my mail-order wife" as he called her, he learns. It comes slow. He can't manage to put into use the Spanish proverb his father gave him: "Break your mare in easy and don't try a year's riding in a week."

A bear near kills him. The woman, "the stranger," nurses him back. He sees "days when my thinking habits seemed to grow and leaf out fast as corn grows in good weather." In a jealous mood he quotes a whittling neighbor: "No use to try to watch a woman. All you can do is trust 'em."

Jealous, he strays from home, is weeks gone, returns to a silent ranch house, a silent woman who sets a table for him. "The quiet deepened in the room and I got afraid that if I set my spoon down on the table board, it would make a noise like a redwood tree falling in a deep canyon. If I said a word it would tear through that quiet like a gunshot. How could I start to tell the truth if she wouldn't talk at all? I couldn't stand it. That wife of mine. No woman has the right to hold such deep stillness."

The book does have heavy odor—as the earth does, as horses and men do, as leather and smoke and houses much lived in by people who both hinder and help each other. The pioneer cabins had this odor of life. So have the trailers, shacks, and shanties bordering many a war-production plant of this hour. *The Stranger* by Lillian Bos Ross may be worth your time. I put it among books I know I will read again.

Comes now also Hal Borland's toolbox of free verse, *America Is Americans*. He don't know where he's going but he's on his way. You can't prove it's poetry. But a first-class argument can be made that America and Yankee Doodle of this hour is here, and that ain't hay.

Are we a nation, a country, an independent free-going people who ain't going to get lost on the way to the post office? Borland tells us. He sings it, and he don't try to be too technical. From a sod house in Nebraska through cattle-ranching and sheepherding, logging and mining, sleeping under stars or canvas in more than forty states, signed with the navy in the last war, Borland now sits in a Manhattan newspaper office, looks out of the window, sees clear

213

across the curve of the earth to the Pacific, and hopes to find words
for "the unwritten cradle song of a mother," his America.

Our Alaska he gives us in an old-timer saying: "We got just two
seasons here—winter and August—but it's sure a wonderful August!"

The colonel's wife

November 1, 1942

The colonel's wife came home to her old neighbors in the Michigan village where her husband was born and had lived the most
of his life except for his term of service in the last war.

Two years ago she and the colonel went away, and the only news
drifting back was that the colonel had a high, fierce, and responsible post at a port of embarkation, where he is connected with
loading and transport of army supplies, arms, and munitions.

Now the colonel's wife has been back among her old friends and
kinfolk for ten days, and she has been talking freely and gossiping
smooth about the colonel's health, how he likes his work and ad-
vancement, the house they live in, what she reads in the papers
about the war and how it is going around the globe.

But not a word, not a sneaking, slinking syllable about what kind
of supplies, arms, munitions her husband has seen and handled,
nor where they might be going nor how they are shipped nor how
the transport system works and what is good and bad about it—
not a word.

Compared with the colonel's wife the ancient and clam-lipped
Sphinx is a garrulous Plymouth Rock hen that has just laid a
large egg—so far as the revelation of military information goes.

She has a first-rate acquaintance with the archaic Anglo-Saxon
formula whereby the accused man on trial may reply on being
asked "Are you guilty or not guilty?" with the words "I stands
mute."

The nearest she has come to delivering any reliable information
was when she was asked why at this particular time she was leaving
her husband.

That was an easy one she laughed off with "I thought maybe
he was getting a little tired of me, and I'm going back soon as he
wigwags I'm wanted again. We've been together every day for two

years and both of us figure two weeks' absence will make the heart grow fonder."

She is one of many officers' wives who understand the value of silence and the importance of secrets being kept secret.

She knows well that she could talk with interest and charm about many things her husband is doing, small matters that seem to have no particular importance and that don't classify strictly as military secrets.

But she is aware that if she got to talking along that line, the first thing she knows she might be edging over into points where she can't possibly be too shut-mouth.

So by saying nothing at all she slips past any and every danger of saying too much about the precious supplies, arms, munitions committed to her husband and his associates for loading and transport overseas.

One of her old neighbors suggested that possibly the colonel has a habit of not telling her any more about the war than she can gather from the newspapers.

This raised the question whether it would be likely that the colonel and his wife could have breakfast and dinner together and sleep in the same room together for two years—and being pretty good pals, as all who know the couple are aware—and the colonel not tell his wife this and that and dese, dose, and dem which would make very live newspaper items, which in fact might be so alive as news that some newspapers would call up the censor's office and ask for the green light on printing such items.

Some of the neighbors had not done any thinking about the possibilities in this field. They agreed that enemy agents seeking military secrets would make it a point to hunt for any such wives of army and navy officers as are free-spoken, who like to talk about what important and fascinating actions and decisions their husbands are engaged in. The neighbors hoped and believed such officers' wives are few and far between, scarce as hen's teeth.

One neighbor quoted some old Roman as saying "I have often regretted my speech but never my silence."

In Washington a while ago I met a Harvard man who works in the naval laboratory, which we might say swarms with naval secrets.

"Every week," said he, "I handle papers, envelopes, folders

215

marked 'Confidential' or 'Secret.' And I pass them along to where
they are wanted—as fast as I can—without reading them unless they
are in my special field. I want to be carrying as few naval secrets
as possible. There are times when what you don't know won't hurt
you."

Election as usual

November 8, 1942

The democratic system, the form of popular government known
as republican, spoke. From coast to coast during a world-shaking
war, with the deeper sacrifices and the actual agony yet to come
for this country, an election came off. It would not be easy for an
advocate of some other system opposed to ours to argue that we
have not shown our customary form. The good order at the polls,
in the main, the usual ways of voters casting their ballots, and the
customary ways of afterward counting those ballots—it was the
same like always in peacetime.

One reason for taking notice of this here and now is because
there were accusations, reports, and ill-born predictions that in
this present November there wouldn't be any November election.
Out of the clear blue came these muddy prophecies nourishing fear
and making sick hope sicker for those who believed there might be
something to such forecasts. Any and all who last year could bring
themselves to believe that elections for Congress were to be out this
November had to believe along with that particular crazy notion
that as a nation we were already deep sunk in dictatorship.

When the showdown came, when the election proved to be decent, quiet, and orderly in the usual and old-fashioned American
way, the false report, the scare prediction, uncovered itself as a
paper tiger, merely a scarehead monster, which has happened before in American politics.

At midnight of election returns, blackout serenaders in San Francisco could have faced toward Washington and shouted, "God
reigns and the government at Washington lives!" with no lower
percentage for profanity than there might be in singing "Praise the
Lord and Pass the Ammunition."

Millions of voters in the past two years have had their lives uprooted and transplanted. The army and navy, the war-production plants, the new taxes and rationings, the changes in big business, the wrecks and salvage of small business—these made unrest and migration on such a scale that this campaign and election were a test. We passed it. "Believe you me, it could have been worse, brethren and sistern."

What the citizen soldiers far away on the fighting fronts of several seas and continents are thinking and saying about the latest election might be important if those fighting men were not so pressed and harried by more immediate questions of supply, transport, strategy, combat. They know their big political say-so is to come after the hard trials and tough going of winning the war. In the inscrutable aftermath of the war the returned veterans will be in the thick of political action making up for these days when they have to forget politics while every day remembering the Axis they face and fight.

Of course, it does happen to be the case that one of the greatest of proven American soldiers, who would like to keep out of politics, nevertheless finds himself continuously forced into political decisions and statements. Reports that can be accepted as completely reliable, which the present writer accepts with no reservations, indicate definitely that General Douglas MacArthur regards himself as a warrior first of all and secondly and thirdly a soldier and a man of war, while a career as statesman and politician is the least of his thoughts.

He was sorry that during the fierce fighting and heavy anguish of Bataan he was suddenly erected into a political figure and required to answer questions a soldier hates to hear with a long hard unfinished fight ahead of him.

MacArthur sees his destiny in that Pacific area where he is now fighting. He appreciated the compliment and had his regrets about those who proposed he should be brought to Washington and be given high command over all the American military and naval forces round the earth. His present job has challenge enough without trying to look beyond that day when he has promised he will go back to Bataan. Those who have used his name in connection with the Presidency or with high command at Washington have done so on their own initiative. If they had consulted his wishes, they would have learned that he prefers silence.

217

Artists of the people

November 15, 1942

Some who treasure the memory of George M. Cohan and value his lifework have had an odd little anecdote for many years. He was still in short pants and was going to make his first appearance on a stage and speak his lines and do his stuff for an audience. He stood on tiptoe and couldn't quite reach his eyes to the curtain hole where the actors size up the audience. His father held him up while the boy looked over the main floor and the balconies. Then the boy George M. Cohan lifted his face toward his father and others, who heard him say with all the confidence and self-assurance you could ask, "I can fool 'em."

Of course, if he had been in training under some of the dramatic critics who didn't get his true measure for more than a score of years, instead of saying he could "fool 'em," he might have exclaimed: "The art of the stage rests chiefly on the creation of illusions and I have no misgivings." This would have been much more correct and elegant than the colloquial "I can fool 'em."

In later years, grown-up and completely confident, Cohan once looked through the hole in the curtain at an audience, then turned to fellow players: "Any day I can't fool those babies!"

For himself Cohan could never be free from suspicion at being termed an "artist." More often he preferred to speak of the theater as "the show business." He was fooling 'em when he tried to definitely classify himself as "just a song-and-dance man," though he knew he was singer, song-writer, dancer, vaudevillian, playwright, producer, actor, eminent citizen, and patriot.

The American people through their Congress bestowed on Cohan a medal for a great marching war song he wrote, our equivalent of the Soviet Union's bestowal of the decoration naming a man as "A People's Artist." Cohan created folklore that still sticks around in many such fragments as "What's all the shooting for?" or "Give my regards to Broadway" or "My father thanks you, my mother thanks you, my sister thanks you, and I thank you." For months and years after he, as "Little Johnny Jones" in a Midwest Corn Belt town, had sat under a spotlight and recited "Life's a Funny Proposition after All" people would be thinking about it and refer to it and quote from it as they never did with Hamlet's "to be or not to be" lines.

Those who have care, anxiety, or love as related to art for the people, the free art of a democratic people, might look to it if they feel superior or upstage in considering George M. Cohan and his lifework. He loved people. He sought to please them as a showman, as "just a song-and-dance man." He knew the right flickering instant to bring out the American flag so as to set the galleries cheering and whistling, and adopting his nickname of "grand old flag" for the national emblem. When he got through with it, the flag had some kind of nameless and glad dignity. What he did with the flag was always more than just a stunt. He didn't set himself up as an instructor in patriotism, though he did stir some humble hearts with a feeling that "Yankee Doodle Dandy" among the nations of the earth had personality, power, and meaning.

It is good-by now to George M. Cohan of Manhattan and Broadway. And in spite of George W. Norris of Nebraska and the Great Plains saying farewell and lights out, we refuse to believe it is curtains for him.

"It is the end of the road," came the heart cry of Norris on news that he had failed of re-election to the United States Senate. Later came that further heart cry "Why should they hate me?" Still later will come his realization that they don't hate him, but rather that they are just now suspicious of themselves and incidentally suspicious of everybody else.

As the years have passed, Norris has slowly allowed himself less of hate and more of understanding regard for his fellowmen. He never did talk like a regular hell-bent radical. He prefers understatement. He likes building. His practical judgment, rooted in long experience—and the sensitive heart of him so close to the people—these are not going to be lost to the country just because he no longer addresses his remarks to the United States Senate. Many of us will listen and take heed to his words whether he says them from Washington or McCook, Nebraska.

And Adolf Hitler? His finish comes when? A second slow reading of his Munich speech of November 9 gives an impression that he feels less sure of himself as orator and propagandist than at any time since he wrote *Mein Kampf* in 1924. Some kind of a wave of unrest is running over Germany around the question "Why are we

219

fighting so far from home? Can't we defend Germany a little nearer home borders?"

The Nazi Leader's answer is lame. And not hitherto has he paid such special attention to "that chief crook [*Oberstrolch*] Roosevelt," who is "without doubt the chief gangster we have to face."

Poor timing goes with this Shicklgruber sentence: "If Roosevelt today executes his attack on North Africa, with the remark that he had to safeguard it from Germany and Italy and so on, one need not lose any words about that lying phrase of that old crook." And this seems to be where the "New Order of the Greater German Reich" in ward-alderman style goes in for dirty work at the crossroads as though the White House don't know how to take it.

Embarkation-port jitters

November 22, 1942

At one of the embarkation ports they tell about a young Filipino off a boat that had been torpedoed and sunk.

"You were on deck when it happened," said an inquiring officer. "Now tell us just how it looked to you when it happened. What did you see and hear?"

With a slight pause between two words came the answer: "Boom. Swim."

The boy knows his verbs. He is a "Spik" who can speak. If he had been an imitation instead of the real thing, he would have said, "Sighted by sub, sunk by same," instead of "Boom" for what the torpedo did and "Swim" for what he did.

Also at this embarkation port, if you should make the rounds you might hear of the secret-paper burner. Every well-equipped office, station, post, or bureau of the army of enough importance to be receiving secret papers about what to do next or where to go from here has its nice little secret-paper burner.

A little sheet-iron affair with a sweet little smokestack, it looks like a tiny wood stove shrunk till it isn't much bigger than the common electric bread-toaster. In our military establishment now there are thousands of these in use, and every day they are fed several tons of secret papers.

In nearly every case, when a secret paper arrives, so soon as it is read it is fed into the burner.

The best place for some kinds of military secrets is in the heads of trusted and worthy men rather than typed on irresponsible paper that unless burned may tattle and blab—so goes the theory of the handy little stoves that make ashes of precious inside information.

Any secret paper, of course, seems important till you read it. Then it may turn out to be petty and ridiculous. In some cases the supposed secret paper merely tells what everybody knows. Then again a single sheet of paper may almost shake and cry over the fate and possibilities it involves. "Burn it" is the order. Burn it and lessen the risk to priceless cargo and to living men.

When you see before your own eyes some of the men, docks, derricks, and ships, working on the most colossal loading, hauling, and delivery job ever undertaken in the history of mankind, it makes you more sober no matter how sober you were before.

The men on this job, their first name is worry. The one of the Four Freedoms least easy for them to manage is freedom from fear. And any time a reporter should get too enterprising with details about how and what they fear, he would be on the edge of blabbing military secrets.

When you are an officer, with humps of gnawing responsibility on your shoulders, and you are on a spot where you are expected to make reports to the public, quite often perhaps you would find yourself saying, "In case of doubt, say nothing."

There is a nice sound to Elmer Davis, the OWI head, saying, "The public is getting whatever our military people know as fast as they know it, limited only by genuine consideration for military secrecy."

It is quite likely Davis has been learning from the armed services while they have learned from him. Certainly the army and navy heads could well study the frank self-effacement and the shining candor of Mr. Davis regarding the two-month withholding of news of the sinking of three United States cruisers in the Pacific. Mr. Davis has the tone of one of President Lincoln's letters to General Grant in saying: "That was my fault as much as the navy's. I knew about it as soon as they did."

Can you hear that cornhusker tang in his voice as he says it?

Americanized Japanese

November 29, 1942

With the passing of George M. Cohan came revival of the anecdote of his Japanese butler who on being asked what he would do if he and Mr. Cohan met as enemy soldiers in war, said he would shoot and kill Mr. Cohan.

Then he was told how Sam Harris's Japanese butler said that in case of war if he with a gun faced Mr. Harris with a gun, he would oblige Mr. Harris by laying down his gun and letting Mr. Harris shoot him to pieces. Mr. Cohan's butler cut loose with one short word of wrath and derision that might be politely paraphrased as hooey, arkymalarky, or bunk. He snorted his scorn that any Japanese could do anything else than kill his non-Japanese soldier enemy.

When a little story like that is too perfect as a story, it may be that it doesn't mean a thing unless we check as to whether Mr. Cohan and Mr. Harris had Japanese butlers, whether Mr. Cohan's butler just naturally hated to hear anything quoted as coming from Mr. Harris's butler, whether Mr. Harris's butler had whimsical ways and supposed they would understand by the way he spoke and grinned that he couldn't mean exactly what he was saying, whether the two butlers from association with men in the show business had learned what lines to speak that might make good theater.

At Camp McCoy, Wisconsin, the troops would agree to the foregoing. For the troops there compose an infantry battalion, a combat unit, whose members are American citizens of Japanese ancestry.

Some had fathers who journeyed from Japan to the Hawaiian Islands. While working on sugar or pineapple plantations the fathers became lonely for women. They studied photographs of women back in Japan, each picking one who looked good to him, and she was sent for and arrived at the islands to be known as a "picture bride," one of thousands of "picture brides."

Now not a few, but many, of these soldiers at Camp McCoy are graduates of the University of Hawaii or other American institutions of learning. Most of them were under fire at Pearl Harbor and have seen months of service in fortifying the islands and making ready for any possible repeat of December 7, 1941.

"These boys have all heard bombs fall, and none of them will turn back unless he is told to," says their commander, Lieutenant Colonel Farrant L. Turner, who reckons their loyalty as absolute. They have impressed their Wisconsin neighbors with their behavior and speech, not to mention their baseball team. As to their future service or why they train in Wisconsin, the army is noncommittal. The youths themselves ask only to be sent to any fighting front, hoping eventually to get back to Hawaii.

The present writer, in this connection, recalls a conversation with a member of the department of anthropology of the University of Hawaii in 1934. During the summer of 1933 this professor, interested in studying "man as an animal," toured Japan. Particularly he looked up a few of his old Japanese acquaintances, Hawaiian-born. And they told him they were not accepted as regular and loyal Japanese citizens.

It had become a tradition in Japan that any who were born in Hawaii and brought up under American influences in American schools had thereby lost place and face as true Japanese. They were refused the trust and confidence put in native Japanese and regarded themselves as aliens. And why not? Are not the Japanese commissioned officers at Camp McCoy, Wisconsin, veterans of many years of service and unquestioned loyalty under the Stars and Stripes, sworn to destroy the power of that Son of Heaven, Emperor Hirohito of Tokyo?

Those now ruling Japan have for years had their phrase "thought control." This goes deeper than any such words as "education" or "propaganda." In fact it is hardly possible to go any deeper in shaping a nation of people for empire, war, and bloody adventure than to control their thought. Those not schooled in Japan and properly controlled in thought in the very homeland and soil of the Rising Sun—these cannot be trusted. Even if their fathers and mothers were born in Japan, they are under suspicion as to what they think, what they believe, and what they may do in a crisis.

One morning in March of 1934 I gave a talk, readings, and songs for the student body of 2,200 in McKinley High School in Honolulu. The Japanese boys and girls were ten to one of the Filipinos, the Portuguese, and the Negroes. And they were solemn or sober, mildly amused or rollicking with laughter, at the same places in the program as were the American audiences on what is called the mainland. Their language, as they spoke, was Americanese, slangy

223

with point and meaning, like the army men at Schofield barracks or the navy men at Pearl Harbor. They seemed to be thirsty to learn of American traditions.

The principal of McKinley High thought it interesting that more than once a Japanese boy or girl had spoken or written of "our ancestors who came over in the *Mayflower*." That was going as good as Will Rogers with a strain of Cherokee in him saying "My ancestors didn't come over in the *Mayflower*, but we was there to meet the boat."

Anyone who bets on the future service of the 100th Infantry Battalion of the 2d Army, in training at Camp McCoy, Wisconsin, will not go far wrong.

Sleigh bells in the snow

December 6, 1942

What have we learned? Flame and death out of the sky over Pearl Harbor one year since—and have there been lessons?

Yes, as a nation and a people we have been going through changes, some of them hard to take, but it may be that we know ourselves better as human beings and we know each other better as neighbors because of what we have had to take.

Then, too, there are the things we didn't have to take, things we threw in because it was a time for throwing in, without asking any questions. When they translate the American word "volunteer" into certain European languages, the nearest they come to getting its meaning is in the two words "free and willing."

We have seen conscription, taxes, rationing, wherein we didn't volunteer but the government told us how and when. In the main, considering what a big country we are and how many scattered millions have been told how to regulate their lives, the war measures have worked out fairly well. In the main, we have "volunteered" to go along, "free and willing." If any real minority had wanted sabotage and mutiny, we would have heard from them. Some measures have moved slowly, because as a people we like to take our regimentation slowly, telling ourselves and each other just what we are letting ourselves in for and what we hope to do about it when the crisis, the emergency, becomes something else again.

Have we gone to school this past year since Pearl Harbor? Have we learned about metals—tin, bauxite, magnesium, harder and lighter metals for airplane armor—new plastics for a thousand useful ends—and rubber, our little old friend rubber? Yes.

And transportation? Have you heard engineers and designers talking about how ignorant we were only a year back? Mr. Kaiser and his demon assembly lines had yet to come. The fleets of sky freighters were not yet a demand and an imperative necessity. Not until the war ends and we begin meeting the challenge of peacetime living, not until then can we try to fully understand what man and his machines can accomplish any time there is will and vision.

We have learned that man's productive powers are vast, from hybrid corn to sky boxcars, from the simple jeep to the almost miraculous photoelectric eye. Many a thinking man offers his guess that when the waste of war is to be followed by a new economics of peace, we can have whatever it is our will and vision to have. If we won't get what we want, it will be on account of we didn't know how and what to want.

We have learned that American youth is not soft. More yet, we have learned that the youth of this hour on land or sea can perform with epics of valor and endurance equal to the best and highest told of in the ancient classics.

We have learned to be a little sad and a little lonesome, without being sickly about it. This feeling is caught in the song of a thousand juke boxes and the tune whistled in streets and homes, "I'm Dreaming of a White Christmas." When we sing that we don't hate anybody. And there are things we love that we're going to have sometime if the breaks are not too bad against us. "May your days be merry and bright—and may all your Christmases be white."

Away down under, this latest hit of Irving Berlin catches us where we love peace. The Nazi theory and doctrine that man in his blood is naturally warlike, so much so that he should call war a blessing, we don't like it. It's got gremlins and worse in it.

While we proceed with our job of making war terrible to the enemy, while we move forward toward killing enough Nazis and Japs to end the war, the hopes and prayers are that we will see the beginning of a hundred years of white Christmases—with no blood spots of needless agony and death on the snow, with no lurking ski troopers in white uniforms on the white snow spitting the merciless music of machine-gun rain and hail.

Where there is will and vision men and women may hope. They may even dream of a century of white peace where treetops glisten and children listen to hear those sleigh bells in the snow.

Chaplin and Johnston: Troubled Men

December 13, 1942

"I am an actor and a producer," said Charlie Chaplin to some friends in Chicago. "I can go on a strike against myself. And I can lock myself out and defy myself to do my worst against me."

As a business manager, a director, a boss, a big-shot executive, Mr. Chaplin is in a class by himself among those American employers who have never failed to meet the pay roll, and furthermore never drifted into the red as a free and independent commercial enterprise.

As the investor and producer, Mr. Chaplin, he hires the actor and employee, Charlie, and when an industrial dispute arises between these two they call in a third party consisting of Charlie Chaplin Himself in Person, who tells one and all where to get off at.

In this triple role of Labor, Management, and Government, Chaplin has come to understand whether the right is all on one side and the wrong all on the other side as between labor and management.

At the Salute to Russia meeting in Orchestra Hall, Chaplin was announced as a speaker and suddenly appeared on the platform, as though he had been poured out of a horn or a tube in which he had been hidden.

There he stood in tuxedo and white waistcoat, the audience rising to stand, applaud, cheer, while a world's great and beloved actor stood half-bashful and then did, with perfect grace and timing, a thing not so easy—his right hand moved to his lips and threw them a kiss.

Then he put his notes on the speaker's stand and began his abrupt speech wherein nobody, not even Chaplin, knew what was coming next.

It was a stump speech—or as Dr. Jacob Buchbinder said later, "A stump speech to end all stump speeches."

He filed the little declaration, "I am not a pro-Communist." Then he declared himself independent of "anti-Communist propaganda" which had fooled and misled so many of the supposed experts and predicters. They expected a Russia of low morale to be broken and shattered by the Nazi war machine—like Hitler, knowing little of the gigantic war production and the amazing fighting stuff to be later shown by the Russians. Perhaps some credit for production and morale shown in the battle of Stalingrad should go to the Communist system, and in any view, said Chaplin, "Russia is fighting for Communism—let's face it. They like that system extremely well."

The producer, director, and leading player of that motion picture *The Great Dictator* recalled our depression with bread lines, millions of unemployed, youth without a future, mountains of oranges spoiled for the market with good gasoline poured over them. "What an indictment of the twentieth century! No wonder it produced a Hitler, an ulcer that burst in our faces! I don't want to go back to that."

What, then, does Chaplin want? "I want change. I don't want the old rugged individualism—rugged for a few and ragged for the many."

The Russians are "godless." So Chaplin hears. "But I think they must have eternity in their souls to fight and die as they are fighting and dying. Anybody who dies for an ideal must have some religion. To fight and die for nothing just doesn't make sense."

The will and the desire to make a better world—this mainly is what is needed. The plans and the programs will take care of themselves if there is the resolve that there must be change.

An anxious man, a troubled man, a tragicomedian, the Orchestra Hall audience heard that night. As a pantomimist on the screen he has for thirty years spoken in an international language to more peoples of the earth than any other living man. Everywhere they know Charlie, his shoes, pants, hat, cane. And Charlie sees them as wanting change.

In the preceding week we heard from that curiously moderate man, also an anxious and troubled man, who is president of the Chamber of Commerce of the United States, Eric A. Johnston of

227

Spokane, Washington. He spoke of the jobless millions, closed banks, foreclosed farm mortgages, of the depression, and the people demanding action. "But with the acid animosities of the depression still etched on our minds, will we be wise and tolerant and efficient enough to cope with the complexities of our civilization when victory is ours? Will management be ready to meet its community as well as its business responsibilities?"

So Mr. Johnston, who speaks for the business element that sees the imperative need for community as well as business change, names three things private enterprise must look to when the war is won.

"First, we must provide employment at just compensation for the American people.

"Second, we will be charged with the tremendous task of actually building the better world pledged by America, so that we will be assured of continued peace and prosperity.

"Third, we must manage even better than we ever have before, so that the progress of our country and its people will continue uninterrupted.

"But can we provide employment for most of our people after the war? If private enterprise can't, we might as well understand now that the American enterprise system and many of our freedoms will be extinguished."

And we may hope and trust that neither Mr. Chaplin nor Mr. Johnston will in the aftermath to come be remembered as a voice crying in the wilderness.

Legend of faith

December 20, 1942

The roof gone, the walls gone, the City Temple of London, England, stands black, burned, broken.

The land under it is still there though the building is hardly worth putting together again.

Once a place of worship, song and ritual, now it is a wreck and shambles, a reminder of dive bombers.

Dr. Weatherhead, the Reverend Dr. Leslie Weatherhead, used to preach there and has faith he will again stand in the pulpit and

228

read from a Bible of how charity vaunteth not itself and is not puffed up.

Dr. Weatherhead tells a story, a timeworn legend, a guaranteed antique of a fable:

When Jesus had finished His work on earth He met near the Gate of Heaven the Angel Gabriel.

And Gabriel was troubled, more than anxious, asking Jesus if He had made plans to be sure His work would be carried on far away down there on the earth.

Jesus answered: "I have given the message to Peter and John, to Mary and Martha. They will tell others and so the message will spread."

And Gabriel doubted. "Suppose the fishermen forget and go out, like always, to throw their nets for fish? Or the women, what if they take up their housework of sewing, mending, washing, straightening the rooms—or suppose they tell the friends and the friends forget to pass along the message? What other plans are there, O Lord and Master? Hast thou made none?"

And Jesus stood quiet with a lighted face: "I have no other plans. I am counting on them."

"Am I my brother's keeper?"

December 27, 1942

One of the oldest disputes known among men is around the point of whether the question "Am I my brother's keeper?" is a better guide, help, and gauge through life than the proverb "Every man for himself and the devil take the hindmost."

Of course, during the Christmas season when the Northern zones have the shortest span of sun and the longest stretches of night, when the clock of the year says "From now on there will be a little more light every day until way next June when summer begins," —in this season it has become a custom and a habit, a convention sacred as lighted candles half-seen through frosted windows, to answer Yes to the question "Am I my brother's keeper?"

I had heard in my rambles so much windy talk here and there about the Brotherhood of Man that I knew I must have been looking for something a few years ago when some Canadian brother let go with the declaration: "We must come to realize that the Brotherhood of Man is no idle dream of a moonstruck visionary, but a plain and humiliating fact."

What that Canadian meant by that saying would need explanations, diagrams, charts, analyses, and elucidations accompanying each analysis, for those who would sniff propaganda lurking behind it that proposed the wreck of whatever is still solid and holding in the established order.

The Roman Catholic versed and familiar in the ways and teachings of St. Francis of Assisi nevertheless would know right off what the Canadian was saying.

So would any regular member in good standing of the Methodist Episcopal Church who has heard a worth-while sermon on what the founder of that denomination had in mind and heart when he saw a fool and a souse, pie-eyed and reeling into a gutter. All that Wesley could think of was "There but for the grace of God goes John Wesley."

It is good for any man to think back and count up how many different kinds of fools he has been.

And furthermore it is not a bad exercise for a man to sit quiet once in a while and watch the workings of his mind and heart and notice how often he can find himself favoring five or six of the seven deadly sins, and particularly the first of those sins, which is named pride.

Not so bad on the part of those antique theologians, who saw that gluttony is bad, envy is bad, sloth is bad, and no other of the seven sins is so bad and deadly as pride.

A certain degree of self-respect, self-reliance, belief in the sacredness of one's self, is, of course, a necessity. But not pride, show-off, not the kind of place and power there is no need of our wanting to gnaw and eat in the heart.

And there are moments of crises for soldier or civilian when as a person and a human being engaged in an assigned task and duty, he must say: "If you don't look out for yourself, nobody else will. I'm the only one of my friends I can count on. I'm for Me, Myself & Company. What counts most is what you got under your own hat."

That last one sure was in the mind of a tail gunner on a Flying Fortress at New Guinea. He is back in the United States of Amer-

230

ica now explaining to navy flyers the Japs he has met in action while earning his silver star. Having seen three years of service, he is somewhat a veteran. Seven men of his squadron were killed at Pearl Harbor. And as that squadron came to an airfield they wrecked at Lae, the first seven bombs they dropped had written on them the names of those seven lost at Pearl Harbor. Twenty-four years old, pink-cheeked, clear-eyed, modest, quiet-spoken, he told of this and that obstacle and hazard. Not one moment of brag or bluster or buildup in what he had to say to a lieutenant commander asking him questions.

Going down an elevator in the National Press Building in Washington, a lieutenant commander said to me, "Didn't you just feel like you wanted to reach out your arms and put them around him?"

The common man through a Vatican prism

January 3, 1943

One headline over the news story of the latest address of Pope Pius XII to the world read "Pope Assails Peril of Godless State." That perhaps was as live and accurate as any of forty other headlines that could be written after a slow and careful reading of the address. There are desk men who would have been pleased to write a headline reading "Pope Asks Crusade for Common Man" and then cite a dozen passages that speak directly in behalf of a justice, dignity, security, and opportunity rightfully due the common man but not generally accorded to him.

The address began with the sweeping and inclusive salutation to "My Dear Children of the Whole World." It quoted a watchword: "I have compassion on the multitude." It spoke of sympathy due to those in error. It warned against and condemned "the various forms of Marxist socialism," repeatedly condemning "state controls of the whole field of public and private life, even going into the realm of ideas and beliefs and of conscience." Some hurried readers vaguely felt that European and Asiatic totalitarian governments were meant in one passage. And among such readers those who have been and are now appalled at the workings of the New Deal in this country there was a feeling of being at home in a familiar atmosphere in this passage reading:

231

"He who would have the star of peace shine out and stand over society should reject every form of materialism which sees in the people only a herd of individuals who, divided and without any internal cohesion, are considered as a mass to be lorded over and treated arbitrarily."

Those who have known good workmen having pride in craftsmanship, looking with pleasure on the product of their labor, their personalities growing and shining rather than shrinking and losing natural color because of conditions on the job, recognize the good though ancient doctrine regarding "the moral nobility of work." The Russian cohorts at and behind the Stalingrad front would solemnly attest the truth of these propositions of Pope Pius XII: "All work has an inherent dignity and at the same time a close connection with the perfection of the person; this is the noble dignity and privilege of work, which is not in any way cheapened by the fatigue and the burdens which have to be borne."

Thus mention is made of "fatigue" and of "burdens" without including the hazardous occupations, now so multiplied in the war-production industries. Some of those in overalls, helmet, and goggles, living in trailer camps or crowded barracks, or taking two hours and more every working day in rides on pack-jammed buses—can it be reasoned that they too embody some element of struggle and endurance worth praise? And without erecting monuments or bestowing awards and medals, can we find the values of an important inscription in the statistical summary reported November 20, 1942, by the National Safety Council? The sentence goes like this: "The number of United States workers who have died in the battle of war production since Pearl Harbor is seven times that of United States soldiers who have been killed on the actual fighting front."

One theme came in for repeated variations in the Pope's message. "The fateful economy of the past decades, during which the lives of all citizens were subordinated to the stimulus of gain"—what have we in such words? And what guilts and complications are involved in the strange cadences of one sentence beating a hammer time of a conscience searching itself? It reads: "What is this world war, with all its attendant circumstances, whether they be remote or proximate causes, its progress and material, legal, and moral effects—what is it but the crumbling process, not expected, perhaps, by the thoughtless, but seen and deprecated by those whose gaze

232

penetrated into the realities of a social order which, behind a deceptive exterior or the mask of conventional shibboleths, hid its mortal weakness and its unbridled lust for gain and power?"

You may read this question twice. Then you may write the answer on a single sheet of paper, using both sides of the sheet. Then you may decide to write a book, if you can find the time. Then you may also decide it will be interesting to watch the forthcoming sessions of the United States Congress and see if you have difficulty in picking those moments when on the floor of House and Senate or in committee rooms or in caucuses the motive of "lust for gain and power" is at a minimum or is as completely absent as it is among the front-line Marines at Buna or Gona.

One prediction as to this Congress is safe. Those members whose names and words will have dignity when their records are studied by later generations will not be many. Only a few will not seem either pathetic or ridiculous.

Of all but a few it will be noted: "How sad they couldn't disentangle their personal malice, their smaller and private ambitions, from their better and more decent driving motives!" Of a few in both parties it will be written: "They worked hard, gave all they had of care, toil, and vision, and they prayed often not to be rash with their mouths."

And these few will be men whose minds have in degree been tantalized by the extent of dream and reality, hope and possibility, lying behind the potentials set forth by Pope Pius XII: "Besides a just wage which covers the needs of the worker and his family, the conservation and perfection of a social order which will make possible an assured, even if modest, private property for all classes of society, which will promote higher education for the children of the working class who are especially endowed with intelligence and goodwill, will promote the care and the practice of the social spirit in one's immediate neighborhood, in the district, the province, the people, and the nation, a spirit which by smoothing over friction arising from privilege or class interest removes from the workers the sense of isolation through the assuring experience of a genuinely human and fraternally Christian solidarity."

233

Our global thinking changes

January 10, 1943

More and more the flat maps of the globe are not so good. The sphere of earth on which we live fools us when we flatten its curves and try to calculate an air route from Chicago to Stalingrad.

That was quite a day in the earlier time of man when he found that by sailing in one direction and never turning back he would in due time come back to the place on the earth where he started from.

From then on the real navigators had a globe with instruments and mathematical tables for calculations in longitude and latitude.

Everything was circles, and when you could locate either the North Star or the Southern Cross, you could find what circle you were on and sail for the circle of the ship's destination.

Until this idea of a round earth got spread far and wide, men imagined the earth flat, and believed that even if it could be proved that the earth was round, how could you prove that all the people living on it wouldn't just naturally slide off into the empty and circumambient air?

There were even a few cases of men being locked up and handled as lunatics because their teaching the earth was not flat went against other older and more respectable and more highly approved teachings.

The law of gravitation was heard about, one more idea that helped make it more clear why there is no danger of the human family some fine morning all sliding off the planet in a calamity and a disaster that would make newspaper headlines never heard of before except for the simple fact that the headline-writers would have slid off too, along with everybody else, publishers, copy boys, rewrite men, teletype operators, and those ingenious birds who know how to repair the ticker tape if it gets stalled.

Men came to see that the earth is magnetized, that what goes up must come down unless it has what it takes to resist the pull of the majestic and sleepless magnets of the earth.

The flat-earth thinking fell back into the past and the global-earth thinking came, and there were for the first time world trade and world trade routes, global colonial dominions and the use and exploitation of designated global "spheres of influence."

And the terms of that global-earth thinking were held to sea routes, where the ships clung to the waters and a man seriously mentioning the ship leaving the waters for a sky route was taken as crack-brained or dreaming about a future too far away for any immediate practical purposes—to railway routes where the cargo hugged close to the land and a boxcar in the sky was a thwarted lesion of a loose convolution under the top pan of the skull—and to canals, mules, camels, caravans, wagons, wheelbarrows, Malemute sleds where the driver no more than the dog ever expected to see the sled acquire wings and propeller and go cavorting in the domed azure high over.

Ships were ships, and they held themselves to the sea and to the sea routes, and what global thinking we did then had to include the fact—and navigators, statesmen, even warriors, seemed to believe it a fact not likely to change.

And a smooth, well-regulated transcontinental railroad, that too was a fact blessed in iron and sealed with the oath of a golden spike—and boxcars on the ground were sure hard enough to handle and keep going without bringing us a horselaugh by the suggestion that one of these days we might haul freight faster and cheaper by taking the boxcars off the legal right of way on the ground and lifting them into the equally legal right of way in the sky.

Yes, it is still another kind of global earth that we now use in our thinking about sea routes or land routes of world trade, and in our thinking about colonial dominions or "spheres of influence" for the exchange and delivery of raw materials and finished goods.

The airship, the vessel that disregards old sea and land routes because it needs no water for its hull to rest on and requires ground only for take-off and landing, this is the revolutionary we have harbored and nurtured and brought along till it means something else again than its creators had expected, making claims for itself and its service and utility, claims so imperative they cannot be denied.

The seagoing liners and freighters, of course, will be with us a long time yet. They have their uses. So do the hurtling aluminum streamlined railway trains and those nice mile-long strings of boxcars hauling freight. But they can never hold the traffic controls they used to. Their routes are too fixed and frozen. They can't make the overnight schedule changes always possible in air traffic. Their development has come to its peak, while that of the airplane, from the proposed little sky jeeps to unheard-of supercargo carriers, takes on such variety and proportion that we know its role in the future is to be colossal.

Our postwar world, which will be a shape partly created by global air navigation, will find itself experimenting with some form of a political world structure, global political codes, not clearly foreseen now. There may even arrive an era of universal good feeling when it is recognized that all men who fly are brothers. This would be a step beyond the time within the memory of many men when it was supposed that all who flew were just flying fools.

Fighting youth and their future

January 17, 1943

Several million of the finest of American youths a year from now will be flyers and ground-crew mechanics whose lives are spent in, on, and around planes.

Many million others of the finest youth of the United Nations likewise will be flying planes or tending, grooming, lubricating, repairing, inspecting planes.

What will become of this host of youths when the war ends is a pleasant speculative thought if you like to think in terms of conjecture, possibility—and ventures into the unknown.

The work these young men now do comes so near completely absorbing their waking time and thought that they have few moments, few hours, for discussions and decisions as to what may become of them when the war ends.

In the months spent in learning how to fly and how to bomb targets and get away and how to intercept or brush off interceptors, there is little or no time for thinking what the next world society may be like or what kind of an industrial or political order will take shape in the home country when the war is over.

And having spent their period of learning and having moved into active service, their schedules permit them even less time to study what statesmen, politicians, journalists, and bystanders have been saying about a world society after the war—and what the critics and opponents of those spokesmen are saying.

236

One reason why they are giving such a good account of themselves is precisely because they know their lives and the excellence of their service depend on their forgetting just about everything else except how to perform the special duties and exact tasks assigned to them.

When they exercise concentration, they prefer to practice in their minds what they are going to do in any one of a thousand given situations where quick thinking is wanted, and where their personal lives and their country's victory depend on how they have learned to handle themselves and their delicate and often whimsical mechanisms of war.

The pilots, bombardiers, radiomen, and gunners, and not forgetting the ground-crew men, they may find time, some of them, for reading fragments or hearing broadcasts of discussions dealing with their own country and its role among the United Nations after the war.

And they know well and they know deep that their job now is not in that field, and for this hour the thought and the action, the schemes and the decisions, are in the hands of others.

Every one of them who rates as good, decent, and regular would never forgive himself if a mishap should come to his plane or squadron because his emergency thinking had been at fault, because his mind had not operated as a proper co-ordinating unit.

What kind of jobs they will come back to when the war ends, and the colossal armed forces are demobilized into individual civilian units—on this they can guess, speculate, and joke.

What sort of an industrial setup there will be in America and how it will be related to a new world society, with Britain, Russia, China, and the others of the United Nations in some form of collaboration and unity not now known and not now possible to know—on this too they can guess, speculate, and joke.

Yet as certainly as the war does end they will be coming home, from foreign fighting fronts, from domestic training camps, by the millions in these United States, by the millions in Britain, Russia, China, these young flyers, these tough and cheerful youths of the ground crews.

And returning with them will be the millions of others, many having seen harder service than the air fighters, youths of the tank crews, antiaircraft outfits, infantrymen, each of whom understands twelve different weapons for shooting and killing—millions of technicians—trained for emergency thinking in the crafts and co-ordinations of modern mechanized war.

What they will be wanting, what they indicate as their will with relation to America's future, what they by reason of indifference or lack of interest wish to let happen—this will be one of the largest controlling factors shaping the course of the American nation and the next world order.

Beyond the limits of violence

January 24, 1943

How long the war will run, whether it can end this year, whether it ends next year or the year after, we will hear continuing discussion of these questions, because of the many anxieties and hopes involved.

The morale of the German people, the German Army, the chances of their cracking, discussion of this will continue.

And German morale will be related to that of the Nazi party and the Nazi leaders, that of the Storm Troopers expected to put down in fast order anything like armed revolt, and that of the Gestapo and its spies and secret operatives by tens of thousands.

With every day that passes now, however, in fact with every hour, things get worse and cannot help getting worse with the Nazi top dogs.

Several points of advantage they once had working for them keep slipping away from day to day, till in due course they will reach zero and will know what it is to be worse off than when you have merely plenty of nothing.

They had in 1940 and early 1941 prestige, name, reputation, after their blitzes that gave them all of continental Europe except a few parcels they hadn't tried for. Then came their test. They were to show in the conquered countries what they meant by "The New Order of the Greater German Reich," a blueprint of the future so curiously and colorfully exploited in their propaganda that it finally came to be mentioned in America as "the wave of the future."

And what came? Efficiency? Better management? Superior production? The integration of raw materials, machines, and labor over the entire continent of Europe into a fine co-ordination never before seen?

Hardly. Those claims were blah. That propaganda was chin music. Those high pretenses, fortified by books and booklets, deluxe illustrated magazines, apostles of Kultur, emissaries, salesmen, and spielers, were a screen, a front. Outside of their military establishment, made possible mainly by the traditions, morale, and special aptitudes of the German army and navy men, the Nazis were seen to be hoodlums rather than organizers, clumsy robbers and wanton butchers rather than bringers of a new day and a bright future.

They wrecked in Denmark an industry that was a model for the whole world in production of eggs, poultry, butter, cheese, sending to German kitchens and dining rooms the meat of pure-bred cows, bulls, hens and cocks, that the Danes, with the most careful breeding, cannot re-establish in another generation.

Norway was straddled and strangled, Poland knifed and ravished, Holland and Belgium pressed down and choked pale, France raped and laughed at, Czechoslovakia split four ways and given the Lidice once-over.

What does it add up to? Whither lead these things? What hope might lie back of them?

Well, part of the hope lies in the fact that the Nazi butchers, hangmen, rapists, and exploiters have a theory that violence can accomplish purposes violence has never yet been known to achieve. Once about midyear of 1942 they gave it out that sabotage and revolts would be handled with increasing "implacable violence."

Yes? Having killed one million people and failed to get cooperation, you go ahead and kill another million of people, and, in case that doesn't get you what you want, you kill and kill, and after you have handed out enough of death, death, and death, things will come your way.

That is the theory. It is that simple, bold, bald, incalculably cruel and inconceivably ignorant.

Meanwhile, such killing business takes time, care, skill, ingenuity, and requires basic minimum expense. Those to be slaughtered must first be rounded up, after which must come the decisions whether they shall be hanged, shot, tortured, or starved in a concentration camp, or otherwise done away with, and "otherwise" is often a special procedure giving a queer, crazy fun to the sadist Nazis.

The breath of life having been extinguished in any given instance, the clothing of the doomed one, however tattered and reeking, must be economized to the service of the Reich, after which must come some disposal of the corpse.

How to bury them, when, where, and by whom, must be considered and decided as a measure of hygiene and to guard against disease and pestilence that may operate even against Nazis, inasmuch as the typhus bacillus and other bacilli practice no discrimination as to race, color, or previous servitude.

A mean business? A low and horrible work to be doing? And for the killing of millions of people far behind the war fronts there has been requisite the time and the services of how many Storm Troopers, Gestapo sleuths, and professional man-hunters? And as the months pass those creatures who hunt and kill by a system consider that day lost bringing them no fresh necks to be broken, no prime rebel youth for a bullet.

A corruption goes on in them. They begin to rot. A certain small minority of them have the austere chill of zealots to whom no change comes, but for the most of them a rotting process slowly transforms them to subhumans. Their motives get tangled with at any cost getting what they desire, whether it is promotion, loot, money, women, girls, drink, or any conceivable fantastic, exotic pleasures.

It is known that the Gestapo High Command has to shift the ordinary rank-and-file troops of occupation every so often, because where they stay some of them come to like the human beings they are supposed to regulate, ride, and shoot if need be. Cases are known of soldiers in occupation areas broken mentally and physically under the strain of carrying out orders having to do with wrecking the families and homes of decent people born in a homeland they loved, now taken over by outlanders.

The administration problems of the Nazi regimes are too vast for their High Commands. While they try to run a war with one hand they try with the other to repress, control, and guide for their Nazi ends a dozen countries with landscapes and languages all different.

The first and last word in their manual of instruction is violence. "Obey, or we kill!"

Of one of the ancients who had the Nazi idea it was written: "He created a solitude and called it peace." And that is practicable in a single province. It has been done. Rome wiped out Carthage and its population of 200,000 and called it a day's work. But the whole teeming, swarming, heterogeneous population of the continent of Europe is something else. Every day for the infamous and besotted Nazis it gets worse.

What was George Washington's course?

February 21, 1943

"We forget or have never learned that Washington had the support of only a patriotic minority in the building of this nation." Thus last summer wrote the foremost biographer of Washington, adding: "There were at times more native-born Americans in arms and fighting on the side of the British than Washington could ever muster for his own troops."

When Rupert Hughes began his researches that led to his writing more extensively about the life of Washington than any other man of this or previous generations, he didn't expect to find some things that crept and slithered out of the record. And having found them, he didn't shrink from presenting them, even though the Daughters of the American Revolution cried aloud that he was doing them wrong, them and their forefathers.

From the bitter hills of Valley Forge, from an army headquarters amid winter huts where soldiers nursed the frozen cracks of their bleeding feet, General George Washington, the father of his country, wrote of the times and the men in these words: "If I was to be called upon to draw a picture of the times, and of Men; from what I have seen, heard, and in part know I should in one word say that idleness, dissipation, and extravagance seem to have laid fast hold of most of them. That Speculation, peculation and an insatiable thirst for riches seems to have got the better of every other consideration and almost every order of Men. . . . Party disputes and personal quarrels are the great business of the day whilst the momentous concerns . . . are but secondary considerations."

Amid this greediness, corruption, laxity, and lack of faith, what was Washington's course? He was a sportsman and a country gentleman who could have isolated himself in comfort, yet he quit his big plantation, his spick-and-span Mount Vernon home, the games and dances, the cotillion parties and the horse races—and he left this ease and fun to become a leader in what was partly a cruel civil war, and a war that seemed lost or half-lost up to the last battle. "He loved riches," writes Hughes, "and was one of the wealthiest men of his day; but he gave up everything for the cause. He did not see his home for six years and he endured bankruptcy for his nation."

Among American businessmen of this hour and this crisis a roster could be made of those who are throwing in all they have, whose effort and whose devotion is of the same cloth as that of George Washington.

In an honor roster of such businessmen, it would be found that they are, each of them, neither hate-ridden nor fear-bitten, that each has something of the sportsmanship and the faith that carried Washington and his loyal associates.

The hate-ridden who make a domestic business of their hate and peddle it for political and journalistic profit, the fear-bitten whose personal necessity seems to dictate that they should infect others with fear and foreboding—they were known to George Washington in war and peace. And we will have them while the war lasts, though their real carnival will not begin till men, hoping they are somewhat sane, try to reorganize the insane aftermath of war.

"There are evils worse than war and war brings all of them," says one of our modern proverbs, and it means to include the gyrations and outcries of the hate-ridden and the fear-bitten.

As a postscript having nothing to do with the foregoing, we might hope that sometime the Irish, the Poles, the Germans, the Bohemians, the Italians, the Argentines, the Portuguese, and the Greeks may have their part in the Civil War of the 1860's set forth as adequately as the Swedes have their case stated in a book just published titled *Swedish Immigrants in Lincoln's Time*. Its author, Nels Hokanson of Evanston, Illinois, is a businessman turned scholar who knows his onions, also his Swedes. The Irish and the Germans, of course, were far more numerous than the Swedes, and of their contributions to American life in that earlier generation more adequate statements are wanted.

We quote herewith from the foreword to Hokanson's book: "Who was the first Big Swede to land in America? The answer is one of many odd facts fished up from obscurity. His name was John Printz and he weighed four hundred pounds and served as the governor of the first Swedish colony in North America and the colonists didn't like him so very well and when the government at Stockholm refused to send him the troops he asked for he packed up and headed right home for Sweden. So he was not much of a Big Swede after all."

What has posterity done for us?

February 28, 1943

An Irish bull is any figure of speech that gets tangled with odd numbers and doesn't add up.

"No sooner would he land on an uninhabited island than he would have his hands in the pockets of the naked savages."

So runs one of the classics. Another one hoary with verdigris and lichen goes like this: "Mr. Speaker, I smell a rat. I see him floating in the air. But I will nip him in the bud."

And you take it or leave it. One dusty specimen hides a gleam of sheer wisdom in the folds of its nonsense: "What has posterity done for us?"

Very illogical this is supposed to be, because posterity is the next generation after us, the present generation, and it amounts to asking "What have those not yet born, not yet breathing, not yet named and alive, ever done for us who now this hour are strictly born, breathing, named, and alive?"

In dealing further with such a question, we might say that posterity is the unborn who will stem from us, the living. And before so very long, certainly in due time, all of us, the living, will pass to the heritage and majesty of grassroots and gravestones.

In that future time, when the present has become the past, those now unborn will be the living, who stemmed from us. Also, looking back, we might say with absolute precision that a time was when we, who are now the living, were then the unborn. In that period we had neither breath, nor names, nor life—strictly we were posterity.

And there were those who had anxiety, love, dreams and hopes, about us, about posterity. Many a one was heard to say, "I couldn't have gone on if it wasn't for the children." Many another suffered and toiled and took wounds and even a hard death with the repeated hope "We won't see it, but our children will."

The fellow who likes to chirp "I'm for Me, Myself & Company" as though he means it and as though it holds some guiding gospel truth for him, this is the fool who gives you a fishy eye if you happen to ask whether a man has a double debt to the past and the future.

Bob Trout of CBS interviewed a woman in Hilton, England, and we heard her telling of her nine children and her husband, all gone away from her for the duration, seven sons and two sons-in-law fighting to the tune of "There will always be an England." She spoke with calm and sanity as though she had the strengths of a serene earth in her. The future to her is holy and posterity sacred and the matter beyond argument.

Like her in faith and tenacity were many of the pioneer mothers who said they were doing with little in the hope that the next generation would have more.

What has often been called the American dream would have been a mirage and a flimflam if in the earlier and foregoing generations there had not been anxiety, love, dreams and hopes, ranging around posterity, the generations to come.

In many a document, speech, or letter between the Declaration of Independence and the Emancipation Proclamation may be found the expression, the forecast and prophecy, that the transaction at hand was not for the soon-dead calendar date of today but for a vast and immeasurable tomorrow. That the gentlemen of the Congress might know whom he thought he was working for, George Washington phrased it in two words: "unborn millions." And President Lincoln took occasion to remind the members of Congress that the record, meaning the personal voting and speaking record of each, in the trial of fire and blood through which they were passing, would be available for reading and study by "the latest generation," meaning the farthest posterity you might imagine.

So often the heavy rag-paper prints of a century and more ago speak of how a new highway, discovery, invention, or some freshly proposed idea, method, or principle, is to reach far across the future and touch and benefit "the remotest generations." They were talking about posterity. Even if posterity had done nothing for them, they hoped to be doing something for which posterity would thank them.

Tomorrow belongs to the children

March 7, 1943

Henry Clay, nicknamed "Handsome Harry," trained hard to be President. He hoped for the White House and never reached it, though leaving us his alibi "I would rather be right than President"—one enemy saying definitely he could never be either.

Also back in his time, more than a hundred years ago, Henry Clay one day rode along a wilderness road in Kentucky. And he stopped his carriage. Then, stepping out, he crouched, bent on his knees, leaned forward, and put his ear to the ground.

Asked why he went through this action that seemed queer or theatrical, he replied, "I am listening to the tread of unnumbered millions to come."

He was under the intoxication of the American dream of his day, of tomorrow's children moving out to the Great Plains and beyond into the flaring sunsets farther west.

Nebraskans several generations later, far from the frontier Clay knew, finished a noble architectural poem and fixed on their new state capitol at Lincoln the inscription: "Honor to pioneers who broke sod that men to come might live."

By their slogans and mottoes the earlier generations made clear their belief that any new world gained and held would come by toil, struggle, hardship, and often by flirting with death.

The Latin motto of the State of Kansas has been translated "To the stars through difficulties" and "To the stars by hard ways."

The Society of California long ago nailed up its slogan: "The cowards never started and the weak ones died by the way."

Each of these belongs in any study of the "American rhythm" and how the past and the future interlock in the way they pronounce their little cry "Let's go."

The American flyer over Tunisia who saw his target pass into the range of another and radioed the message, "Go ahead, Super man, he's all yours," had the old urge and bright accent.

Barney Ross, the battling Jew who held three prize-ring championships and enlisted in the Marines overage, who took three wounds at Guadalcanal and arriving at West-coast American soil went on his knees and kissed the ground of his country—Ross said it wasn't patriotism; it was something in his heart beyond words.

To Barney Ross his country is worth dying for, is worth men alive now giving their lives for the sake of their country in the years, the centuries, to come. For him, America *is*.

The quality of clairvoyant dream, the hushed murmuring of sacred music that many find in the Gettysburg Speech, has to do with its solemn salutations to "these honored dead," men no longer numbered among the living, and a debt owed to them by those alive, breathing, and holding a resolve "that these dead shall not have died in vain." And thereby tomorrow's children, the unborn, posterity, shall know the benefits of "a new birth of freedom."

The present anxiety and questioning about what kind of a world we shall be leaving to those coming after us—this is good to see.

The generation of youth to whom shall be handed the somewhat changed and reorganized postwar world—you can't read 'em and weep, you can't even read 'em. They have not yet had time to instruct us on their answers to the now common questions, "What are we fighting for?" and "What kind of a world peace do we want when the shooting stops?"

Tomorrow belongs to the children—yes. Which means that they and their children will take their own peculiar directions dictated by events now not known to any prophets well accepted.

The living might plan and blueprint a world for the unborn, who on becoming born and grown to man-size would decide to forget the arrangements made for them while they were unborn. Starting in on their own, they might shape something else. With respect and affectionate regard for the elders and ancestors, they might do what they want to do in their time, acting under wills, theories, and compulsions not clearly understood by the Founding Fathers.

This has happened. Across history several times precisely this has happened. Tomorrow belongs to the children. They will mold that tomorrow with care and wisdom. Or they will muddle and while

246

muddling some may look backward saying "There is plenty of precedent."

There are careless generations who drift, dawdle, decay. Still others leave tall landmarks of discovery and culture, setting targets of achievement at which no succeeding generation can take a horse-laugh of derision and belittlement.

Mei-ling—look at her and listen

March 14, 1943

During the long period of peace before the present war began, we gave the Chinese kerosene, bullets, Bibles, various articles of commerce, besides religious missions. And the Chinese gave us the radish, the soybean, silk, poems, paintings, proverbs, egg foo yong, gunpowder, Fourth of July fireworks and firecrackers, not to mention labor gangs for the Pacific railways.

And now in March of 1943 we can say that perhaps nothing yet from China has ever come to a deeper welcome than the woman Soong Mei-ling, wife of the Chinese leader Chiang Kai-shek. She spoke of freedom and democracy in words and voice so that no one could doubt her belief that what she wants she wants for the Family of Man over the entire earth.

There she stands. We look at her. Or we listen. She represents money. Or rather her father and her family are known for riches in multimillions. Money, however, is about the last thought as to Madame Chiang.

What woman over the earth has for six years been closer to heavy misery, high responsibility, and hard work, terrific decisions every day, agony by truckloads and death and devastation over thousand-mile areas of burning villages and bombed cities? Only China among the United Nations counts its dead and gazes over its scorched plains, like Russia, in aggregates of valor and toil that justify her quoting "The difficult we do at once, the impossible takes longer."

The wonder of this little woman ought to stay with our country a long time. Her speech in Madison Square Garden could well be folded into any school or college textbook on politics, ethics, literature, the art of discourse and speech. Not that she has any particularly new approach in style, but that few moderns, if any, are as good as she in the best of ancient styles which are simple, which open the heart and let it pour.

What will we make of the future after "the hideous blood-letting" of the present? She sees the wisest minds of all corners of the world pondering. "And the wisest of all reserve their opinion." For herself she would venture "Never again must the dignity of man be outraged as it has been since the dawn of history."

A little diamond lantern, an emblem out of China, forms the button of her high standing collar. Any lantern ought to go good on Mei-ling saying "Exploitation is spiritually as degrading to the exploiter as to the exploited."

The small, intricate diamond brilliants she wears sometimes in her ears remind beholders of Chinese puzzles. And we could name offhand six or eight Congressmen and one Congresswoman who are not merely puzzled but annoyed and alarmed at any American voice presenting Madame Chiang's viewpoint: "All nations, great and small, must have equal opportunity of development. Those who are stronger and more advanced should consider their strength as a trust to be used to help the weaker nations to fit themselves for full self-government and not to exploit them."

Her tongue and mouth have a perfection at chiseling syllables. She is a marvel at timing her pauses and making each word count in relation to what goes before and comes after. Yet she doesn't know how she does it, any more than Ty Cobb knew which one of his eleven ways of sliding to second he was using.

A speech is good in these days if it is a safe bet that it says something definitely that will be holding good ten or twenty years from now. That goes for dynamic little Mei-ling.

She has been instructed by America when she was a schoolgirl in the State of Georgia, where she practiced the Southern drawl. She added to her instruction when she was exposed to the Yankees of New England at Wellesley College. She has deep wells of feeling about Wellesley. So deep is this feeling that when she was introduced to a Wellesley audience it wasn't easy for her to begin speaking. The first slow words came: "Strong emotion tends to make one inarticulate." Then she took a long wait and got hold of herself. The wife of the Generalissimo of the armies of the Chinese Republic would not be doing so well as one more Wellesley girl letting herself go with a good cry.

Yet who might have been more truly authorized to show tears and shake with sobs? She comes from mountains of grief, from valleys of desperate hope and action.

Two key words from her have sunk deep in many of her hearers: "co-operation—and humility."

Those words alone would save the postwar world if they could be spread into a wide enough understanding. She visions a world of global lives and global nations from now on. Whether they want to or not, they must be neighbors. They will make decisions whether to be good neighbors or bad.

Mei-ling invites one and all to see what they can make of the words "This whole world must be thought of as one great state common to gods and men." To some, that's just preaching. To others, neglect of it foreshadows the global war that may follow this one now fighting.

If we can be sober, patient

March 21, 1943

Voices, mouthpieces, organs—we have them. We listen to them. We read them. We take it and like it. Or we wonder what to make of it.

You might with little risk to your immortal soul and its eventual dwelling take oath that at least one-tenth of one per cent of the absentees in the munitions plants knock off for a day or two once in a while just to see if they can figure out any ordinary case in the day's news like that of Senator Robert Taft of Ohio crying aloud over the American landscape that Elmer Davis, head of the Office of War Information, had "commandeered," or seized by legal force and decree, the big radio networks for a Friday-night broadcast to the whole country.

Here was a man who before he headed OWI rated as the highest-paid, farthest-throwing, hardest-hitting newscaster in the business. The networks welcome him. His smooth and cool Hoosier-twanged voice is good for whatever ails people, and if nothing ails them it's good for that. And instead of $40 a minute for broadcasting, like he used to get, what is his pay now? Not a cent, nothing, plus the ingratitude and unjust vociferations of Senator Taft, whose father's judicial decisions were better grounded.

Among voices, of course, there is the priceless Madame Chiang, who leaves us in a few days now hoping we will cherish those words "co-operation—and humility." And those who missed the Washington, D.C., Constitution Hall speech of Governor Harold Stassen of Minnesota, in print filling four newspaper columns, would find him using a style of approach worth looking at.

"Good God!" cried one reader of this Stassen speech, "this man doesn't hate anybody—except the enemy—and he gives them every sporting chance they could ask."

The postwar world—Stassen gave his slant at it, what to do and how to do it. Part of it ran like he was telling a class of high-school boys and girls about civil government, police, schools and education, how you must have 'em in Minnesota now and how in the postwar world over the earth you must have 'em—or another global war busts loose.

A tough job with political tools and military arms Stassen sees ahead. If we can be sober, patient, and reduce anger and malice to a minimum, we stand a better chance at working out something new and good for a coming generation to build on. Some of us can hold only genuine affection for a political leader with malice toward none of his own political party rivals and no odorous innuendoes, no carefully worded little stink bombs, meant for others who have different notions about how to reorganize and set going the shattered and burnt human world we face when this war ends.

For current history in this present hour the reader is recommended to see, when it is soon released to the screen, *The Moon Is Down*. When Steinbeck wrote the book, he puzzled some people who couldn't see that Nazi officers in an occupied country have varying theories on how to put the screws on the conquered so as to get industrial production. Such readers now have the puzzle cleared up.

The technique of conquest is not so easy. You tell 'em in Nazi style to work the mine and get out the ore. Maybe they don't hear you. So you tell 'em again. And they hear you. And they understand what you want. Yet there's no production. So you shoot a few. And maybe that doesn't help. Then you shoot more. And about then a mining works is dynamited so it will take two months to repair and get going. Then you shoot more and more. And after a while it may dawn on you as a Nazi conqueror that the dead are unconquered and unproductive. No book of rules from Berlin will help.

"The flies have conquered the flypaper," might serve as subtitle for this motion picture. It is Steinbeck's story done for the screen with intelligent co-operation. Nunnally Johnson wrote the script, Irving Pichel directed, the leading players and the extras all threw in and all deserve salutation, along with Twentieth-Century Fox.

After the Nazis have clamped their awful claws on one town in Norway a struggle begins between them and the people. The word "freedom" weaves through many lines. Are you wanting that word to be made more crystal-clear for you? *The Moon Is Down* will help. It is good to see this picture, a cinema psalm of the terrible price and beauty of human freedom, going to a world audience. It will surely be shown secretly in Norway and France, openly in Chungking and Casablanca and Moscow, winning reverence from men and women who have witnessed agony in behalf of liberty.

Does it have a spot where boy meets girl? Yes, indeed. In fact, two boys meet girl. One marries her. The other doesn't. Both die. The girl gets over the border to Sweden. It is a nice change from the chocolate eclairs we are fed up on where boy meets girl and there is not a flicker worth thinking about afterward.

Among the greatest newsreels ever seen is the current release of *The March of Time* presenting a portrait of the Soviet Union at war. We have heard how a hundred and fifty Russian photographers started at dawn at different places covering the fighting fronts, how thirty of these cameramen met death in their work of making this record. No reportorial word descriptions could possibly deliver us such on-the-spot impressions as this screen rendition of current history.

One lone little woman from China

March 28, 1943

Not in the history of this country has there been a tour by a woman visitor from another country so dramatic, so darkly momentous, as what we have seen in recent weeks in the journey of one lone little woman from China.

What she has been saying is not quite up to what she has been trying to say.

After reading President Lincoln's message to Congress, December of 1862, a London *Spectator* commentator wrote of "the mystical dreaminess" to be found in Lincoln's picture of an American Union of States becoming a light to the world, and "The thoughts of the man are too big for his mouth."

Lincoln couldn't get it said fully and adequately, because great hopes and dreams are immeasurable and they include horizons where people are willing to struggle, suffer, and even die for the sake of issues that are mystical and vast.

So now we have been listening to a little woman whose thoughts are too big for her mouth—in this hour of chaos.

A later time will come, however, and events will justify her words and frame her sentences in fresh lights and make some of her declarations and predictions carry the sound of terrible warnings.

One of her sisters married Sun Yat-sen, founder of the Chinese Republic, a student of Lincoln who urged his people to take counsel of Abraham Lincoln as one figure near to holding the secrets and hopes of democracy and popular government.

As some of us heard her at the Chicago Stadium last week, she seemed to be trying to make herself the voice of the many millions of Chinese who have died for their hope of an independent republic of free people, joined in co-operation and humility with other free peoples.

There were moments when she seemed to be summoning nearly her last reserves of physical strength, as though implying "God helping me, I must get this said to you people of America even if death takes me where I now stand."

By merely hearing Madame Chiang speak we don't get her message. She is vastly implicative. Reading one of her speeches carries us on into meanings we didn't get from her spoken words. These speeches, soon to be published in collected form, will constitute one of the classics of the literature of democracy and free peoples.

If it should happen that after this war the guidance and leadership are such that again in another generation or sooner there comes another global war, her book will read like an infinitely sad music of dreams lost in a welter of personal follies, personal ambitions, and personal greeds. Her two high words, "co-operation—and humility," will come back like ghosts no doors can shut out.

"Goodwill and desire for co-operation will do as a starting point," she counsels, "but left to themselves, they will make little headway."

She has heard of soft soap and moonshine, of dreamers blamed for idle dreaming, of hopers and rainbow-chasers. And she wishes that some of those who don't see eye to eye with her at all might get her picture of herself as she would like to be, her words running:

"Invariably the great spirits in human relationships have honesty and imagination—honesty in appraising themselves, first, as they see themselves; second, as they think others see them; and third, the imagination to place themselves in others' positions while appraising themselves. The first two, being subjective, cannot be all-sufficing; the third, an objective approach, is needed to complete the picture."

She would like those Americans she seeks to convince to think of her and her fellow believers as tough-minded, telling it in these words: "To translate faith into reality, you and I must recapture faith in our fellow man in the spirit of your pioneer fathers who forged in the van of the movement westward and forward in cutting across the wilderness and endless forests. We should march onward with staunch hearts and steadfast wills in the cultivation of what William James calls tough-mindedness—tough-mindedness while searching for rectitude and truth in the triumph of a just and permanent peace."

And naturally enough, she knows for sure that some who pride themselves on precisely this quality they term "tough-mindedness" refuse to string along with her in her last words before shaking the dust of Chicago from her gleaming slippers and heading for the West coast and her last speech to America at the Hollywood Bowl. And those last words? They go like a little psalm and read like this:

"Let us then together resolve to keep on fighting in the faith that our vision is worth preserving and can be preserved. For is it not true that faith is the substance of things hoped for, the evidence of things not seen?"

The new world will be air-minded

April 4, 1943

We hear about hindsight being more sure and easy than fore-sight? Of course it is. When Babe Ruth hit a home run, those who bet he would had foresight. They saw him hitting it before he stepped up to the plate. And when other times again they bet he would wham out a homer, and he didn't connect and they lost their bets—what they had then was hindsight.

When our responsible War Department strategists passed on to the divisions of procurement and supply in 1940 and 1941 their plans calling for tanks of various sizes, thousands of little land bat-tleships moving on caterpillar tractors, they hoped they had fore-sight. They could foresee tanks wanted for fighting on several fronts in Europe, Africa, Asia, and the Pacific. So they believed logic backed them in their demands and requisitions for tanks. So the word went out and the orders were issued and on farmland areas here and there sprang up new plants for the manufacture of tanks while in several spots, some of them notably in the automobile industry, the conversion was from motorcars to tanks.

When they finished their new setups of machine tools and the tanks began rolling off the assembly line as completed units, those tanks were loaded on flatcars and hauled by rail to seaports. From the rail terminals these tanks were moved to docks where mighty derricks lifted them to the decks of freight vessels. And as the lines of freight vessels moved out of the harbor into the open sea, joining a convoy, they were guarded by many guns, destroyers, sub-chasers, planes, having, too, the help of a variety of scouts and patrols.

Then what? Then they took their chances. What the toll has been, of men, ships, tanks, and other property lost, we do not know, and properly that information should not be given to us now if it lends or leases to the enemy any aid or comfort. The official an-nouncements have come, however, that the losses are heavy, and during the months immediately ahead one of the gravest points of danger is enemy submarines.

Suppose, however, that the responsible strategists of the War Department had in 1940 and 1941 ordered one-half or one-fourth or even one-tenth as many tanks. Suppose they had reasoned that the production forces given to tanks should in the main have been given to bombers. What would have been the advantage? Certainly one gain would have been that the moment a bomber was finished it could say to a finished tank: "Now they don't have to bother with me any more. I carry myself to where I am wanted. But you— you tank, you—they're going to lift and haul and sweat and cry and agonize before they ever get you to where you're wanted. And even when at last they do get you where you're of some use, it will take weeks, maybe months. But me, the bomber, I'll be where they want me in just a few days and nobody worrying."

Perhaps when some of the brass hats get around to their memoirs many years from now they will be saying that maybe they should have given a little more priority to bombers and a little less to tanks.

Why bring this up now? Why mention such a matter at this time? Because it goes back to the old question of who is air-minded and why.

Not only in the discussion of how to win the war now is there relentless need for stress on the fact that in a global war the first and most important requisite is air power—and no part of the war can be won where air dominance is lost. Furthermore, in the discussions of the world after the war, must be the picture of an earth family of nations whose people fly, who travel in passenger Clippers above the clouds over oceans and continents, who haul super-cargoes in sky freighters.

In any attempt at a parallel or comparison of the thought and feeling of the American people in 1943 or 1944 as against 1918 and 1919, the question must be raised whether the people know and understand why a national isolation that looked possible twenty-five years ago is now something else again.

Now in every geography class where the teacher is not dead from the neck up the students hear that from where they sit it is only sixty hours of air travel to any spot of the earth they might want to visit.

Now in hundreds of news bulletins each week the mind is impressed with how small the globe has become and what close neighbors are the nations large and small.

Now so many men and women have had the experience that only a preposterous fool considers it a distinction that he has crossed the Atlantic ocean by airway in twelve hours or less.

Yet nobody, not one of them, sitting at the Paris Peace Conference had ever looked out of a window and looked down to see the white rolling mist of clouds above an ocean.

Now nearly every neighborhood in America has its boys who ride or grease and groom aircraft that takes oceans in its stride.

A terrible adventure and a new one

April 11, 1943

The question comes often: Will the ending of this war be followed by the same kind of useless feeling so many of the people of this country had in 1919? And quite often the answer comes as though it is the same kind of a war and can possibly have the same kind of an end with the American people in the same kind of shifting moods as to our taking a wider hand in world affairs—or not.

We hear this sometimes out of a sincerity we cannot doubt. At the same time we can have our doubts as to the information, the evidence, and the historical basis on which such an answer is founded.

Perhaps first of all certain questions should be set forth. And to the extent that sincere seekers can agree on the replies to such questions, they can help each other move toward better understanding of what we must face and grapple with as the war drags on toward its end.

At the end of the last war, is it not correct that we disarmed Germany and took from her certain disputed areas of territory and there was no march to Berlin—and the peace terms gave Germany humiliation rather than shame as compared with the present German-occupied countries, where the Nazi conquerors have imposed shames beyond shame? And is it not correct to assume that the last twenty years would have been vastly different if Germany in 1918 and after had been bled, devastated, sacked of her resources and sucked of her sustenance by the methods the Nazis have used and are using in Poland, France, Norway, eastern Russia?

Those who assume that this is correct are many—and more than a few of them are hard, unforgiving, and they can't consider for a moment any such peace as that of 1919. This underlies the announced purpose of the United Nations that this time it will not

256

do to merely disarm Germany and strip her of a few areas of territory and leave her fairly free to work out her immediate future, as in 1919.

When the granitic French Prime Minister Clemenceau, who earned the nickname "Savior of France," wrote his book titled *The Grandeur and Misery of Victory*, he forecast the return of Germany for another attempt at conquest of its neighbor nations. That was where the misery of victory gave the grandeur a flat taste. And could Clemenceau have foreseen the Nazis taking over Germany and ruling it more absolutely than ever did the Hohenzollerns, would he not have left out all mention of grandeur in connection with victory and titled his book merely "The Misery of Victory"?

What misery we are to have following our victory this time will be definitely and unmistakably misery—but different from 1919 and that aftermath. For we now face the fact that this war will cost high in part because our aim is not merely to disarm Germany and mildly punish her. Now the purpose is to break the power and to wreck and shatter the whole Nazi-controlled government of Germany. What to do with the wreckage, the smoking ruins, the death stench, is not yet clear in the plans of the United Nations, and we have yet to hear what the present and further "exploratory" discussions are to reveal.

But the depth, intensity, and undiminishing voltage underlying this motive take this present hour beyond comparison with 1919. Of course the American people will have shifting moods, and they will move this way and that in response to changing events these years of 1943 and 1944. But they will shift to a willingness to compromise and make a treaty with some German authorities whatsoever only when a condition not now conceivable as fact should arise.

That would be a condition where both sides, all contestants in the war, had fought and wasted and bled and wasted still more, till the war was a stalemate and a draw with further fighting seen as useless.

Before Pearl Harbor such a stalemate was conceivable. It could be imagined.

Now the facts, the foretokenings, the weather signs, all say that whether the war runs long or short in time, German national power will be shattered and the Nazis given "death and dust."

It is a terrible adventure, and a new one for the American people. We didn't have it last time. It will be quite different, with some of the music good to hear and some not so good.

Poets major and minor

April 18, 1943

The Easter season will not see a broadcast of Stephen Vincent Benét's radio play *The Strangers at the Stone*. Death took him after he had a title for the play and before he could get it onto paper.

Homer Fickett, the radio director who had hoped to see this Easter play produced, told me of how Benét was getting ready to write it, at his side a Bible with markers at the pages holding verses to be quoted. Fickett was impressed by a physician's judgment that Benét, for years a sufferer from arthritis, died from the more immediate cause of overwork. The war, the American dream, human and international solidarity after the war, these shook his bones and writhed in his heart.

His body twisted so that he shambled rather than walked, Stevie Benét preferred to call his malady by the old-fashioned name "rheumatism" instead of the more stylish and modern word "arthritis." When I saw him in Fickett's office last December discussing a Christmas play, there was a sweet pathos in the wry smile of his mouth when he spoke of how the doctors would be able to fix him up all right "when they find out the cause." Three or four times he smiled in pleasant irony about how his rheumatism would be gone "when they find out the cause."

Norman Corwin mentions Benét as a fighting propagandist: "More than once in the past three years when an anti-Axis free-American program piece was wanted and we asked Steve Benét to help, he threw in, asking no pay."

Like Archibald MacLeish, Muriel Rukeyser, Alfred Kreymborg, Edna Millay, Struthers Burt, Gene Fowler, Ben Hecht, and other American poets, Benét threw in with what he had. Sometimes it was good and again not so good. But because of the time element, because if you get there with too little and too late you lose the war and eat dust and ashes, Benét and those of like viewpoint let their writing for the moment go forth for the moment, hoping a little good might come of it, and keenly aware it will not do to wait, revise, wait longer, revise yet more.

There is a sheer loveliness of timing in that Chinese proverb "The dawn does not come twice to wake a man." Of course, it now happens to be the case that two or three major American poets believe the foregoing to be more or less tommyrot and fuddyduddy. They have held themselves and they go on holding themselves in foxholes of safety and silence. They have the safety that goes with taking no risk of utterance that later might not look so good. They keep the silence that has the ease of saying nothing about how to handle the world hurricane while it rages.

They fold deep in their bosoms the secrets of why they prefer the record should stand that in this hour they took advantage of the ancient Anglo-Saxon legal custom permitting a witness to say "I stands mute." In a time of terrific storm, unprecedented change, humanity at a crossroads amid endless forked lightning, they have in effect answered the questions "How do you look at it? You with your wisdom and valued contemplations, you with knowledge and time to think things over, what can you tell us? What of guess, surmise, or hazardous and trembling thought can you offer us beyond those awful undetermined horizons?"

Their silence for the hour constitutes their reply for the hour, the cryptic often heard from the politician in a pinch, "No comment."

Once among American major poets Ezra Pound rated. Now he's out. Now the magazine *Poetry*, which first published him, names him renegade, betrayer, and Fascist outcast forever and after that for a thousand years, his old editorial associate, Eunice Tietjens, telling him to hunt sackcloth and ashes, to get a shave and go soak his feet in salt sea brine.

"Ezra Pound: Lord Ga-Ga" runs the title of an article by William Carlos Williams in the magazine *Decision*. "Once you have respected, admired, and loved a man," writes Williams, "there will always remain in you a residuum of affection, even when through the deprivations of age and other defects of the intellect he finally goes ga-ga. It is proper that you should continue to admire him for his positive achievements. But after all you cannot for that go on swallowing his imbecilities into infinity. If you care for him, you should show them up."

He sketches Pound as once alive, then dying though still ambulant and vocal, failing to find what he wanted of culture and recognition first in America, then in England, and when the French gave him the brush-off he tied up with Italy and Mussolini. "He reached Italy and his apotheosis at the hands of a bigger fool than he."

Whether the Department of Justice will indict Pound for treason depends on a legal viewpoint under consideration as to whether his broadcasts from Italy to America have the element of overt acts that incite to violence. Certainly the military performance of his former fellow citizens in North Africa now has him guessing as to where he will move unless he decides he will take his chances as a prisoner.

Jefferson's surest memorial

April 25, 1943

For those who, like the present writer, are neither lighted with enthusiasm nor dusty with disappointment over the Thomas Jefferson Memorial just dedicated in Washington, D.C., there is sweet consolation and enduring satisfaction nevertheless. For the fame of this man can last beyond either mediocre monuments or mistaken judgments. The books holding his speeches, writings, and state papers—there they stand. Cold facts, specific data, speculations and hopes around democracy, the people, the American dream, the Bill of Rights—often he says it with music, in a cadence of words that quietly sing.

Under the red hair of his head and in his right wrist that could manage a violin bow with skill ran melody and passion. In any high and wide definition of poetry Jefferson rates as a bard whose written lines have taken possession of his countrymen. His companions, the men who knew him close-up early in the American Revolution, they must have seen something far out of the ordinary in him. Otherwise they wouldn't have given him the assignment to write a document that would answer for their own people and the peoples of the world the question "What are we fighting for?" The members of the Continental Congress saw that when in the course of human events it becomes necessary for a people to tell why they are fighting a war, it is an advantage to find a writer who can say "We hold these truths to be self-evident," and then get down to cases, as did Jefferson in the Declaration of Independence.

So wide-ranging is Jefferson that good men of both political parties claim him and cite chapter and verse. When after two terms as President he left the White House, for the time discredited and lacking as good a name as he once had, he met his Virginia farmer neighbors and asked them what wrong he had done, and "Whose ox have I gored?"

Time passed, and his name shone again and once more his words were kept, cherished, studied. In the one field, for example, of free speech and a free press, perhaps no other American, whether in the realms of politics, journalism, law, or philosophy, has equaled him in statement and analysis pointed up so sure and basic that it holds good for one crisis after another, including the one that now roars with endless discussion.

Not yet has come a first-rate, long-range biography of this man. Such a book is much wanted, truly needed. Young people especially should have at hand the story of his life for what they can learn from it. The younger Abraham Lincoln studied his Jefferson, and in later years spoke his thanks for what the always smoldering Virginian had given him. For those now lacking time to read the thousands of pages of collected Jefferson writings there is available a Jefferson cyclopedia where his thoughts are indexed as to farming, fertilizer, politics, newspapers, vegetables, and liberty.

In the speeches and writings of Lincoln there are direct tributes to Jefferson, the man and his ideas. Also there are spots in Lincoln utterance, as in the Gettysburg Speech, where he quotes Jefferson— "All men are created equal"—without naming the author. A free-ranging commentary on where Lincoln got his style as a writer would bring in Jefferson with quotations from Lincoln that could be set alongside of Jefferson sentences so nearly parallel that we feel sure of the elder Virginian's influence. Some parts of Jefferson's thought Lincoln absorbed so completely that they became part of him and he didn't care whether his listeners found Jefferson or Lincoln in what he was saying. Twice in political addresses Lincoln paraphrased Jefferson, as Jefferson in turn had found the main thought in Voltaire, who probably took it from some one of the ancients. Jefferson wrote it in a letter to Roger C. Weightman, June 24, 1826. It reads:

"The general spread of the light of science has already laid open to every view the palpable truth, that the mass of mankind has not been born with saddles on their backs, nor a favored few, booted and spurred, ready to ride them legitimately, by the grace of God. There are grounds of hope for others. For ourselves, let the annual return of this day [July 4] forever refresh our recollection of these rights, and an undiminished devotion to them."

Earth-shaking events to come

May 2, 1943

Earth-shaking events are to come. We say that now in early May of 1943 as though we have not already seen the earth shaken for several years by an international revolution of global range taking us toward horizons too smoky and shifting to read.

What we expect now for a year and two years or more is action that will begin to make more sense out of the vast conflict. We are somewhere in the middle of the war, months past what Churchill termed "the end of the beginning." How long the middle of the war will be, at about what time we may reach the beginning of the end, this no one can forecast. For the first time in history immense labor battalions have worked to make the continent of Europe one consolidated colossal fortress. And it is getting almost too simple to say that the war ends when a break-through into that fortress is followed by the capture of it.

Yet every American truly alive finds his mind occupied at times with the question of what the actions to come this summer will do to the mind and feeling of the American people. We have poured out money and thrown in toil and sweat resulting in materials and armament. Yet our blood and tears are still to be given. In the sense that our allies Britain, Russia, and China have borne devastation and agony, our heavy effort and sacrifice is yet to come.

When the next of kin in the United States of America will have been notified of a half-million casualties on the various fronts, some things now taken easy in our stride will be taken differently. If and when such casualties reach or pass one million, many things now done and said will be no longer done and said.

Nothing we can part with, nothing we can say good-by to as though in silence dropping fresh red rose leaves into a salt sea wash, nothing of material and practical contribution, is to be mentioned for comparison with the pouring out of the blood of our picked and chosen youth on altars dedicated to national existence and the rainbow hopes of the Four Freedoms.

Death carries majesty. The dust of vanished youth can be sacred. The phantom of a good fighting man can come back asking "How goes the flag I fought for? Has any man's dream of a better world been helped?"

Meantime while the earth rocks in new combat zones over other continents, sudden realities emerge and deepen motives already operating in our hearts and blood. The Japanese authorities do not yet know what resolves they steeled and what purposes they laid open and lashed by their announcement they had tried and executed death sentence on American flyers.

The millions of American workers who are to see that extraordinary screen story and document *Desert Victory* will be drawn nearer in feeling to the battle fronts and will realize more deeply how and why the munitions, armament, airplane, and shipbuilding plants are a living and vital part of every battle. The Eighth Army of Britain under General Montgomery, by performance already rated one of the greatest armies in history, is become a tradition so bright and gleaming that many now take pride in being joined in effort alongside its desert-dusty banners and bagpipes.

New streaks may show in men. Frank Sullivan, the laugh-maker, the comic, drops the clowning in his latest piece. He takes a two-sentence poem from Willa Cather's novel *O Pioneers.* It reads:

"The heart, when it is too much alive, aches for that brown earth, and ecstasy has no fear of death. It is the old and the poor and the maimed who shrink from the brown hole; its wooers are found among the young, the passionate, the gallant-hearted."

Fighting and home fronts

May 9, 1943

We have heard of the two gentlemen, a long time ago, who fought themselves out of their own overcoats into each other's.

They were so wrapped up in their own mental preoccupations and the peculiar pleasure of being furious at the other fellow that they didn't know what they were doing.

The time to get excited is after the fighting. So we are reminded by a flyer from Guadalcanal who brought down more than a score of enemy planes.

In a dogfight when split seconds count it is something like suicide to get excited.

Timing—precision—cool gunnery work—smooth and swift headwork outguessing the enemy—they go back to practice and instinct.

The soldier who does good work in marching, shooting, handling himself in emergencies as though he had met like emergencies before, he is what we call a born natural, having an instinct for what he is doing.

The soldier who gets to be fast and tough from many workouts, from going through the same movements over and over, his practice after a while becomes instinct.

And whether they get it by natural inheritance and without trying or whether it is by hard work and prayer and deep desire, the good soldier who is really good learns that in combat it pays not to get excited till the action is over.

This is the instruction we hear now from veterans of scores of fast-whirling sky combats.

The quick thinking of the cool head gives a nice pay-off. "It was him or me—and I got him" we have heard and understood. Also "I lost my head and did the wrong thing."

And all of the above and foregoing is not for a flickering instant intended as advice or teaching meant for any men of the armed services. It is presented merely to show what a contrast exists between the combat lads on the fighting fronts and certain varieties of civilians on the home front.

What would we find if we read the files of the *United Mine Workers' Journal,* official organ of the labor union headed by John L. Lewis, during the past three years? Mainly personal anger, denunciation, spleen, malice, misrepresentation, arrogant misuse of the rights of free speech and a free press, very little of the cool straight shooter.

Vast and fixed is the ego of John L. Lewis. It is safe to predict that no matter what the outcome of the present melancholy chaos, and no matter how events show him to have been moved chiefly by personal wrath and a thirst for vengeance that began when he was denied his hope of being nominated for Vice-President, he will never be heard saying "I lost my head and did the wrong thing."

His ego was operating somewhat more than twenty-two years ago when still new in his seat as president of the United Mine Workers of America. He then sought for himself the office of president of the American Federation of Labor.

Samuel Gompers, then president of the A. F. of L., had been kind enough when Lewis had lost place as a U. M. W. organizer, to appoint Lewis an A. F. of L. organizer. Yet Lewis wanted to unseat Gompers. He came to William D. Mahon, head of the Street Railway Men's Union, telling Mahon he had enough delegates at the A. F. of L. convention to elect him president. Mahon told Lewis he might not have enough delegates, the balloting would show, but anyhow he, Mahon, would not string along with Lewis in a fight to throw out Gompers and put Lewis in. In the balloting Lewis lost—and made a record with Bill Mahon and others for ingratitude, treachery, ambition, thirst for place and power, ego almost beyond belief.

Now, as to Lewis, we'll see what we'll see. Those who think the present chaos could have been headed off by proper decisions and actions at an earlier stage of the situation will find themselves on no safer ground than either Horace Mann, the great educator, or Samuel May, the distinguished and belligerent abolitionist. Mann snorted to May, "I hate your doctrine that we should think only of the right and not the expedient," May rejoining, "And I hate your doctrine that we should think of the expedient and not only of the right."

The miners are a heroic folk. In the world-wide labor movements of the past century their record in the causes of human freedom and democracy is pretty good to look at. As a people often mercilessly exploited and degraded in an industry usually sick with its confusions of monopoly and competition, they have more often represented civilization and decency than some of the mine owners who have believed themselves in no sense whatever responsible for some of the ugliest and most God-forsaken towns in the United States.

Lewis has not helped the miners to learn, by practice, the meanings and processes of democracy. They have let him pay himself well for getting them better pay by methods that will look worse as time passes.

Past and present odd numbers

May 16, 1943

Two biographies of Billy Mitchell are before us now. And as we go through them we can see that his case for air power is now well proven. He foresaw what was to happen, from the Aleutians to Tunisia. If he could come back alive for a few minutes to look at what is now happening and to realize that some of the best of it stems from the headstrong agitation he carried on, he might wish to soften the remark he made seven years ago on his deathbed to Colonel Homer Berry, a good flyer with whom he had common memories: "Homer, the American people will regret the day I was crucified by politics and bureaucracy."

If there is a Valhalla, then from some window or outlook there early this May of 1943 Billy Mitchell's face must have lighted to see 300 new-made American fighter planes together in a flight across the Atlantic, losing only one plane crew, in the greatest mass flight of aircraft thus to cross an ocean. And earlier he would have felt that perhaps his contribution was slight but definite when United States Army planes alone wiped out a Japanese fleet of 22 ships, leaving reporters mentally mixed on whether it could correctly be termed a naval battle.

"Has the army got the guts to kick him out?" queried the columnist Frank Kent, while the verdict of the court-martial board was awaited, Kent fearing that Colonel Mitchell "had created a condition that makes his dismissal inexpedient and which will compel a compromise verdict," Kent then as now favoring the past and hoping the future would be the same, flying like the auk which flies backward so as to see where it's been.

266

Mitchell's court-martial legal counsel, Congressman Frank Reid, after the conviction and sentence, remarked: "Colonel Mitchell is a 1925 John Brown. They may think they have silenced him, but his ideas will go marching on, and those who crucified him will be the first to put his aviation suggestions into use."

Of course, the verb "crucified" here doesn't make the required picture, because Mitchell lived on for eleven years, went everywhere in America and Europe, got his message across to the country, had the sane and simple Will Rogers with him, made a name as a bitter and crying crusader, though his smiling lips and beaming warm eyes were those of no croaker nor sourpuss. He talked because he could not keep his mouth shut about needless death and tragic unreadiness to come, saying time would tell, as it did.

And now what? Out of the present turmoil what names of what men are to stand out ten years from now for the warnings, forecasts, they speak now?

Quite likely this fellow Eric A. Johnston, the Seattle businessman, now elected to a second term as president of the Chamber of Commerce of the United States, will in time be shown as not just another odd number. Did he stand on the White House steps one day last summer and actually permit himself to be photographed alongside of those two eminent heathens, William Green and Philip Murray, heads of the AFL and the CIO? He did. And did several members of the Chamber, who have paid a lot of good money in backing the Chamber, write in that they were through and couldn't go along with Johnston's "truckling" to organized labor? They did. Later, however, they came back. But their fingers are crossed.

"We must all work together," says Johnston. "We are bound to have our differences over the right ways of reaching our goals, but we must learn to settle these differences by sitting down together. They can't be settled by name-calling in the press or over the radio."

Now, before the war ends, Johnston warns, is the time for anxiety about and plans against the dangers of unemployment after the war. His voice goes high on this. He sees that what business or the capitalist system neglects to do in the field of jobs for men who want jobs will be handled, at whatever cost, by government.

In decisive tones he tells business America: "Only the willfully blind can fail to see that the old-style capitalism of a primitive, free-shooting period is gone forever. The capitalism which thrived on

267

low wages and maximum profits for minimum turnover, which rejected collective bargaining and fought against justified public regulation of the competitive system, is a thing of the past."

He sees changes coming that can't be stopped, whatever these or those men might wish. He rates capitalism as "a dynamic, evolving structure." Unity of purpose, he holds, can give us "such a degree of well-being as few have dreamed of. The sky is the limit if we will but work together and think daringly."

This new voice of American business deserves complete hearing. He meets the requirements of President James B. Conant of Harvard, who wants to see new-style "radicals" in America. What Johnston is telling business America, financial and industrial America, is as radical as what Billy Mitchell told the army and the navy about air power. To go back to prewar capitalism is to be sunk. A new approach is demanded. Johnston is worth listening to. He has broken from the past.

"Don't solidify it"

May 23, 1943

Once I wrote a piece that purported to give the classic prayer of the editorial writer: "O Lord, give me this day my daily opinion and forgive me the one I had yesterday."

And this got a rise out of the pink feathers of a Florida flamingo fastened to a desk in a cockeyed cubicle where he wrote and had it published that as to the above it is "a false statement."

Very well, then. As to him it ain't correct. And we are sure the good Lord forgives him for thinking the same today as he did yesterday. And if he has moss in his ears and wears barnacles instead of binoculars and spits in the wind finding it comes back in his face, this too must not be denied him.

A truly first-rate and provocative editorial writer like Elmer Peterson out in Oklahoma City likes to wake up in the morning and find his mind a perfect blank so he can murmur: "Wonderful! I don't know a thing! So today I shall ask questions and be Socratic and write on a clean new page what I find out. And if I end with merely asking questions and not answering them that will be all right. Socrates did it. And Henrik Ibsen (than whom which playwright is greater?) once said his dramas mainly were intended to ask momentous questions."

That is my guess about Peterson, because I read a magazine article he wrote that made me change my mind a little. Not much but a little, enough so that I know he walks around Oklahoma City or pails a cow at his farm in the Ozarks occasionally mumbling, "O Lord, give me this day my daily opinion and forgive me the one I had yesterday."

This particular hour of dazzling destinies and crazy crossroads is no time to be petrified and proud of it. You can be petrified, if you want to, and you can rate it a privilege to be petrified, but there is no need to mention it and emphasize it as though you had been born in that Arizona forest of stone where the petrified birds sit in their petrified nests and hatch their petrified young.

I know a columnist who sometimes writes as solemn as the Swedish Lutheran catechism. Then again he writes as fishy-eyed as Artemus Ward and Petroleum Vesuvius Nasby. He has these reciprocals of gravity and nonsense. And only those readers who have the same kind of reciprocals clip his column and carry it around and read it to others who say they prefer Ernie Pyle with his wonderful candor confessing that many another like himself has sat on a rock in North Africa, his chin in a cupped hand, saying "Why the hell am I here anyway?"

I go to the Cosmos Club in Washington and eat with Billy Leiserson of the National Mediation Board. He is the best pancake-turner that ever performed for the street audiences who watched him as he shifted the pancakes from one side to another in the window of a Childs restaurant in Madison, Wisconsin, when he was working his way through the University of Wisconsin.

And he tells me about an airlines president who was making a contract with a labor union and would welcome suggestions and help of any kind. The airlines executive was ready to agree with most anything just so it would not be frozen or petrified. His word was "solidify." In asking Leiserson to work on a tentative draft of an agreement his caution was "Whatever you do, don't solidify it!"

The main result was an arrangement by which two representatives from labor and two from management hold conferences on any grievances that arise. What solidifying they have done so far isn't much and has worked out.

"Cheesecake" is a photographer's slang for the stereotypes of hokum. There are cheesecake photographers with the cheesecake mind, and what they bring in is in a pattern out of yesterday's petrified molds.

There are solidified minds who don't know that there has always been economic chaos and human misery in the coal industry of this country. Strife and sullen strength have always been there, open or repressed. So tortuous and dark is the human past of this industry that the involvements and entanglements now are such that no course of procedure can spell out justice and equity for all concerned. For its bearing on this and future hours when the present fine Pennsylvania anthracite screenings or rough Harlan County, Kentucky, bituminous are cinders and clinkers, this thumbnail commentary is offered again:

"As a people often mercilessly exploited and degraded in an industry usually sick with its confusions of monopoly and competition, they, the miners, have more often represented civilization and decency than some of the mine owners who have believed themselves in no sense whatever responsible for some of the ugliest and most God-forsaken towns in the United States."

George Washington wishes for global peace

May 30, 1943

The blessed and definitely remembered American hero, George Washington, was nobody's fool, neither was he a stuffed shirt nor a Christian gentleman who went to church regularly merely to set a good example. It does not lessen his dignity nor his worth to remark that while he was beautifully human, he knew his onions and could tell a hawk from a handsaw. We come to these observations out of reading the original manuscripts of two letters written by General Washington. With a feathered quill pen he traced across the honest and rugged ragpaper words for this hour a little more important than the general run of what comes off the hit-and-run typewriters of today.

My friend Oliver R. Barrett of Chicago had dug the manuscripts out of his wide ranging and priceless collection. We agreed that Washington is worth reading—now. He saw the earth as a globe

270

with the human family on it. And he saw the global life of man was to be hard and hazardous though like many of us today he had his wishes and prayers for global peace. This he saw possible whenever men should truly try to shape it with will and vision.

At Mount Vernon on September 5, 1785, General Washington's goose-quill pen wrote these lines to be sent to his friend in France, the Marquis de Chastellux:

"Dear Sir: My first wish is to see the blessings of peace diffused through all the countries, and among all ranks in every country, and that we should consider ourselves as the children of a common parent, and be disposed to acts of brotherly kindness toward one another. In that case, all restrictions of trade would vanish; we should take your wines, your fruits, and surplusage of other articles, and give you, in return, our oils, our fish, tobacco, naval stores, etc.; and, in like manner, we should exchange produce with other countries, to our reciprocal advantage. The globe is large enough. Why, then, need we wrangle for a small spot of it? If one country cannot contain us, another should open its arms to us. But these halcyon days, if they ever did exist, are now no more. A wise Providence, I presume, has ordered it otherwise, and we must go on in the old way, disputing, and now and then fighting, until the globe itself is dissolved."

This should go into the *Congressional Record*, also into the standard school readers immediately following the Farewell Message which is read aloud in the halls of Congress each anniversary of Washington's birthday. Alongside the above letter should go one that Washington wrote on the same day to "his Excellency Chevalier de la Luzerne." It reads:

"From the last European accounts we have reason to hope that the clouds which seemed to be gathering in your hemisphere will yield to a tranquil sky, and peace, with all its blessings will spread its mantle over the threatened lands. My first wish is to see the sons and daughters of the world mixing as one family, enjoying the sweets of social intercourse and reciprocal advantages. The earth certainly is sufficient to contain us all, and affords everything necessary to our wants, if we would be friendly and endeavor to accommodate one another. Why, then, should we wrangle, and why should we attempt to infringe the rights and properties of our neighbors? But, lest you should suppose that I am about to turn preacher, I will only add that, with the highest esteem and consideration, I have the honor to be, etc."

Thinking in global terms is no new thing for a President of the United States. Abraham Lincoln capitalized his phrase "the Family of Man."

Mei-ling Soong Chiang, in giving the gist of her own philosophy in the two words "co-operation—and humility," was also summarizing Washington and Lincoln.

Force only isn't worth so much. Force with control is what counts.

As between speed only and speed with control, who wouldn't take speed with control?

Immeasurable self-restraint

June 6, 1943

Benes speaking in this country in 1943 is deeply moving. Four years ago, too, his words threw long shadows.

And how so? And is this some kind of double talk? And why not get down to cases?

All right, feller, and here are cases. Four years ago this little man spoke as the voice of the little people of the world and he is still so speaking. Then President Eduard Benes had stepped out of his place and position as head of the Czechoslovak Republic, a worthy and pretty well run country in this world of many imperfect governments.

He had seen his country and people broken, ravished, bled, the prison camp and firing squad handling much of the brightest youth and the best leaders. And when Benes in Britain and the United States of America spoke of what had happened the words came like those of a man who had tasted deep of the bitterest drink imaginable without his face telling it.

He wasn't blaming anybody. He could have named names and pointed a dramatic finger of accusation. He let it go with quiet intimations that in the storm to come the whole earth would rock and many a big name be rubbed out and many a magnate of fixed importance be flattened under Nazi-shod feet.

272

After four years comes Benes to us again. And again the little man of great hope for the little people. "Immeasurable self-restraint," says he, was needed in the darkness of four years ago—and is now needed in the faint daybreak lights of this hour. Plain t is that he wishes to see in the approaching political and administrative chaos in Europe and elsewhere plenty of "immeasurable elf-restraint."

A powerful France must be reconstituted. Europe needs a strong France. This Benes urges. Close co-operation with Britain will come from his own government, as an exile "sheltered" in London.

And understanding and collaboration with Soviet Russia? This s among first things necessary, even vital. At Versailles it was "a cardinal mistake to imagine that we could devise a permanent peace settlement in Paris when no Russian representatives were invited to the conference table."

Why does the little man Benes sweep some of us along with him, so we have been studying his every word lately? Partly because he and his people made a record fairly good to look at in their measures of political freedom and economic democracy. And because where a large and powerful nation may believe it can get permanent peace by superior strength and sheer armed might, the small nation is more likely to do its thinking around the question of what conditions of fair play, equity, square dealing, might make for permanent peace.

At times our talk gets weird as to how we should put together again the Europe not yet anywhere near finished in its process of falling to pieces.

You meet a sign occasionally in Manhattan that reads "Damages rewoven invisibly." They will take a garment torn or worn and repair, reweave it, so the stitches don't show.

In our new world fabric after the war no one expects to see the damages of the war rewoven invisibly by warriors, statesmen, politicians. But among the men who seem to understand what kind of retailoring is required stands Eduard Benes, he and his immeasurable self-restraint.

Who does a zoot suit suit?

June 20, 194.

Zooter: one who zoots or one whose suit zoots him or whose zoo suits him.

Of course it's comic. And more yet, it's tragic. Like a gargoyle it is. And a gargoyle ain't a new baloney nor a new twist on glo baloney.

One kind of gargoyle is where a sculptor chisels a face. And by looking twice at that face you can tell it says deep under "I don' belong." Either that or "You and who else?" Or maybe "Don't ask me where do we go from here—there ain't any place to go to—no even home."

When Shakespeare put into the mouth of Jack Cade that line, "The first thing we do let's kill all the lawyers," he was shaping an old-time zooter from Zootersville.

When a zooter goes intellectual and writes a book or publishes a newspaper, what comes, what gives? Nothing. Either that or Nothing plus nothing equals nothing. Or, when you believe in something you have to believe it will work and the chances are it won't work, so play safe and believe in nothing.

Or do we have a zooter set, a zooter cult, among the intellectuals, of persons special and satisfied, smug, aloof from the seething, whirling life of the great dark masses of people in the streets, shops, homes, on the farms and ranches, in the harbors and on the seas?

Of course, part of the strong-arm stuff in handling zooters lately is plain old-fashioned gang fighting among boys who don't like each other's looks. Some of it is race riot and lynch-law stuff. Part of it is the scorn of the armed services for boogie-woogie bugs who wear hepcat clothes with a hip drape. As a sign and passing phenomenon it may fade into the mist of yesteryear like hobble skirt, the Tom Thumb golf course, tiddledywinks, yo-yo, or mah-jong.

Of course, the hot-trumpet hero is not to blame. Of course, the flashing, lashing, hot-lips orchestra leader whose trumpet is mean, terrific, blazing with moans of boogie-woogie blood—he, of course, has not added to the bewilderment of any modern fevered American youth asking "What does it all add up to?" Of course, the more hot-lip music we hear, the better we know the answer to

'Where do we go from here?" Of course, Benny Goodman has it
all over Bach. And Harry James says to the shadow of Tchaikovsky
what the rug said to the floor, "I've got you covered," or what the
mayonnaise said to the icebox, "Excuse me, I'm dressing."

The Chicago Times Syndicate—A personal note

The publisher of the *Chicago Times,* S. E. Thomason, and its
editor, Richard J. Finnegan, have seen the foregoing newspaper
columns running once a week from early April, 1941, to mid-June,
1943. They did not know as they printed these pieces from week
to week that they were giving their public—and the clients of the
Chicago Times Syndicate—productions which have a value as permanent literature or historical record. Nor does anybody else know
any such thing with regard to permanent literature or historical
record. Mr. Thomason and Mr. Finnegan do know well, however,
that they came to the present writer saying he had no right to keep
silence during a time of world chaos and storm.

Thereupon they heard from the present writer that he believed
he had a clear and perfect right to keep silence if he so chose—but
he didn't so choose. It did not then follow that a watchtower arose
shedding light over the national scene, bringing order out of confusion. The result rather was a Portrait of a Man in a Fog, at times,
or again the piece of writing offered represented the best lucid
memorandum occurring to the writer for that particular week-end
moment of time.

Much is overwritten. Much would have been better done had
there been no deadline to meet. Much would have had meritorious
brevity and bright gleam had it been put off into some vague period
of an afterwhile when again the same questions would arise: "Why
take a chance? What's the use?"

POEMS: LEGENDS: FOLKLORE

Blue sky over Scotland[1]

(On the news of the landing of Hess in Scotland I picked up a guitar and found myself singing a song which seemed to have the title "Blue Sky over Scotland." The verses go improvisato. Readers are free to swing these or to just talk easy. And there is no statute which provides that they may not shift into the classic.—C. S.)

Down out of duh sky over Scotland who come a tumblin, who come
    a tumblin?
Blue was duh sky over Scotland, high over, blue over, deep blue,
    over Scotland,
Sweet blue, duh sky, when lo and behold, who come a tumblin,
    a tumblin?

Down he come in a parachute, like a big white umbrella open and
    wide holdin him,
Down in a parachute, fallin, fallin, out of the sweet blue sky spread
    out,
Down he come like a good new messenger, like a world series, like
    a wonder.

Out of duh sky he fall like he got business, like he got words to
    tell 'em,
Like he know where he come from in duh mornin, where he going
    in duh evenin,
Like he got answers in his heart, like he got answers on his tongue.

Easy on down she come like a feather, like a flicker, easy on down
    she come,
Like somebody slipped on uh ladder to heaven en Gawd seen him
    slippin on down—

1 The *Nation*, July 12, 1941.

En Gawd says, "Ahm going to let you down easy—keep your shoes shined."

Duh parachute zig and duh parachute zag and Death come a-creepin around,
Old man Death figgerin maybe he goin to pick him up a few bones, white bones.
Like a crow get fooled, like a buzzard get fooled, old man Death got fooled.

Farmerman seen him fallin, farmerman pick up feet and run and run,
Farmerman find him on duh ground feelin where he busted uh ankle, just uh ankle,
Duh wind was nice to him, duh weather was right, duh blue sky nice, so nice.

He might uh busted his neck fallin dat long fall out uh duh big sky high over.
He might uh busted his kneebone, legbone, armbone, thighbone, shoulderbone, headbone.
Farmerman find him layin easy, laughin a little—only a busted anklebone.

Out of duh big blue sky over Scotland, lo and behold he come a tumblin down.
Where from, dey asks him, where from who and why and how—and who? who is you?
Identification tag tells 'em who—bright gold identification tag tells 'em.

Hess is de name, Rudolf Hess, Mistah Rudolf Hess of Berlin is de name.
He tells 'em, papers in de pockets tells 'em, identification tag tells 'em.
Maybe you done heerd about me, his eyes sayin, maybe you done heerd.

Dey gets a nice cyah, cushions and all, and dey handles him easy, soft like.

Ain't his name Hess? Ain't he nice to come down from duh blue sky over Scotland?

We gonna take care of you, Mistah Hess, we gonna be good to you.

In duh hospital dey gives him a room by hisself so he can lay and think and study.

Does he want ham and eggs he gets sugar-cured ham and fresh-laid eggs, one side or over.

Does he like chicken and gravy, coffee with cream and sugar, dey lays it out for him.

All by hisself, in a corner by hisself, in a room dey know where he is dey keeps him.

And dey talks to him easy, dey comes and dey goes talking to Mistah Rudolf Hess.

And nobody know what Mistah Hess sayin, talkin, tellin, outside nobody know.

Many people glad, so glad, Mistah Hess done decide come away fum Mistah Hitlah.

Like old friends dey was, like bosom companions dey was, like David and Jonathan.

Sayin one about duh othuh, "He can have duh shirt off my back."

Now it ain't like it used to be all duh while twixt Mistah Hess and Mistah Hitlah.

It don't look so good like it was in duh good old times dat used to be.

Evvybody asking, "What foh? who dat? how come? why dat gold identification tag?"

People lookin up at duh blue sky over Scotland now, wonderin, studyin, askin,

"Who gonna come, come a tumblin out uh duh sky next? who next, what man come next?

Mistah Hess, what he sayin, what he talkin, tellin, talkin, talkin, talkin?"

Night over Europe[1]

There is night over Europe.
The sun goes down and the stars come out
    and it is night—one kind of night—
    the old eternal night.
Frameworks of fixed planets, familiar forms
    of moving constellations—they come out
    after sundown—saying sweet night—saying
    good-night.
Or the disc of a full gold moon comes up over
    Europe, a young moon giving lights and music
    to singers and lovers.
Or a baby crescent moon sails with its slow silver
    curve of promise to the young, assurance to the
    old.
This is the night that was over Europe, with a North
    Star never failing, with co-ordinations telling men
    to fight and hope.
Now this night comes with smoke and shame, with fire
    and tears between men and stars, between singers
    and the moon, between those hunting the North Star
    and hoping to find it again.
Night and the rats sing, the rats live fat, the rats
    tell the stars nothing wrong, nobody home, every-
    thing looks pretty.
And yet—once in a while—here and there—a rat weeps—
    a rat sits alone in ashes and looks up at stars and
    the moon rolling in smoke—over and over the rat
    cries: "Yes, maybe there is something to laugh at—
    for me it's crying time—and I'll be crying here
    tomorrow and the day after. If you meet anybody

1 The *Nation*, November 22, 1941.

that used to know me, tell 'em you saw me here crying and tomorrow it will be the same. I will be alone here in my own peculiar and personal ashes— crying till the stars and the moon come clean again."

Is there any easy road to freedom? [1]

A relentless man loved France
Long before she came to shame
And the eating of bitter dust,
Loving her as mother and torch,
As bone of his kith and kin
And he spoke passion, warning:
"Rest is not a word of free peoples—
  rest is a monarchical word."

A relentless Russian loved Russia
Long before she came to bare agony
And valor amid rivers of blood,
Loving her as mother and torch,
As bone of his kith and kin:
He remembered an old Swedish saying:
"The fireborn are at home in fire."

A Kentucky-born Illinoisan found himself
By journey through shadows and prayer
The Chief Magistrate of the American people
Pleading in words close to low whispers:
"Fellow citizens . . . we cannot escape history.
  The fiery trial through which we pass
  Will light us down in honor or dishonor
  To the latest generation . . .
  We shall nobly save or meanly lose
      the last best hope of earth."
Four little words came worth studying over:
  "We must disenthrall ourselves."
And what is a thrall? And who are thralls?

[1] The *Free World*, December, 1941.

Men tied down or men doped, or men drowsy?
    He hoped to see them
    shake themselves loose
    and so be disenthralled.

There are freedom shouters.
There are freedom whisperers.
Both may serve.
Have I, have you, been too silent?
Is there an easy crime of silence?
Is there any easy road to freedom?

Freedom is a habit [1]

Freedom is a habit
and a coat worn
some born to wear it
some never to know it.
Freedom is cheap
or again as a garment
is so costly
men pay their lives
rather than not have it.
Freedom is baffling:
men having it often
know not they have it
till it is gone and
they no longer have it.
What does this mean?
Is it a riddle?
Yes, it is first of all
in the primers of riddles.
To be free is so-so:
you can and you can't:
walkers can have freedom
only by never walking
away their freedom:
runners too have freedom
unless they overrun:
eaters have often outeaten
their freedom to eat
and drinkers overdrank
their fine drinking freedom.

[1] The Chicago Times Syndicate, June 13, 1943.

American knowhow

These lines were written as a commentary (in some places spoken between long pauses) for a one-reel film *Bomber,* produced by the Film Unit of the Office of Emergency Management in 1941. The motion picture showed the making of the B-26, army multimotored medium bombing plane, in the plant of the Glenn L. Martin Company in Baltimore. The British have named the B-26 the Marauder, and the Americans nicknamed it Murder, Inc.

I. BOMBERS

One American factory—one of many—
One bomber—thousands on the way.
An angel of death—
Death to those who mock at free peoples,
Death to those who tell the world they are out to wreck the American democratic system.
Hundreds here—thousands—tens of thousands on the way.

II. TEST FLIGHT

Every part tested—every piece of metal tested—
Every bolt, rivet, and welded seam—tested under the pressure of combat conditions.

Off the ground now—for the first time as a complete fighting unit.

Power—power to travel far, dump her bombs and return.
Power to say, "I can outfly and outfight any pursuit ship now fighting over Europe. I am the strength of the people of the free world!"

III. MEN, MACHINES, AND MATERIALS

Here you get her insides—aluminum alloy—light and strong—
Steel, copper, brass—a dozen other metals
Put together like a fine watch.

Wings made strong to hold her high in the air while she delivers—
Each wing built to take all the pounding a superpowered motor can give it.

Here is the fire bath, where the bomber begins to grow.
Born in fire to fight fire with fire.

She is going to have the guts, wind, stamina, to fight and deliver
death—a bellyful of it—to those who are asking for it.
Made of metals tempered and strong—
Woven together—strong—
American mass production, American knowhow . . .
Hands with knowhow . . . minds with American knowhow . . .
These workers—these riveters, welders, drillers—
All these craftsmen have pride, a genuine pride in their share—their
participation in the titanic job we call "National Defense Production."

IV. ASSEMBLY

Parts—more than twenty-five thousand for each ship.
Parts stacked up, waiting to be assembled and woven into a living
destroyer traveling the sky.
We are taking these parts—weaving them into a thing that breathes
and lives . . .
Breathes with the Spirit of America
That says, "Don't tread on me."

Made to stand heavy toil and struggle—
Made to stand shock and storm and heavy travel.
Ready to flank and outflank the enemy.
Packing enough power to climb over the highest antiaircraft barrage.

Everything under control.
From hundreds of subassemblies—
From scores of major assemblies—
These precision-built sections roll into final Assembly.

Day and night . . . twenty-four hours a day . . . seven days a week . . .
Three hundred and sixty-five days a year . . .
Body, bones, and wings roll and join into the form of a finished breathing bomber.

Bombers . . . thousands in the air now . . .
Tens of thousands on the way.

The motor—raw, naked power—a Niagara of horse power—
John Henry on one wing—Paul Bunyan on the other!

Wires—miles of wires link the nerve centers of the ship.
A giant wing spar protects the cables from enemy gunfire.

She packs guns—so many guns the army won't let us tell about it—
A flying arsenal—she's the toughest, fightin'est ship of her size in air.

Here is America strong-hearted—
Keen—aware—alive.

Massive—honest—this wing seems to say,
"You can count on me!"

V. DAWN FLIGHT

Dawn . . . daylight. Over Europe, over Asia—night, black night.
America flies into the dawn.
Bombers for a new day.

"Humanity with all its fears,
With all the hopes of future years,
Is hanging breathless on thy fate!"

Bronze wood

During several days in San Francisco in the summer of 1940 I lived in a room with a white door. On it hung a mask carved of bronze wood by our friend Leon Gelber in a creative playtime mood.

The face was baffling yet very companionable, inscrutable yet easy to be with, ready to smile with pity and understanding, ready to weep in solemn contemplations, as you chose at any given minute.

The face seemed to say it had forgotten things that ought to be forgotten and it is a gift worth having to so forget.

In the same look the face seemed to be saying important things have been forgotten that shall yet be remembered and used and loved. The face seems very ancient in time, as though born in a continent where mankind had origin and began wandering. Yet the face is alive now and will be alive across all coming generations, wherefore it holds the present and the future and is very modern, and postmodern.

In one of his photographs Henry Flannery renders the face mask of bronze wood and you can almost smooth the features as though your hand touched the actual bronze wood. In another photograph Flannery gives it a wild flowing dream quality.

So it seems that both Flannery and I have been haunted by this apparition that came to Gelber's brain with such impact that he had to release it into hard wood of bronze color. As I lived with this mask an impression would keep repeating itself in my mind. It always ran in an outline something like this:

The sky over and the earth under make a room. We are in this room—for a brief moment. Others were here in this room before us. They connect with our being here. They know we are here. They helped put us here. At rare moments we definitely imagine they moan over us or laugh with us from far corners of the room. They are phantoms now. Yesterday they were another sort of reality, actual men and women, bones wearing flesh and breathing.

The impression moves to a second look. In this comes the understanding that all of us in the room are here for a moment about as long or short as the moment covering the time for yesterday's phantoms. That is, each of us in the room will tomorrow join yesterday's phantoms.

At this point any easy mocker may interpose, "You are merely saying that we all have to die," which is too easy and which neglects the point that man—we here in the room—invented Time as a convenience and a utility. The assumption that you die on a definite calendar date may be canceled in the proposition that birth begins the process of dying and any calendar date is mere punctuation.

So here we are in this room—we who are termed the living—with habits of speech, action, violence and quiet, mainly carried on as we got them from the long line of phantoms who once were the living in this room. So heavy is this burden of the past on the living that a vast multitude usually is resigned to a belief that no basic changes should be wished, envisioned, or attempted in the present. The present for them is the past and the future. "We are what our fathers were. You can't change human nature." Yet restless individual and minorities—also inevitable and irresistible, flaming majorities—do plunge headlong on adventures aimed at change. This goes on in the great room. The record of it is called History.

The impression shifts to its third phase. Beyond the room, in a realm for convenience named The Future waits the multitude that will follow those now here breathing of the sky over and the earth under. Nothing is more mysterious in this great room than the host of unborn children, the babies yet to come and be occupants, living residents having names and faces, carrying on with their faiths and aims, their realities and illusions, in what is termed the generations to come.

San Francisco
July, 1940

Youth and pioneers: an ode

Speech at the rededication of Old Main, Knox College, Galesburg, Illinois, June 15, 1937.

Old and tarnished is the saying "Time is a great teacher." Many here today feel that if Old Main as a living structure could speak for itself it might say: "I am a child of time. I celebrate the dignity, importance, and pathos of time. Time used me with snow and rain, wind and frost, rust and rot, till I was falling away. Unless loving and thoughtful hands had come to help me I would have prepared to vanish and become dust in the wind, a shattered form and a forgotten melody, a house melted into thin shadows. Here to my doors have come the feet, faces, and voices of the young. Here at my windows generations of the young gazed out on the world, gazed in on themselves, some asking questions: 'How and why do we live? And while we live what is worth looking at? what is worth listening to? what might be worth dying for?' Shoes have worn my doorsills, sleeves smoothed and softened my banisters, cries and laughter tumbled along my hallways, human associations making me across the years into a breathing instrument."

Yes, Old Main could tell today of the workings of time, how time keeps secrets, how time translates practices and institutions of one age into programs and establishments yet to be tried under hammers and tested on anvils, how time is a destroyer yet a grower and a healer too, how there is no answer to some questions unless in the ancient saying "Time will tell."

Those Knox pioneers of 1837, the year Abraham Lincoln moved from the village of New Salem to begin law practice in the city of Springfield, how could either they or young Lincoln read the fog, the mist, the faint crosslights of the future? How could they know they were a fated bridge generation? Who could tell them they were moving from a society of farmers and land culture into a Machine Age where the claims of a new system of industry, transportation, finance, and its owners and controllers would bring a changed national picture? The shrewdest foreteller among them, in the somber chaos of nearly twenty years later, in his House Divided speech, was to say, "If we could first know where we are and whither we are tending, we could better judge what to do and how to do it."

In the sciences of chemistry and physics then were pioneers restless as any on the Western prairies, beginning to perform the impossible things that until done they were told couldn't be done. Whether you pressed inward to the American mind or outward on the flow of the huge, diverse American landscape, you found personal ambition and greed mixed with love and sacrifice, interwoven with the tantalizing and indefinable American dream. Was a humanity older than Shakespeare, older than the Bible, trying to

292

arrange a new human scheme for the Old World to look at and be glad over? Many said so. It had wonder and mystery. Many who could not explain it at all were ready to die for it.

Time during this inscrutable drama sent fresh generations of young men and women into the doorways of Old Main, sent its boy students out into the agony of the war of the 1860's, saw the plains and valleys to the Pacific filled with networks of human settlements and rails and wires, saw its boy students step forth into the first great World War, saw the Machine Age blend into the motor and power age, saw a national and world economic collapse bring questions in weight and consequence the parallel of the issues threshed out by Lincoln and Douglas in front of Old Main here before twenty thousand people on a raw, windy October day seventy-five years ago.

Now the pilots of the night air mail look down on lighted cities struggling with systems of human culture perhaps more complex and variable than any the earth has ever seen. And these pilots of the night air mail, are they not pioneers as truly as the pony-express riders of the old days? Because the frontier with the free land is gone, are we to lose the word "pioneer"—hard as the wood of an old ox yoke, homely as a one-room log cabin, fierce as famine, flies, and vermin, tough and stubborn as men and plows breaking unbroken sod, mystic as rainbow lights on horizons not yet reached by man? Engineers and inventors harnessing invisible brute forces to do the heavy and backbreaking work formerly done by man—are they not pioneers?

Shall we say across the next hundred years will be more pioneers making headway favoring human solidarity as against war and strife among nations and men, making headway on the conditions to exist between ownership, management, and labor, winning changes toward better terms on which human beings shall live? Yes, there will be generations taking hold as though loneliness and the genius of struggle have always dwelt in the hearts of pioneers, as though the restless and venturing human spirit shall perform again tomorrow with exploits today declares visionary and impossible.

What the young people want and dream across the next hundred years will shape history more than any other motivation to be named.

Youth now living and youth as yet unborn hold the seeds and secrets of the folds to be unfolded in the shapes to come.

None shall look back on this hour and say we did not have hope and faith.

The mystery of justice between man and man, nation and nation, shall take on new phases.

Dreamers of deep sacred dreams, finders and welders, sons and daughters of burning quests, shall come.

In plain work done with honesty, in actions of courage and endurance lighted with inner humility, lighted sometimes with a fine balance of motives as between freedom and discipline, they shall clothe human dignity with new and wider meanings.

Old Main as a living instrument today might be saying: "One thing I know deep out of my time: Youth when lighted and live and given a sporting chance is strong for struggle and not afraid of any toils or punishments or dangers or deaths. What shall be the course of society and civilization across the next hundred years? For the answers read if you can the strange and baffling eyes of youth."

The American fable of the two maggots, one of them getting a nice break

A WPA worker leaves his scoop shovel one night in a WPA truck. And two maggots crawl in and take a long sleep. When they wake up it's daylight and the WPA worker has the shovel on his shoulder heading for his job. One of the maggots yawns, "What's the destination?" and his brother, "Well, maybe there ain't no dog-gone destination."

Just about then the WPA worker shifts the shovel from one shoulder to another. And the two maggots lose their toeholds and fall off, one of them into the deep dark crack of a concrete sidewalk. And when his eyes get used to the dark, he finds there is nothing a maggot can live on, not a toehold for climbing up, and it's cold and he starts shivering as he says, "I'm a hoper and a wanter, that's me—a hoper and a wanter."

And the other maggot, his brother, falls into a big pile of humus and manure with three dead rats and the ripe carcass of a cat, heaven for a maggot. So he eats and eats and five days go by and around his middle there are seams and wrinkles where odd little creepers have come to feed on him and keep him company. And he is kind of proud about this as he says to himself, "You really ain't got class unless you got some parasites."

So he climbs up on the concrete sidewalk and it's a fine summer morning, blue sky with white fluffs of clouds floating along lazy like, bright sunshine pouring down. Now he comes all of a sudden to the deep dark crack in the sidewalk. And he stops and looks down and after a while he makes out away down there—his brother, weak by now. And his brother's knees sag and he is wobbly as he looks up: "Yes, that's you up there, my brother. We was on that shovel together. Here I am down here in the dark shivering and starving. And you up there you're fat and greasy and lousy with prosperity. How did you do it? Tell me—how did you do it?"

And the fat maggot up in the sun leans over and looks down: "Huh—how did I do it? Brains and personality."

Independent versions of this fable have been told by Lincoln Steffens, Jo Davidson, Oscar Ameringer, and I have heard it told using worms, instead of maggots, by the General Passenger Agent of the New York Central Railroad, James W. Switzer, who in 1898 was the seventeen-year-old bugler of Company C, Sixth Illinois Volunteers U.S.A., in the expedition to Puerto Rico when we were both commandos.
Collier's, the National Weekly, September 25, 1943.

Elephants are different to different people

Wilson and Pilcer and Snack stood before the zoo elephant.

Wilson said, "What is its name? Is it from Asia or Africa? Who feeds it? Is it a he or a she? How old is it? Do they have twins? How much does it cost to feed? How much does it weigh? If it dies, how much will another one cost? If it dies, what will they use the bones, the fat, and the hide for? What use is it besides to look at?"

Pilcer didn't have any questions; he was murmuring to himself, "It's a house by itself, walls and windows, the ears came from tall cornfields, by God; the architect of those legs was a workman, by God; he stands like a bridge out across deep water; the face is sad and the eyes are kind; I know elephants are good to babies."

Snack looked up and down and at last said to himself, "He's a tough son-of-a-gun outside and I'll bet he's got a strong heart, I'll bet he's strong as a copper-riveted boiler inside."

They didn't put up any arguments.

They didn't throw anything in each other's faces.

Three men saw the elephant three ways

And let it go at that.

They didn't spoil a sunny Sunday afternoon;

"Sunday comes only once a week," they told each other.

Scroll [1]

Memory is when you look back
and the answers float in
to who? what? when? where?

The members who were there then
are repeated on a screen
are recalled on a scroll
are moved in a miniature drama,
are collected and recollected
for actions, speeches, silences,
set forth by images of the mind
and made in a mingling mist
to do again and to do over
precisely what they did do once—
this is memory—
sometimes slurred and blurred—
this is remembering—
sometimes wrecking the images
and proceeding again to reconstruct
what happened and how,
the many little involved answers
to who? what? when? where?
and more involved than any
        how? how?

[1] The *Nation*, February 10, 1940, under the title "Memory."

Time scheme [1]

Now the almanacs say mid-June 1943
And time goes by on a wool foot wool-shod
And time flits on in a velvet sheen of a velvet mist
While smoke on the moon does changes
And blood on the moon creeps over and under
And time is a row of puppets
And times says fade-me, find-me, blitz-me
And time says, "Yes the blitz, where is the blitz?"

In September before the autumn leaves,
In September and Poland and 1939
Time said, "Yes the blitz, here is the blitz,"
And walls fell in London-on-the-Thames
And roofs fell on the walls in 1940.

Time ran fast and time ran out
Over Vyazma, Smolensk, Kharkov, Rostov-on-the-Don,
Over cool Moscow murmuring "Nietchevo,"
Time saying, "1941 and the blitz for you now"
And the walls fell and the roofs fell on the walls
And lonesome little villages looked up
And saw smoke on the moon, blood on the moon.

Time wore on and time eased out
The days adding up to months
And the months melting into 1942 gone
And cylinders of sweet death like compliments,
Out of the sky and out of nowhere sweet cylinders
Better known as ashcans, eggs to make ashes,
Blockbusters falling on Berlin, Cologne, Essen, Düsseldorf,
Time saying, "1943 and the blitz returns, recoils, comes back."
And summer says how-do-you-do on the Wilhelmstrasse
And June says lead-in-your-guts along the winding Ruhr Valley
And summer says nuts-to-you where the Volga waits
And the Gestapo dossiers are not so good any more
And out of the underground they don't know just who to kill

[1] The Chicago Times Syndicate, June 27, 1943.

And the faces of the already killed float hither and yon
And there are footsteps heard, unheard, heard again
And the sky writing goes on,
Night and day a handwriting in alphabets of fire,
Punctual as a sober old grandfather's clock,
Bright as the precisions of a nice wrist-watch,
A pale moon keeping numbers on dead, on mangled, on homeless,
On walls falling first and the roof falling on the walls
Or the roof falling first and the walls falling on the roof
And time wearing on and time easing days into months
And time saying, "Yes, 1943, and the blitz returns, recoils, comes
     back."

Transatlantic call [1]

Of what are you thinking
And how are your thoughts and afterthoughts
And what are you going to say
When this creative pause comes to an end,
Reichschancellor of the Greater Germany,
Founder of a thousand-year herrenvolk?

When you talked off *Mein Kampf* in jail
And Hess with a pencil put it all down
The book sold and you went to town as a spieler
And later the spotlights played on you in the Sportspalast
And after the purge in 1934 you took to the microphones
Sending your alibi to five wide continents:
About Sudetenland you had remarks more than brief,
About Danzig, Poland, Lebensraum, more and more remarks.
About the Communists, the Jews, plutodemocratic warmongers,
We heard you weekdays, Sundays, Nazi-anniversary days.

What other mouth poured so many earfuls into so many ears?
So many promises, threats, edicts, so much "Do this—or else!"
    Who since time began?
Who since language came born for loose tongues?

  In days that came could you throw a scare
  With a couple of innocent-looking syllables,
    A shrug here, a whisper there?
And you took what you wanted, by the timetable,
According to plan calling the turn correct,
Your guns covering Europe from Calais to near Moscow,
Your hangmen having fun at your order: "implacable violence."

We listened when you let yourself go fast and hoarse
And clipped your syllables telling us who was next,
How the map of Europe looked silly to you
And you would wreck it and fix it new and nice,
From Narvik to Novorossiisk all new and nice,

1 *Collier's, the National Weekly*, September 18, 1943.

How England would fall, not a doubt about it,
How Russia would be hammered to pieces on your anvils
And Leningrad, then Stalingrad, were in the bag
Any time you gave the word for the pincers to press.
And America was a mongrel-bred democracy run by Jews
And America, the U.S.A., was soft and would never throw in.

    Words, language, jargon, did you have it?
    The speech of fright, scare-talk, fear-talk, big-talk,
    That was your line, your technique: it had worked.
    The war of nerves? Why, you had a patent on it.
    With Storm Troopers, Gestapo, Luftwaffe, Wehrmacht
Backing your words, you went to town with tongue and tonsils.
You spoke three words "Heads will roll!" and a million men
Felt of their necks where they might get the headsman's ax.

And now—now we don't happen to hear from you any more.
    Now in a silence of deep caverns,
    Now in a silence of dark cisterns,
The Reichschancellor of the Greater Germany says nothing.
The big wind once blowing now blows no man knoweth whither.

    Of course, what we're doing to you costs us
    And it's going to cost us more and more
    So you too will have to pay and pay.
    And we've counted the cost and we're willing
    And there will be hell to pay, for you, for us,
    And one for sure will be gone when the hell is over—
    The Reichschancellor of the Greater Germany.

Sometimes in the creep of the hour hands
Clocking the summer of 1943
We ask how you will take the pay-off, the rendezvous,
How come you never figured what was cooking,
And how are your thoughts and afterthoughts,
And what are you going to say when your big moment comes
For the founder of a thousand-year herrenvolk,
    You and your hell-bent New Order
Getting hammered to hell-and-gone in round-the-clock blazes,

Getting shattered in shambles of reek and fire—
    And the people, the little people
    Hoping to God for only a hundred years of peace.
They'd settle for that—a hundred years of peace.

    Of what are you thinking
    And what will be your lines
    When again you must speak lines—
Chancellor of the Greater German Reich,
Reichschancellor of the Greater Germany?

The fireborn are at home in fire[1]

Luck is a star.
Money is a plaything.
Time is a storyteller.
The sky goes high, big.
The sky goes wide and blue.
And the fireborn—they go far—
       being at home in fire.

Can you compose yourself
The same as a bright bandanna,
A bandanna folded blue and cool,
Whatever the high howling,
The accents of blam blam?
Can I, can John Smith, John Doe,
Whatever the awful accents,
Whatever the horst wessel hiss,
Whatever books be burnt and crisp,
Whatever hangmen bring their hemp,
Whatever horsemen sweep the sunsets,
Whatever hidden hovering candle
Sways as a wafer of light?

Can you compose yourself
The same as a bright bandanna,
A bandanna folded blue and cool?
Can I, too, drop deep down
In a pool of cool remembers,
In a float of fine smoke blue,
In a keeping of one pale moon,
Weaving our wrath in a pattern

[1] *Collier's, the National Weekly*, September 4, 1943.

Woven of wrath gone down,
Crossing our scarlet zigzags
With pools of cool blue,
With floats of smoke blue?

Can you, can I, compose ourselves
In wraps of personal cool blue,
In sheets of personal smoke blue?
   Bach did it, Johann Sebastian.
So did the one and only John Milton.
   And the old slave Epictetus
   And the other slave Spartacus
   And Brother Francis of Assisi.
So did General George Washington
   On a horse, in a saddle,
   On a boat, in heavy snow,
   In a loose cape overcoat
   And snow on his shoulders.
So did John Adams, Jackson, Jefferson.
So did Lincoln on a cavalry horse
At the Chancellorsville review
   With platoons right, platoons left,
In a wind nearly blowing the words away
   Asking the next man on a horse:
"What's going to become of all these
      boys when the war is over?"

The shape of your shadow
Comes from you—and you only?
Your personal fixed decisions
Out of you—and your mouth only?
   Your No, your Yes, your own?

Bronze old-timers belong here.
Yes, they might be saying:
   Shade the flame
Back to final points
Of all sun and fog
In the moving frame

Of your personal eyes.
Then stand to the points.
Let hunger and hell come.
Or ashes and shame poured
On your personal head.
Let death shake its bones.
The teaching goes back far:
  Compose yourself.

 Luck is a star.
 Money is a plaything.
 Time is a storyteller.
And the sky goes blue with mornings.
And the sky goes bronze with sunsets.
And the fireborn—they go far—
  being at home in fire.

ROAD TO VICTORY

A PROCESSION OF PHOTOGRAPHS OF THE NATION AT WAR, DIRECTED BY
LIEUTENANT COMMANDER EDWARD STEICHEN, U.S.N.R. TEXT BY CARL
SANDBURG. INSTALLATION DESIGNED BY HERBERT BAYER.

GRATEFUL ACKNOWLEDGMENT IS MADE OF THE CO-OPERATION AND PER-
MISSION TO USE THE PHOTOGRAPHS OF THE MUSEUM OF MODERN ART;
THE UNITED STATES ARMY; UNITED STATES NAVY; UNITED STATES DEPART-
MENT OF AGRICULTURE: FARM SECURITY ADMINISTRATION, AGRICUL-
TURAL ADJUSTMENT ADMINISTRATION, BUREAU OF AGRICULTURAL ECO-
NOMICS, EXTENSION SERVICE; UNITED STATES DEPARTMENT OF THE
INTERIOR; OFFICE FOR EMERGENCY MANAGEMENT; TENNESSEE VALLEY
AUTHORITY; TIME-LIFE, INC.; PM; ASSOCIATED PRESS; INTERNATIONAL
NEWS PHOTOS; ACME NEWS PICTURES, INC.; PRESS ASSOCIATION, INC.;
UNITED STATES STEEL CORPORATION; ASSOCIATION OF AMERICAN RAIL-
ROADS; SAMUEL GOTTSCHO; ROBERT YARNALL RICHIE; PATRICIA DYETT;
ARTHUR FELLIG ("WEEGEE"); HANS GROENHOFF.

Road to Victory has come and gone and yet stays with us. Talk
about it and discussion of it will go on. Here the still photograph
steps out, moves and speaks, chants lonesome or sings in choral.
Here a procession of photographs marches, makes its report to the
nations on the American people, their home front and fighting
fronts, our wartime America.

It carries faith and expectancy that the modern genius of man
can go far and is beyond defeat or conquest, in line with the ancient
proverb "The fireborn are at home in fire."

For quite a while yet there will be discussion of the Road to Victory show and what it might be pointing toward in the teaching of
history, geography, love of country, and understanding of humanity.

The show opened in May of 1942, a procession of 150 photographs requiring the whole second floor of the Museum of Modern
Art in New York City. Only the careless, tired, sleepy, or absent-
minded took less than a half-hour to walk along the floors and
ramps and see the entire show. Many took an hour or two hours.

And some went away haunted and came back to make sure and keep what they had seen the first time or to go farther and find things they had missed the first time.

Running six months in New York, it moved on to Cleveland, Chicago, St. Louis, and has been scheduled for San Francisco, Portland, Oregon, and many other cities. One replica of the exhibit sailed for England and was sunk by a submarine. A second one that sailed reached London, pleased and instructed large audiences, and has gone to other cities in the British Isles. Another went to Honolulu and will go to Australia and other parts of the Pacific. Still another started in Colombia, South America, for travel southward, and a second replica, shown first in Uruguay, toured northward. At one embarkation port the army has put the show into regular use among troops waiting for transports. And in pocket form Road to Victory is in continuous use among the armed services at home and abroad.

So Road to Victory has gone to town. Here and there you might say it has become a legend, with people who have never seen it talking as though they had. Still others who did see it talk so as to make it something beyond what it was in fact. They voice an imponderable theme of American dream and human hope that wove itself through the marching photographic murals. They heard a poem with music and horizon haze in it.

It began with David H. McAlpin, a Trustee of the Museum of Modern Art in New York City, and his suggestion in September of 1941 that a large-scale photograph exhibit on national defense might be worth while and that he would see it got the necessary support. Shortly afterward, Monroe Wheeler, Director of Exhibitions at the Museum, gave Edward Steichen full leeway in producing such a show, placing at Steichen's disposal all the resources of the Museum.

So Steichen in October of 1941 leaves his Umpawaug Farm, near Ridgefield and Danbury, Connecticut, leaves its rocks and rills, its woods and templed hills, its tens of thousands of delphinium plants, its house of glass walls overlooking pond lilies where giant frogs croak in August midnights, its waterfalls leaping tall boulders, and one skyline where every spring the mystic white shadblow says greeting to hard-rock palisades over winter gone and summer nearly come in.

Month on month for six months Steichen plows his way through piles of photographic prints, handling more than 100,000 prints in departments of the Federal Government, in the photographic files of newspapers and magazines and individual cameramen.

On December 7 came the unforgettable Pearl Harbor attack and with the United States of America on a war basis with a changed national unity, the aim and the main idea of the exhibit was to make a portrait of the American people at war. In January the United States Navy gave its newly commissioned Lieutenant Commander Steichen a special assignment to assemble and direct production of the exhibit for the Museum. In April of 1942 he had, with patient handling and plenty of turmoil, picked and chosen and at last cut down the pickings and choosings to 150 photographs. Over 90 per cent of these had been supplied by the departments and agencies of the United States Government, the largest number coming from the Farm Security Administration, the Army Signal Corps, and the Navy Bureau of Aeronautics.

These final 150 photographs Steichen arranged in sequences, "each room a chapter, each photograph a sentence," starting with the naked primeval continent, moving through food and war production, with fighting men from training periods on to combat fronts. From room to room and up and down ramps that circle and wind, the spectator walks meeting murals from three by four feet to ten by forty feet in size, the subjects ranging from the comic and earthy, bringing smiles and laughter, on to the big spaces of wall presenting Shasta Dam and Boulder Dam. In the latter one visitor saw "a combination of Rheims Cathedral and Niagara Falls."

In April of 1942 Steichen lays out on the floor of his Umpawaug house the groups of photographic prints that are to make up the sequence of the exhibit. Then he holds me to a promise that I would do my best at writing the captions or text for the photograph sequences and we go to work, for some twelve days. Steichen gives me, as best he can, his impressions of how 8-by-10-inch prints will look when "blown up" into 8-by-10-foot or 16-by-20-foot murals. And I write, sometimes desperately, first one and then another text, till we have a framework of words, a stream of commentary and announcement that moves in tempo and theme with the flow and change of the marching murals. Sometimes the text for a group or sequence was rewritten five or six times. Steichen is no slouch of an editor; he wangled, joked and threatened better texts out of me

han I would have believed possible. The enlargement of the prints
o mural size went on while the text was written and the rooms and
amps were being completed for the exhibit.

Never before was such a march of mural photographs. Here is
nan and what man hath wrought, here too the sea and the face of
he earth, and the American people in their productive and fight-
ng phases. Steichen's faith in his America runs deep. The photo-
,raphs he chose present a people and a country who have strengths,
ights, and faiths to wrestle with any dark destinies ahead.

As Road to Victory, after its six months' run in New York, went
o Cleveland, Chicago, St. Louis, and other cities, it left an impress,
ind around several questions made its points. The people, as such,
is designated in the Constitution and in the utterances of Jefferson,
.incoln, and other revered figures, are worth looking at. And
America, the United States of America, stands rugged and challeng-
ng here, lies fruitful, inviting, and lovable there, and as a piece or
domain of global earth is worth the faith and the fighting of men.
n will and vision the present generation makes grand comparison
vith any of the earlier generations that necessity and destiny hurled
nto hard and terrible conflict. Something like that stands out from
he array of photographic prints that shape a massive portrait and
.n epic poem of the United States of America at war and on its road
o victory.

The human factor stands out, with faces, feet, shoulders, torsos,
elling their stories. And beyond this look and this very smell of
vhat is human lies the thought that the word "victory" in the title
neans not merely winning a war over enemies outside the United
States of America. It means further the conquest of ourselves in the
ense of the old verse "He that ruleth over his own spirit is greater
han he that taketh a city." What through war we have learned of
uuman solidarity and national unity, what lessons we have gained,
vhile making war, of the values of co-operation and humility, these
ve can hope to carry over into peacetime for victory in the fields of
vider personal freedom and of advances in national discipline and
lomestic welfare.

Road to Victory informs and then goes beyond information.
Steichen's selective skill, his sagacity among masterpieces, his eye
'or enduring values in a photograph, are represented here in faces
ind places of a haunting quality. These faces and these places will

be here after the war. Peacetime victory waits only the will and vision of men. Heavy and terrific mass production, performances of invention and workmanship still regarded as marvelous, countless acts of devotion where the idea was service—these can have a future. Man does not stop. Man goes on. Tomorrow is a day. Tomorrow belongs to the children. The word "breath-taking," so often used to describe Road to Victory, came in part because the murals give terrific testimony to the production genius of the American people. What they as a people truly have the will and vision to desire, to want, to achieve, either in material goods or in new lights and goals of culture, they can have it and nothing can stop them. The possibilities loom. The chances beckon. Something like that hovers in a blue-and-white mist of implication behind Road to Victory. It leaves you with a quiet hangover to the effect that humanity is worth loving and the plain people are going places and life in this day and time is easily more than 51 per cent worth living.

Never before was a generation of men with its significant faces and places registered and presented as in this strange and intricate panorama. Anything like it out of 1776 or 1861 or 1918 would be equally priceless.

The generations pass. The nation lives. And this will be so for as long as some saving remnant of humanity has victory on its face and in its eyes. More than a remnant and much of its good work in our times is caught in the camera record Bruddah Steichen assembled from the fine labors of his fellow craftsmen.

THE FOUR FREEDOMS

(Message to the 77th Congress, January 6, 1942)

In the future days, which we seek to make secure, we look forward to a world founded upon four essential human freedoms.

The first is freedom of speech and expression — everywhere in the world.

The second is freedom of every person to worship God in his own way—everywhere in the world.

The third is freedom from want —which, translated into world terms, means economic understandings which will secure to every nation a healthy peacetime life for its inhabitants—everywhere in the world.

The fourth is freedom from fear —which, translated into world terms, means a world-wide reduction of armaments to such a point and in such a thorough fashion that no nation will be in a position to commit an act of physical aggression against any neighbor—anywhere.

FRANKLIN DELANO ROOSEVELT

In the beginning was virgin land and America was promises—and the buffalo by thousands pawed the Great Plains—and the Red Man gave over to an endless tide of white men in endless numbers with a land hunger and no end to the land they wanted—over the eastern seaboard through the Appalachians moved this human tide of pioneers and home-seekers—out among the spreading arteries of the Mississippi waterway system—out to the Rockies and beyond to the long sunsets of the West coast.

Grain to the skyline and beyond.

Wheat makes bread and bread breaks hunger—bread is the renewer of life.

The earth is alive. The land laughs. The people laugh. And the fat of the land is here.

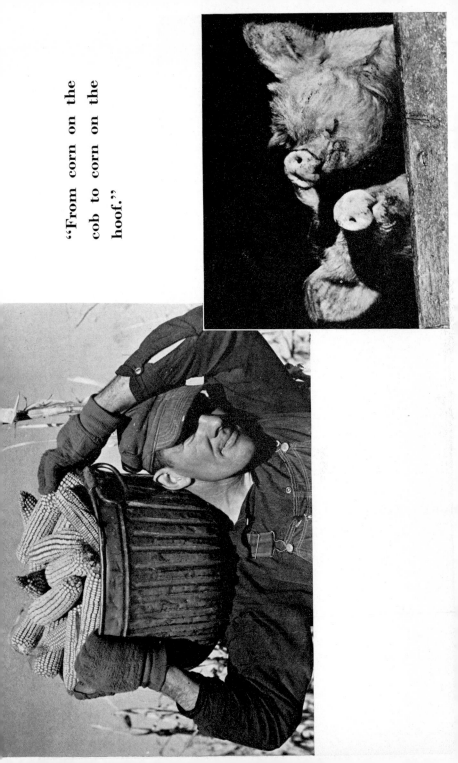

"From corn on the cob to corn on the hoof."

Many people, many faces, in their homes, their home towns, their churches, shops, schools where books say their country is "the last, best hope of earth."

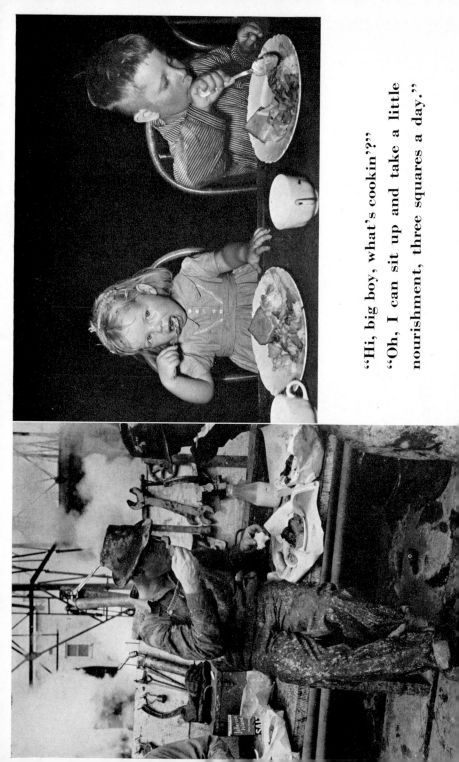

"Hi, big boy, what's cookin'?"

"Oh, I can sit up and take a little nourishment, three squares a day."

Power dams, generators, transmission, to water desert farms, to control floods, to bring light and power to homes and factories—horses, billions of horses, hauling,pounding,boring,drilling, lifting—electro-dynamic wild horses tamed to help man, locked in concrete, singing through overland wires, the live kilowatts go where man wants them for the day shift or the night gang.

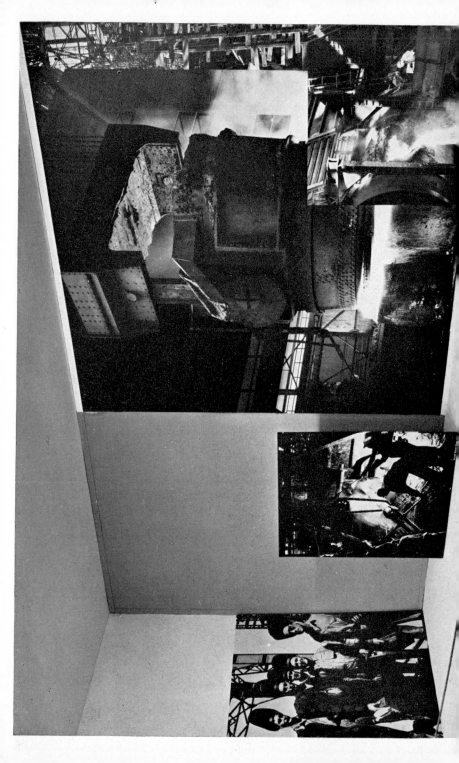

"The men behind the man behind the gun," they dig out ore from deep down in the dark, they shoot the oil wells, they chase the slag out of copper, steel-driving men they drill and twist deep rock, they hammer steel bars for rifle and cannon, they rivet the steel sheets and sew them tight with steel buttons to meet storms or torpedoes—listen, they clank and boom the mighty song of steel—the breath of their assembly lines is in miles of tanks—their thumbprints are on bombers over five oceans.

"War—they asked for it—now, by the living God, they'll get

"December 7, 1941"

"Two Faces"

Country boys, big city lads, home town fellers, they're in the Army now — behind a jeep instead of a plow — engineers bridging a river, chutists in the sky, skirmishers on the land, troopers on sea transports — into sea fog and land smoke—into the test of fire. . . . Trouble shooters, millions stepping along now, millions more on the way — killers in khaki riding smoke wagons—ready for long war or short —trouble shooters in the first round-the-world war.

Silence, yes.
Let them have silence.
Call the roll of their
names and let it go at
that.
To long sleep and deep
silence they have gone.
Deep among the never
forgotten.

Silence, yes.
Let them have silence.
Call the roll of their names
and let it go at that.
To long sleep and deep silence
they have gone.
Deep among the never forgotten.

Smooth and terrible birds of death—smooth they fly, terrible their spit of flame, their hammering cry, "Here's lead in your guts."

Loads of death, tons on tons of annihilation, out of the sky and down down down on the enemies of the free world—killers with wings—dropping polished cylinders to let loose tornadoes of hell and ashes on the hideouts of the "New Order."

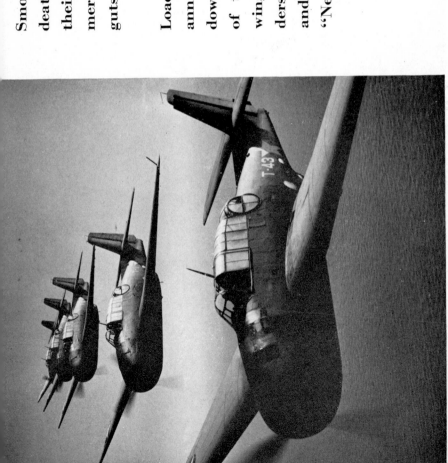

Fog-gray sea or mist-green, sun-silver water or storm salt and spray, daylight or midnight, two bells or eight bells, tropic sea or arctic, antarctic or equatorial, the Navy knows them all. Colossal the Navy—and paradoxical—hairy-chested and many-armed yet glinting its gun-barrels with astronomical precision and split-second timing—turbine web-feet on the open sea, submarine fins undersea, plane wings overhead. Hunting the enemy, slugging, pounding, blasting. And always chores we got with tenders, oilers, tugs, smoke-screens, with harbor submarine nets, minelayers, mine-sweepers, torpedo and depth bomb—heavy chores with endless patrols and long breathing convoys, caravans of the sea. "In the Navy you get every snootful of the sea there is."

Below:—Japanese cruiser is blasted by Navy dive bombers in the battle of Midway.

THE MARINES' HYMN

From the Halls of Montezuma
To the shores of Tripoli;
We fight our country's battles
In the air, on land, and sea;
First to fight for right and free-
* dom,*
And to keep our honor clean;
We are proud to claim the title
Of United States Marine.

The Merchant Marine seamen—have they held their own? Have they done their best with whatever they had? Have they stood up against the Nazi undersea wolf pack? Have they taken torpedoes and tasted black oily smoke and soaked their skins in black oils floating the open sea? Have they lived on rafts, drinking rain water, eating raw fish and turtle till they were picked up? Have they made a record for wit, understanding, struggle, so that landsmen wonder at them? They have. Yes, they have.

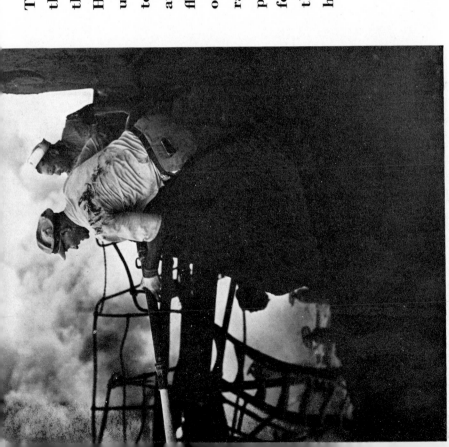

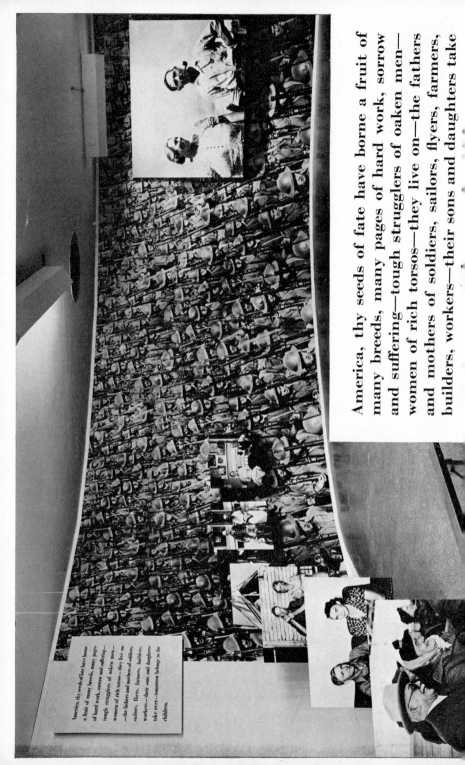

America, thy seeds of fate have borne a fruit of many breeds, many pages of hard work, sorrow and suffering—tough strugglers of oaken men—women of rich torsos—they live on—the fathers and mothers of soldiers, sailors, flyers, farmers, builders, workers—their sons and daughters take